Safer Investing in Volatile Markets

Safer Investing in Volatile Markets

Twelve Proven Strategies to Increase Your Income and Financial Security

CAROLANN DOHERTY BROWN

with ALLYSON DOHERTY BROWN
and MICHAEL DOHERTY BROWN

Dearborn™
Trade Publishing
A **Kaplan Professional** Company

This publication is designed to provide accurate and authoritative information in regard to the subject matter covered. It is sold with the understanding that the publisher is not engaged in rendering legal, accounting, or other professional service. If legal advice or other expert assistance is required, the services of a competent professional should be sought.

Editorial Director: Donald Hull
Senior Project Editor: Trey Thoelcke
Interior Design: Lucy Jenkins
Cover Design: Scott Rattray, Rattray Design
Typesetting: the dotted i

Published by Dearborn Trade, a Kaplan Professional Company

Printed in the United States of America

02   03   04   10   9   8   7   6   5   4   3   2   1

Library of Congress Cataloging-in-Publication Data

Brown, Carolann Doherty, 1946–
    Safer investing in volatile markets : twelve proven startegies to increase your income and
financial security / Carolann Doherty Brown.
        p.   cm.
    Includes index.
    ISBN 0-7931-5148-1 (7.25x9 pbk)
    1. Portfolio management.   2. Investment analysis.   3. Stocks.   4. Investments.   I. Title.
HG4529.5 B745 2002
332.024′01—dc21

                                                                                    2001007549

Dearborn Trade books are available at special quantity discounts to use for sales promotions, employee premiums, or educational purposes. Please call our special sales department, to order or for more information, at 800-621-9621, ext. 4455, or write to Dearborn Financial Publishing, 155 North Wacker Drive, Chicago, IL 60606-1719.

Dedication

This book is dedicated in loving memory to my wonderful husband, Paul, the best God had to give, and to my parents, Milly and Henry Doherty, to Gemma Cardillo, a great friend, and to Casey Logan, a wonderful young man who deserved to live a lot longer.

It is also dedicated to the loves of my life: my children Allyson and Michael Brown, my Aunt Rose, and Mary Brown.

All profits from the sale of this book go to the Paul R. Brown Memorial Fund.

CONTENTS

If you were invested in the market in 2000 and 2001 and found it frightening, then this book is for you. *Safer Investing in Volatile Markets* is for investors who didn't like the market's roller-coaster rides and wished they had more control.

Too often investors think that they have only two alternatives: "Grin & Bear It" (better known as "Buy & Hold") or "Panic Selling." There is a third alternative, however: "Taking Control." We show you 12 strategies that let you take control, increase safety and returns, and offer great profit potential, strategies that enable you to *get out on time and exit gracefully.*

Learning to exit gracefully is a lot more fun than roller-coaster rides.

There are no perfect investments. There are no perfect investment strategies. But there are far better strategies than just watching your assets erode (Grin & Bear It) or getting so nervous that you sell at the bottom (Panic Selling). My 12 strategies will not work all the time for all people, but history has shown they do work most of the time. Each of us is unique, with different time horizons, risk tolerances, and goals. What works for one may not work for others. I show you how to review alternative strategies and evaluate how they fit into your overall financial picture.

If you are alert to changes in the market, employ sensible strategies, and are willing to take reasonable profits, then you can do well in almost any market. But if you believe the market will go up forever and even for a brief moment discard or set aside sound strategies, then you can get hurt.

If you think back to November 1999, November 2000, and September 2001, you will know why having good, solid *exit* strategies is important and why we cannot let emotions take hold. The extreme volatility on the upside in 1999 and on the downside in 2000 and 2001 will have an impact on the market for years. It is hoped that watching the market the last few years has taught investors a valuable lesson.

In 1999, as we approached the new millennium, the whole world feared the impending doom of Y2K and the potentially damaging consequences of a global meltdown. Top priorities were keeping technology companies solid, making sure that companies had updated computers, telecommunications, and power supplies, and that banks and companies were Y2K compliant.

But in 1999 the market was becoming overvalued. All the indicators we use to measure value were showing that the market was too high and warned us to invest in safer, value stocks. But the money was in high-growth stocks. Because growth stocks offered excitement, the media focused on growth. Everyone was talking about the new rules, the new paradigm, saying that values didn't matter anymore and that there were no limits to how high the market could go. Almost everybody wanted the hot new companies, and everyone became an expert on technology stocks. Investing seemed so easy, and many investors became their own online broker, abandoning financial and retirement planning and the building of solid portfolios. They focused instead on finding the great fast-moving companies. They looked at the rewards, the upside potential, but seldom the downside risk. It was exciting listening to financial news shows, talking about stocks and the new millennium, and it seemed the party would never end. Analysts hyped the fast-moving stocks into an ever faster whirl. There was an overabundance of buy recommendations but little advice on selling and exiting the market.

The year 1999 was golden for the Nasdaq 100 index, an unmanaged index of 100 stocks used to measure growth stocks. It returned over 85.6 percent, but things just weren't right. All of the investing activity in technology was skewing the real profit picture. Only a handful of stocks were doing well. As the Federal Reserve started to raise rates in 2000, the party came to an end. Even though interest rate increases are one of the best predictors of pending doom, most investors ignored them and failed to exit the market in time.

Federal Reserve Chairman Alan Greenspan kept saying the economy was healthy—too healthy! On the surface the economy looked too good. Who knew that the markets were doomed? Anyone who watched the valuations knew! But even if we knew the market was overvalued, many of us still could not pull out. Even if the market fell, it was hard to believe that it could not come back quickly as it had done so many times in the past. If the Federal Reserve Board didn't know, it was probably impossible for anyone else to know that we were entering one of the worst economic falls in history.

Content Summary

Safer Investing in Volatile Markets explores strategies that have historically outperformed traditional "buy-and-hold" strategies. The strategies explored here can help investors exit gracefully from the market, avoiding emotion and panic selling. They give you ideas on how to enter the market and how to increase income and safety by avoiding downside risk, along with ideas for how to stay in the stock market with peace of mind.

When I was five years old, more than anything in the world I wanted blue eyes like those my two sisters had. I prayed and prayed and prayed. When I woke up on my sixth birthday with my same brown eyes, I was crushed. My mother tried to console me. She said, "You have so much that you should never pray for anything more. Pray instead that you do not lose what you have." If you are an investor who wants to strive for more and outperform the market, there are six strategies for you. If, however, you are an investor who follows my mother's advice and wants to earn good returns without losing what you have, there are six strategies for you. In life, as in investing, there is probably room for both.

Why This Book?

I am writing this book now because all the rules and strategies I knew screamed loudly to get out of the market in 1999. However, those rules were quickly being rejected and becoming unfashionable. But had we paid attention to those rules and strategies, most investors would have fared very well during the last few years. Those old valuation measures, old protective strategies, and old control strategies were valid. I am writing this book to remind you to always have some protection in your account. No matter what the media say, no matter how different you think the world might be, no matter how great things look, *always have exit strategies.*

Look at valuations, not media hype. Don't let one big event risk hurt you. When you do get hit badly, don't panic, don't sell out. There are better alternatives—and this book shows you those alternatives.

More important, this book shows you ways to get out of the market before a big fall and before small losses turn into big losses. It shows you disciplined ways to take profits and also how to stay in the market for the good times. It shows you ways to insure your investments while you are holding as well as strategies for making money even in flat markets. It shows you successful strategies that have worked for decades and how to avoid letting one bad month turn into years.

1997: After one of the worst point drops in the Dow on October 27, 1997—554 points—the market rallied so quickly the next day that everyone forgot about the drop. Because I thought no one would be interested in a book on safety, I put this book aside. But after the recent dramatic market fluctuations, a new interest in safer investment strategies has emerged.

My clients gave me permission to tell some of their stories, but I have chosen not to use their names. Although the names may not be true, all of the stories are.

When I started this book in 1997, my husband was alive and I was blessed to share my life and build a family with one of the brightest, kindest men I ever knew. He had an incredible memory (he won so many Trivial Pursuit games when he was in the navy that they finally barred him from playing so that someone else could win).

Paul edited my newspaper columns, newsletters, and books over the years. I would write bullets and he would fill in the text, correcting the grammar and so forth. Most important, he would fill in the dates. Without his memory, I couldn't rely on the accuracy of some of the dates for the stories about my clients and seminars. Paul had the great memory in the family. I was a mathematician, but I do remember the people well. Their stories allow you to see how investment strategies operate in the real world. These people greatly influenced my view of risk, and I think that they will also help you to better understand risk.

I also relied heavily on my two children. Even though my daughter, Allyson, has two master's degrees, she knows little about finance, and so she read these chapters over and over to find information that was too difficult or overwhelming for the novice investor. Thanks to her, I think this book is a tool for novice, intermediate, and, in many instances, expert investors. My son, Michael, who is a broker and financial advisor, verified the statistics and data. Most of my statistics are from Ibbotson Associates, which is one of the most popular and reliable sources of market information. Janet Rochon, Ann Knoll, and Marilyn Goldman helped with the editing. Ann is a contributing editor of *Money* magazine, and Marilyn was the publisher of *Tidewater Virginia Business* magazine.

I cannot end without a special thank you to my wonderful friends and family, especially those whom I forgot to mention in the acknowledgment. Every day they reinforce in me the belief that money is not everything but friends and family are.

ACKNOWLEDGMENTS

I have been blessed with so many wonderful, supportive people in my life—my family, friends, and especially my children. I almost hesitated thanking them here because it seems so slight a way to say thank you for all their support, but here goes.

To my children, Allyson and Michael, of course, you know how much I love you.

To my wonderful Aunt Rose, and my mother-in-law, Mary Brown.

To my great siblings, and their families, Mary Lionette, Joan O'Leary, Betty-Ann Nutter, and Will Doherty. My wonderful nieces and nephews also: the Dohertys, Danny, Tony and Kathy, Megan and Bruce, and Tara; the Nutters, Kathy and Mariann; the Lionettes, Robert, Christopher and Kathy, Katy, and Jamey; the O'Learys, Megan, Jason and Helen, Paul and Patrick; the Gaudreaus, Evan and Lee; and the Browns, Lauren and Kristen.

To the Browns, Nancy, Sue, Bobby and Jane, David, and Betsy, and Don Harper, as well as the McElhineys.

To my dearest friends, Marie D'Eramo, Pat and Dave Donohoe, Ellen and Mark Rosenthal, Barbara, Mike, Tim and Penny Sikorski, Marilyn and Dan Goldman, Tanya and Maurice Miller, Susan and Graham Smith, Pat and Tip Jennings, Ruth O'Leary Miller, Lin and Bob Logan, Ginny and Ed Hopkins, and Diane and Rob Beaver.

I also would like to thank some of my great clients and friends, from whom I learned a great deal and often share their stories with you. To Sue and Jack Jobe, Henry Krevor, Kappy Leonard, who taught me that it is better to have great people in your life and lose them, than to live without them, and Ira Janowitz, who left us with his wonderful family, Donna, Adam and Lindsay. Ira not only taught me to hold on when things looked the worse, but also introduced me to some incredible people: the Rabins, Bronskys, and Schulmans. To Mimi Rankin, Mary Cahill, Paul Janov (thanks for helping to get my Ali home from Guatemala), Mary Nell Roosendall, and Mike Landauer. Also thanks to Ed Ohlert who helped with the President Reagan story.

To my extraordinary staff, Sheila Camara, Janet Rochon, Vicki Zipkin, Sharon Snyder, and Christopher Robert.

To Mark Rappaport, Athol Cochrane, and Jeff Suyematsu for their valuable contributions to this book.

Lastly, I would like to thank all my wonderful radio listeners for all their support and contributions to the Paul R. Brown Memorial Fund.

Thank God, I didn't win an Academy Award, I would be up there forever. Although I am grateful that I have so many wonderful people to thank, I fear that I am forgetting someone. I realize the best part of writing a book or winning an award is the opportunity it affords to thank those you care about. Thank you.

CHAPTER 1

Panic-Free Investing

During my junior year in college, I traveled to Donegal in the northern part of Ireland in search of my family roots. I convinced a few of my fellow classmates to come with me on what we had hoped would be an exciting adventure. I had heard stories all my life about how my great-great-grandfather, James Doherty, came from Donegal to the United States during the gold rush. He struck it rich and was able to buy a castle in Ireland. As it turned out, the castle was nothing more than a pile of ruins—somewhat like my dreams of finding stories of exciting ancestors. Donegal was beautiful as we traveled down its narrow country roads, but we could barely see the landscape because of the constant rain. However, two things we could see clearly in every place we visited were Doherty pubs and Doherty funeral parlors. Apparently the Dohertys had a talent for drinking and dying. As we traveled, we never once heard any exciting stories about my great ancestors, and soon I began to doubt the Doherty's legendary talent. Buying ruins and limited ventures in drinking and dying were not exactly the kinds of stories I expected or wanted to repeat.

It wasn't until a few years ago when I had a surprise family reunion for my dad that I appreciated the skills of my ancestors. I invited Dohertys from all over the world, and I was so impressed with them: bright, articulate, and multitalented and from many diverse backgrounds. I shared with them the story of my long-ago trip to Donegal and my embarrassment at having to admit I was a Doherty, a name permanently associated with drinking and dying. As I finished, one of my cousins scolded me for my embarrassment, pointing out that our ancestors were, in fact, pretty smart! They had picked the only two recession-proof industries: drinking and dying. I realize now that my cousin not only taught me an important lesson about life but one about the stock market as well. In life and in your job, make yourself indispensable, and in the stock market do the same. Stick with those companies and strategies that in good times as well as bad are needed and reliable.

To reduce panic we need to find and invest in *indispensable companies,* the companies that supply necessities. All portfolios need some investments or investment strategies on which we can rely, strategies that reduce stress and allow us to sleep at night. We need investments that, in spite of whatever may happen, will survive. They might be dull. We might not be able to brag about them at cocktail parties and feel part of the fast track, but we will always be certain they'll be there. *They are investments and investment strategies that have limited market risk, inflation risk, interest rate risk, and credit risk.*

Although we are constantly searching for outstanding strategies, there is no one perfect strategy. Each of us is unique and each of us needs a combination of strategies that suits our own unique situation.

12 Strategies

During the market volatility of 2000 and 2001, most investors felt they had only two alternatives: Grin and Bear It (buy and hold) or Panic Selling. However, other strategies have been successful in adding safety or outperforming the S&P 500 in most markets.

Although these strategies have been around for years, we hope to show you new twists to most of these strategies to accommodate the increased volatility in the market. Most important, we hope to show you that safety does not mean avoiding risk. *Safety means controlling and understanding risk.*

Avoiding risk is not safety—safety is controlling risk.

When I was preparing to teach my first college economics class, the dean reminded me of the three basic tenets of teaching. First, begin by telling the class what you are going to tell them. Second, tell them what you want them to know. Finally, tell them what you just told them. So in this chapter I start by telling you a little about the strategies.

Building a Strategy and Trading Off Risks

The next two chapters focus on setting realistic goals and building safety into a portfolio by learning to control risks. We look at the different types of risk you must consider and how you can benefit from risk. But before you can benefit from risk, you have to understand it.

Too often we assume that only stocks have risk. We understand market risk but neglect to pay attention to other kinds of risk, such as interest rate, credit, opportunity, inflation, and event risk. Many investors assume that owning government bonds is the ultimate route to safety, but that assumption can be dangerous. Bonds have credit risk, opportunity risk, inflation risk, and also interest rate risk.

Interest rate risk can be more dangerous than market risk. In the 1980s, I met Harriet, a poor elderly woman who lived in the slums of Norfolk, Virginia. Her husband had passed away in the 1970s, leaving her a $10,000 life insurance policy. This was the only money she would ever have to invest. Someone told her the safest thing she could do would be to buy a government bond and so she did. She earned $690 a year in income. To her, that was a lot of money. When I met her, she was ill and close to death, and she wanted to sell her bond to help her only daughter. However, that "safe" $10,000 U.S. government bond she had bought was worth only $5,200! No one would pay her $10,000 for a bond paying only $690 a year when one could buy bonds paying as much as $1,400 a year. Interest rates had gone up dramatically in the eighties, and the value of Harriet's bond fell proportionally. Her bond had no credit risk, but it had extremely high interest rate risk. When she found out, Harriet sat there crying, repeating over and over, "But this is a government bond." I wanted to hold her and tell her to hang on, that it would be fine over time and she would get her money back. But it could be 18 years before she got her money back, and time for her was measured in weeks and days, not years.

Even if she could wait until the bond matured and the government guarantees fulfilled, she would always suffer *"opportunity risk,"* the risk of missing the opportunity to earn much higher income, as high as $1,400. As each day passed, the bond was worth less and less. She stopped coming by to check on its value. Months passed, and I never found her again. I never knew what happened to her, but what I did know was that interest rate risk is a true risk, as dangerous as market risk.

Risk comes in many different disguises: inflation, interest rate, credit, opportunity, and event as well as market. There is even a risk associated with holding a physical certificate instead of letting a bank or brokerage firm hold it. What if it is lost? What if Harriet's daughter didn't know where it was hidden? Chapter 2 explains all of these risks and how you can protect yourself and benefit from them.

Strategy 1: *Guaranteeing Your Investments*

The first strategy—*guaranteeing principal*—allows you to stay in the stock market without fear of losing your principal. It combines investments with indexes, stocks, or funds to ensure that all your money will be returned at a predetermined time. If you didn't like the roller-coaster ride that occurred the last few years, then this is a strategy for you. Learning to guarantee your principal reduces stress and panic selling and makes investing rational instead of emotional. Although this strategy doesn't strive for the greatest returns, it lets you live and enjoy life instead of being stressed over the day-to-day movements in the market.

Strategy 2: *Stopping Losses with Stop Loss Orders*

In 1987 my husband, Paul, was stationed in Puerto Rico and claimed we had the perfect life. He was a carrier pilot, a commanding officer of a navy squadron in paradise. My children had the opportunity to play every day in the beautiful sun of Puerto Rico within the safety of a military base. We fell in love with the Puerto Ricans and the relaxed lifestyle. I was able to sit outside working on my computer from a home satellite office while gazing at the Caribbean. The market was soaring, and life was perfect. That was until I learned the tax laws in Puerto Rico were different from those in the states and my clients would be taxed in Puerto Rico because I was based there. I was forced to commute back to the states each week to avoid Puerto Rican taxes on my accounts. The year 1987 was a great one for the market because of a broad market rally. It seemed as if nothing could go wrong. But because I was commuting and out of the office so much, I needed automatic programs in place to take the worry out of big market falls, so I started to use *stop loss orders* religiously. Normally, I set the stop losses at 10 percent away from the current price, but because we had done so well that year, in October I moved the stops up to 5 percent away. The next day, I headed home. When I got off the plane, the market had fallen 109 points, and most of my stocks had been sold out. I felt embarrassed and called all my clients. I had just sold them out of one of the best bull markets in history. I promised them I would head back on Monday and buy back all the stocks.

I went back on Monday, but when I landed in D.C., I found the market had fallen by over 508 points, one of the worst one-day falls in history. On Friday, I looked naïve, but on Black Monday I looked like a genius. The stops had worked better than I could have ever planned. I sometimes think how lucky I was, but one of the reasons the stop losses worked so well was because they were automatic. There was no second-guessing and no emotion. We had set targets and worked with them. Limiting losses is critical, and stop loss orders can often help limit your losses. Stop loss orders don't work as well anymore, however, because the markets are too volatile, but there is still a place for them. Such a strategy can help you assess how much risk you can handle and get you out of the market before your losses become so large that it takes you years to recover.

Strategy 3: *Insuring Yourself with Puts*

There are times when investors just can't handle any downside. The third strategy for risk-averse investors is to use *market insurance.* The insurance will not protect you from inflation risks or opportunity risks, but it does offer a high degree of safety from the risks of the stock market. There are no perfect investments, but this is one of those strategies that is close to perfect for risk-averse investors who feel panic-stricken when the market falls.

Strategy 4: *Generating Income and Increasing Safety with Covered Calls*

There are times when investors want some protection but don't need the maximum protection that insurance provides. *Covered calls* provide some protection but can also increase income from your stocks. I introduce several different uses of calls and option strategies that may reduce your risk in the stock market by 10 to 20 percent. Don't get nervous when you hear the word o*ptions*. The options, or calls, discussed here are for the faint of heart and are used to *increase safety*. Covered-call writing involves contracts in which investors promise to sell their stocks at higher prices in return for premiums (money) paid to them. In later chapters I show you how to use options to increase returns but here the focus is on safety. Because different markets require different call strategies, I show you how to determine the best strategies for you.

Strategy 5: *Wearing Collars for Maximum Protection*

Collars are among the best strategies for protecting you on the downside while offering maximum safety. Although collars limit upside potential, they do assure limited downside risk so you can wear "collars" instead of "straight jackets." These strategies are for those who are nervous about short-term volatility in the market. Chapter 8 explains how to combine the strategies you learned in Chapter 6 (puts) and Chapter 7 (covered calls) to increase your returns and safety and reduce your costs. Although collars are strategies for risk-averse investors, even aggressive investors can find them useful in volatile markets as an exit strategy or to hedge a profitable portfolio.

Strategy 6: *Dollar Cost Averaging by Selling Puts, or Going for the Gold*

Selling puts offers the potential for some of the highest returns. Puts are promises to buy stocks when they have fallen. They can be used to increase safety through *dollar cost averaging* or putting fixed amounts of money into the stock market at regular intervals. But they can also be very risky and often have tax consequences that may minimize their attractiveness, so they must be monitored constantly.

As important as safety is, many investors seek to increase returns. If you can increase returns with additional safety, you have the best of all worlds. Selling puts, if used carefully, can be a way to get into stocks you want to own at a 20 percent discount. They can also be used as a way to increase returns. Although there are many strategies—straddles, spreads, collars, and so on—for which puts can be used, the presentation here is a simple one for investors who want to learn how to dollar cost average and purchase stocks at a lower price. It is a strategy that pays you for your patience and allows you to still make money while waiting for stocks to fall.

In the mid '90s, I wanted to buy Texas Instruments. It was trading at a price higher than I was willing to pay, so I sold a put, promising to buy it if it fell 10 percent. It never fell to the price at which I agreed to purchase it, so every three months I sold more puts. Finally, after years of selling puts, I made more money than if I had purchased the stock in the first place.

Unfortunately, not all "put selling" has such a happy ending. If not used carefully, it can be dangerous and destructive. Pat K. saw his account grow from $200,000 in 1996 to approximately $2,000,000—almost entirely by using puts. But then in 2000, his account fell in less than four months from $1,975,000 to $66,000! Pat has given us permission to tell his story and show you how he created such wealth and the mistakes he made that led to his losing millions of dollars so quickly.

Strategy 7: *Seeking Value and Teaching Old Dogs New Tricks*

Although growth strategies historically have outperformed value strategies, several approaches to value investing exist that increase returns as well as decrease risk. Although many investors gave up on value in the late 1990s, they are starting to look again at some of the tried and proven strategies that worked in the past. There is a new awareness that at different times *value strategies* work better than growth.

We examine several strategies—Dogs of the Dow, the Top Ten, and the Triple Play—as well as some ways to add even more safety and income to these strategies. All of these strategies have proven successful in many different markets, but you need to know when to use them.

Strategy 8: *Seeking Growth with PEGs*

The debate over value and growth has created a need to evaluate stocks in more than a single way. The tools and criteria used to evaluate value stocks are not applicable for growth stocks. Historically, finding growth stocks, especially midcap growth stocks with *price-earnings to growth ratios* of less than 1 can lead to returns of 19 percent or more. However, when PE to growth ratios (PEGs) are higher than 3, returns often become dismal and even negative. PEGs seek to find the best growth stocks.

Strategy 9: *Allocating Assets with a New Perspective*

Traditional asset allocation programs use colorful charts that suggest allocations between cash, bonds, and stocks. However, these simplistic allocations often don't offer the best protection or the potential for higher returns. *Asset allocation strategies* can add safety and balance and can often increase profitability relative to the market, but the traditional practice of allocating assets among stocks, bonds, and cash no longer works. Asset allocation strategies must now include inflation hedges and deflation hedges as well as value and growth investments and various levels of PEs, PEGs, betas, correlations, and standard deviations. (For those of you new to investing, don't be put off by the terminology. We provide the definitions you need as we explore these strategies, which are a lot simpler than they often sound.)

Asset allocation strategies should include investments that move in the opposite directions of each other. You need some investments that go up while others are falling. If done correctly, asset allocation can lead to peace of mind and performances that may match and even outperform the S&P.

Strategy 10: *Timing*

Timing is a strategy that has gotten terrible press over the years and probably rightly so. For years the prevailing theory was that timing was not important; rather, it was "time in the market" that mattered. However, time out of the market, or "time-outs," can also increase the potential for better returns. This strategy tends to be difficult for many investors to employ, and it is not tax efficient.

Timing at its best. If over the last 71 years you could have been in the market on every positive month and out on every negative month, your ten thousand dollars would have grown to *over nine billion dollars*. Yes, that is correct; it is billions of dollars! I hesitate to even mention something like this as it is impossible to have that kind of crystal ball, and most timing experiences have been pathetic at best. However, since studies have often shown that successful timing strategies can return twice as much as a buy-and-hold strategy, it is certainly worth considering.

Strategy 11: *Sector Rotation*

Probably one of the most successful investment strategies for increasing returns is *sector rotation:* moving investments from various sectors as the economy changes. Value Line reviewed many different strategies in the late '90s and discovered that sector rotation out-performed buy-and-hold and timing strategies. It found that average returns on buy-and-hold strategies for an S&P 500 index were 11 percent from 1973 through 1994. Market timing strategies, if done successfully, earned over 27 percent. But best of all, a successful sector rotation strategy yielded over 34 percent!

It is obvious that for those investors seeking higher returns, sector rotation is something to be considered. However, the more elaborate technical forecasting strategy requires an investor who is willing to pay attention to hundreds of variables. In short, a crystal ball would be nice, but without that, you need to invest time and attention. For the average investor, forecasting sector rotation strategies is not only cumbersome but often leads to failure. We will, however, show you sector rotation strategies that the average investor can employ without the more complicated forecasting strategies.

Strategy 12: *Tax Balancing to Increase Return; Location, Location, Location*

One of the easiest and safest ways to increase returns is to use some very simple, commonsense approaches to investing in the correct tax vehicles. Yet some of the biggest mistakes involve investors who neglect the tax ramifications of portfolios or who invest in all the wrong places.

Real estate agents frequently say that it isn't what you buy but where you buy and that the three most important things to remember for investing in real estate are *location, location, location.* Placing financial investments in the right location is also critical. The right investment vehicle saves on taxes, enhances trading ability, increases returns, and makes estate planning more attractive.

About the Format

At the beginning of each of the strategy chapters, you'll see a key and summary describing the type of investor best suited for the particular strategy (e.g., risk averse, aggressive, etc.), the safety of the strategy, its potential for high returns, and its tax consequences.

- The strategies with the highest safety have five stars (★★★★★).
- The strategies that have the potential to make the greatest returns have five dollar signs ($$$$$).
- Some strategies are very simple to employ but others need a bit more attention. The simplest strategies have five stars (★★★★★), and the more difficult have fewer.
- Some strategies are very tax efficient with few or no tax implications. Those that are the most tax efficient will have five dollar signs ($$$$$). But strategies that have large tax consequences have negative dollar signs (−$). If a strategy has $$$$$, you may want to consider it for a taxable account, but one with −$$$ is a warning that the strategy is best suited for an IRA or a tax-sheltered account. Some strategies will be tax neutral and may or may not impact your tax situation depending on how you use them. Those usually are designated with +$−$.

CHAPTER 2

Building a Strategy

Are you the person whose instruction booklet on a new bike says "Stop! Warning! Read the instructions first!" but you ignore the instructions and proceed anyway? Your bike might work fine. On the other hand, some day when you need your bike most, an improperly placed screw may fall out so that not only is your day ruined but your safety is also impaired. This chapter is that instruction booklet that most of us ignore and throw away. But unlike most instruction booklets, this chapter is possibly more important than the book itself. Some readers will like it because they will see some of themselves in it and will be able to relate to some of the situations. Others will want to get right to the strategies, feeling the prelude is irrelevant. But unless you already have a good sense of your risk tolerance, know how to make risk work for you, and have a good handle on your financial plan and goals, you should read this chapter.

You need to know where you are going before you can get there.

What This Chapter Is About

This chapter explores the various types of risks and shows you how to control and benefit from risks.

There are all kinds of risks, but if you know how to control them, they can work for you. Risks, in and of themselves, are not necessarily bad. It is when we don't understand risks and don't know how to protect ourselves from them that they become dangerous. *Risks can actually be beneficial.*

If there were no risks, there would be no chance for returns better than risk-free investments, such as Treasuries. If you are going to benefit from risk, you have to understand how to trade one risk for another. Each risk section is followed by a list of *solutions* for controlling the numerous types of risks.

We also show you how to set *realistic* goals (and the time mapping associated with them). *Risk tolerance and goals are the foundations of your financial plan.* Without the plan, you won't know what strategies will best suit your individual needs. You may be able to throw away the instruction booklet when it is some simple, unimportant item, but when it is something as important as your financial future, you need to start with the basics.

Understanding Risk

Do you really understand how much risk you can handle, how much downside your account can sustain before your dreams and goals are destroyed? Do you know when you will be able to add money and when you will need to withdraw funds and how the timing of those events will impact your savings plan?

How much of a fall is too much? If you were invested in the S&P 500 from March 2000 to March 2001 when it fell almost 27 percent,* or in the fall of 2001, you may have a pretty good sense of how much risk you can take. If you were invested in the Nasdaq index[†] or the over-the-counter market when it fell from 5,132 on March 6, 2000 to a low of 1,387 on September 21, 2001, or more than 72 percent, you probably do understand risk. How much were you down? How long will it take you to make up your losses? What kinds of returns are needed to bring you back from these big falls?

- If you were down 20 percent, you need to come back *25* percent to break even.
- If your account fell 30 percent, it needs to rally *42* percent to come back to even.
- If it fell 40 percent, you need a *66* percent rally to bring you back!
- And if it fell 50 percent, you need *100* percent to return to even!
- But even worse, if it fell 80 percent, as some of the popular technology stocks did from March 2000 to March 2001, you would need a home run, or *400* percent, a quadruple to bring you back *to even!*

Did you "feel the pain"? If you didn't suffer big losses during these corrections, you may not have as good an idea of how painful it is to drop 20 percent, 30 percent, or even

---

*The S&P traded at a high of 1,553 on March 20, 2000, and a low of 1,136 on March 26, 2001.
[†]You cannot actually trade the Nasdaq, an unmanaged index of 5,000 U.S. and non-U.S.-based companies, but you can trade indexes such as the QQQ that represent it.

40 percent; but I think it is important for you to consider how you would have handled it. During the Vietnam War, the U.S. Navy would send the pilots to "survival schools" before sending them to Vietnam. They would simulate imprisonment by the Vietcong. The logic was that the pilots and the navy needed to understand how much pain each man could handle before he was sent into combat with secret information. I am not sure it is important for all of us to "feel the pain" and to have suffered through the Nasdaq crisis any more than you had to be in New York in September 2001, or in a Vietcong prison to understand the pain.

You do not necessarily need to feel the pain, but you do have to understand it.

If you invested $10,000 in the QQQ, which mimics the Nasdaq index, on March 20, 2000, it was worth a little over $2,750 on April 2, 2001. You would have lost almost $7,250, or 72.5 percent. Many of the big Internet funds, as well as AT&T, Lucent, Qualcomm, and many more "safe" stocks were down 70 percent or 80 percent or more! Enron, at the time one of the largest energy companies, fell from $90 in 2000 to 25¢ in 2001. How long do you think it would take to make up an 80 percent loss? Let's assume the Internet funds do great and you could earn 30 percent a year in the future. How long would it take you to come back to even?

It would take 6 years at 30 percent just to break even. But 30 percent returns are extremely unlikely. What if the returns were only 12 percent a year, which is more typical of the S&P's historic returns? At 12 percent, it would take almost 15 years to break even. Could you hang in there that long? Often investors say they will change to safer investments as soon as they get back to even. Can you hold on that long without becoming stressed, ruining your dreams, or postponing your goals? What if the market doesn't go straight back up or there is another correction in the meantime? Then how long would it take you to break even?

I am not trying to be dramatic or to frighten you, but most of us cannot wait. It would mean putting too many of the important things in our life on hold. There is no foolproof way to get good returns without downside risk, but if you cannot or do not want to sit by and watch your assets disappear, then you need damage control.

You should not avoid investing in the market because you are afraid of the risk; instead, you should control the risk. Avoiding risk does not equal safety— controlling it does.

Having some hedges, some market insurance, and some safety allows you to minimize and control the downside so you don't have to wait for strong rallies to make up for big losses. Sure, the market could earn 30 percent and make up those losses quickly, but ask yourself if you really want to live waiting and watching, hoping and praying for the market to bring you back. Or would you rather have control over your own finances and your own life? If you can't handle wild swings and rides, then you need to learn strategies that allow you to share in much of the market's appreciation but avoid a lot of the downside and panic selling.

Determining Your Own Risk Level

Because you are unique, a good investment for your neighbor may be a terrible investment for you. Your age, tax bracket, personality, health, risk tolerance, and time horizon all play a role in the investments and strategies that you should select.

No set package of strategies or investments is suitable for everyone. When you select your strategies, think of yourself as a portfolio manager rather than a money manager. Portfolio managers work with individuals, building specific investment packages for their unique situations. Money managers work with money, building packages that may or may not be suitable for most investors. Money management gives everyone the same package. But if you are not the same as everyone else, you may need a portfolio that is unique to you. I show you how to be your own portfolio manager and how to build a financial plan to suit your special needs.

Financial Plan

By far the most important step in achieving your goals, controlling risks, and avoiding losses is to have a financial plan. Most investors spend hours trying to analyze hot stocks but only minutes evaluating insurance, asset allocation, strategies, tax minimization techniques, and other critical issues. Not only is analyzing stocks difficult and risky but also not worth the time because most studies show that *stock selection* accounts for only 6 percent of a portfolio's return.

Bottom-up versus top-down approach. When investors use a bottom-up approach, that is, spending most of their time researching and attempting to find great stocks instead of focusing on overall planning, they often lose sight of their goals and where they want to go. Instead, investors are better served with a top-down approach—that is, looking at their overall needs, where they want to go, determining what asset classes (real estate, bonds, stocks, etc.) they want, determining appropriate strategies and sectors, and only then worrying about individual stocks.

Think of the top-down approach in terms of a person going on a trip to Alaska. The person maps out where to go, makes a list of needs, and then goes shopping. This person goes to the winter clothes section and buys hats, mittens, winter jackets, boots, and the other items on the list. This is the *top-down approach.*

Now think of the person who just won a free trip and immediately goes right out shopping. Wonderful things are on sale, bargains are everywhere, and this person buys and buys—hats, bathing suits, boots, sandals, and anything else on sale that looks good. Great things at great prices! This is the *bottom-up approach.*

With the top-down approach, you know where you're going, you make a list of what you need, and then you look for it. Whether you are in Alaska or entering retirement, you have what you need and you get there on time.

Bottom-up investors buy great stocks at great prices but not because of their ability to achieve goals or relate to other investments in their portfolio. The bottom-up investor ends up in Alaska with bathing suits and lots of great items, but probably arrives late and finds he or she doesn't have what's needed to survive the cold.

Bottom-up investing can be an excellent approach for professional managers, especially managers of mutual funds. They are dealing with one small part of the picture; they are looking for value, stocks on sale. They don't have to worry about your specific needs. But you do, and you are looking for more than bargains; you are looking for securities or items you can use. If you look for bargains, you could end up with nothing but telecommunication stocks that may appreciate years down the road, but what you may need is income today.

Before you set out on your financial trip, take the top-down approach: know where you are going, what you need, and then invest in those securities that fit your needs.

Spend your time wisely. Most *studies* show that it is the overall plan, including the investment strategies and *asset allocations* that account for over 92 percent of the success of a portfolio.* Spend your time on the overall plan, where it really matters most! Your insight will be most valuable when you're planning your risk tolerance and goals, but when it comes to analyzing individual stocks, it is unlikely you will have unique insight that surpasses that of the pros. Rely on analysts and research such as the Value Line Investment Survey or Standard & Poor's Stock Reports to analyze stocks. Not only do they have easier access to company executives and information, but they have large teams of experts in various sectors. They often hire doctors, engineers, and manufacturers as consultants who evaluate the technology, new drugs, and the like. Unless you have access to that kind of expertise, leave the analysis to the consultants and pros and concentrate on the overall plan.

Start with the top-down approach: Set your goals, your time map, your risk tolerance, your asset classes, the proportion in each class, your sectors, and then select the stocks that fit those categories. Use the recommended stocks as a starting point, and then select the ones that suit your risk levels from those recommended stocks and investments. You will have to determine the entrance and exit points that are most suitable for you, but the basic stock research is not as important as the sectors, the market, the timing, the style, and the strategies. You will have enough to worry about, so leave the least important and most difficult part to the analysts.

---

*Brinson, Singer and Beebower, "Determinants of Portfolio Performance: An Update," *Financial Analyst Journal,* May/June 1991.

Set reasonable expectations and set exit and entrance points that are dependent on your unique risk tolerance. For most investors this top-down approach is more likely to lead to a plan of great strategies that will improve your income, your returns, and your safety. However, even before we can consider strategies, you need to know who you are and where you want to be 5, 10, 15, 20 years down the road. You need to understand how and when the strategies fit into your plan. Not only are your destinations unique, but the paths to getting there can be very different for different people.

> **Having a plan does not assure that you will get everything you want or need in life, but with a plan the probability of getting what you want is much greater.**

Creating a Plan

"If you don't know where you're going, you'll wind up somewhere else.
—Yogi Berra

The first step in building a portfolio is to have a plan.
What is a financial plan?

- It is a list of your goals, your dreams.
- It is a time map that illustrates outflows and inflows stretching out over your life and the life of those you care and provide for.
- It is a quantification of your goals.
- It is an analysis of how much risk you can handle.
- It is a list of strategies and investments that can get you where you want to go.

Write it down. Make sure you write down your plan so that you can monitor and analyze it. You are going to want to revisit it annually to make sure you are on track and that you are truly where you want to be. Be the buyer who goes into the store with a shopping list instead of the impulse buyer. It may be more fun to shop without a list, but it is too dangerous to invest without one.

> **A financial plan is a road map of where you want to go.**

Goals

Setting goals is the first step of your plan. What *are* your goals? Have you really sat and thought about them, written them down, and tried to quantify them? Usually it is difficult to quantify them, but I will show you some tricks that can help.

Although I usually assume men and women have similar needs when they invest, I have found over the years that when you ask men what their goals are, they usually give it to you in dollars or percentages. They may want to achieve a 20 percent return or they may want to have a million dollars when they retire. Women, on the other hand, usually state their goals in terms of life events. They want to retire at a certain age, help their children go to school and provide a nice wedding, take care of their parents, or emphasize other life issues. Men and women usually want the same things, but they express them differently.

It doesn't matter whether you start with quantifiable terms or qualitative ones, but you need to express your goals both ways.

Goals can be stated in many different ways.

- Peace of mind
- Stress-free life
- Educating children
- Healthy retirement
- Happy marriage
- Vacations
- New home
- New car
- Emotional independence
- Financial independence
- Avoid poverty
- Set up an educational trust
- Set up a charitable trust
- Minimize taxes
- Keep up with the market
- Outperform the market
- Achieve stability and consistent returns
- Keep up with inflation
- Outperform inflation
- Achieve a target return (e.g., 8 percent)
- Preserve capital
- Minimize estate taxes
- Avoid losses

There are some goals that money can't solve. Finding a spouse may be a goal that has little to do with money (unless you are a gold digger). But having a nice wedding can be a financial goal. You might not think of a super vacation as a financial goal, but without the money and a plan, it may never happen.

At first glance some of the goals listed above may not seem quantifiable. Emotional independence may seem to have little to do with financial goals, but often it relates to your ability to take care of yourself and survive on your own. Thus it is tied to financial independence, especially true for women in poor marriages who may be forced to stay in an emotionally painful situation because they lack financial resources. You can start by using current dollars for now, but later you will need to get a better handle on what you need in future dollars. I included tables in the appendix to help you convert present values into future values, or dollars, and to show you how much you need to save, at what rates, and for how long to achieve your dollar goals.

Date Needed	Goals	$ Needed	Future Value	Savings
1. _____	_____	_____	_____	_____
2. _____	_____	_____	_____	_____
3. _____	_____	_____	_____	_____
4. _____	_____	_____	_____	_____
5. _____	_____	_____	_____	_____
6. _____	_____	_____	_____	_____
7. _____	_____	_____	_____	_____
8. _____	_____	_____	_____	_____

- Write down the five most important things you want in life or five goals.
- Try to list them in the order in which they will occur (i.e., emergency funds, children's education, retirement, estate planning).
- Now write down all the necessities you need—taxes, insurance, and the like. (If you are wealthy and these are part of what you consider operating and maintenance expenses, you can skip them.)
- Next, list your other goals.
- Highlight the most important and necessary goals (realistically you may not be able to save enough to achieve all your goals, so you want to focus on the most important).
- Now estimate how much money you will need to achieve those goals or the most important one in today's dollars. (See the appendix and find the future value of your goal or goals in the future value table and the How Much Do I Have to Save? table.)
- Place your distributions from and contributions to your savings on a time map. I like to do it on graph paper and make the arrows proportional to the amounts. A simple visual can be a big help.

Time

Build a time map. Start your plan by building a time map that includes your goals, when you want to achieve them, how much you need for them, and how much you have to save today to achieve them.

The time map is just a visual tool; the dates and amounts don't have to be exact but should be realistic. Look for clusters where several distributions or large amounts of money are needed in very close periods.

Assume you are 38 years old with a three-year-old child, A. A simplistic time map for you may look like the one in Figure 2.1. In reality, you should work on a larger spread-

FIGURE 2.1 Time Map

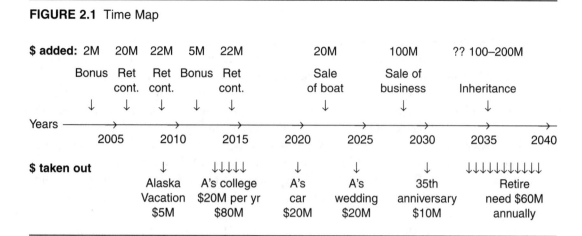

sheet with better estimates of contributions in and out. *Contribution* is abbreviated on our map to *cont.*

    Understanding goals and having a time map does not necessarily guarantee that you will achieve all you want or need, but it helps.

    According to a Bureau of Labor Statistics study done in the 1980s, over 90 percent of Americans will not be financially independent when they retire. That means most Americans will have to depend on the government, their children, their families, or charity to live a decent life. Most of us assume it will never happen to us, and we further assume that it is the person who was poor or lazy all his life who will retire in poverty. That is just not true.

    Most people do not want handouts. They want opportunity. They want independence and the ability to care for themselves and those they love. They want to be in control of their own l life. Sometimes we let the stock market take us on a ride, letting it control us as we ride it down, cross our fingers, and pray for it to rally. Then we watch it fall again, rise again, and feel that over the long run the best strategy is to grin and bear it, better known as buy and hold. Or worse, we avoid the market altogether or sell in a panic. We assume the market is out of our control. But it's not the market that is out of control it is usually ourselves. We have to be in control, set targets, set strategies, and have a plan to get in and out of the market on our terms, not the market's. As investors we need to take control so that we will be self-sufficient and independent.

> **Poverty is more than money and lack of opportunity. It is fear, stress, and lack of financial independence.**

> **Poverty means fear and lack of control. Wealth means independence and control.**

> **Grin and Bear It is the worst strategy. The next worst is Panic Selling.**

Taking Control

Three women and a cat. Many years ago, I met three women through my seminars. All were poor and in their 80s. They were a little bitter that they had been dealt such a terrible hand in life. But these were good women, women who in different circumstances would have been givers. They wanted to be givers, but instead they ended up takers on the receiving end and hating it. They were proud and refused welfare, wanting to be independent. But they couldn't be, and it frightened them.

Marie was the first one I met. She was a widow who had no savings and was receiving less than $200 a month from Social Security. She did have a house, a small one, and it was debt free. But even with a debt-free house and a little Social Security, she was unable to get by. She also had a cat, a cat that I would learn to hate, love, resent, and sometimes threaten to take to the pound.

I met Emma shortly afterward. She received a slightly larger Social Security check, almost $650 a month, and had a little over $2,000 in savings. However, her rent was going up $25 a month, which may not sound like a lot to you, but it meant Emma's going without heat during the winter and electricity in the summer. She barely got by before the rent hike, and it was going to be impossible after it. If she dipped into her savings, it would soon be gone and her dignity with it. She needed her savings which represented to her more than just money. It was her security, her sense of self-sufficiency. Emma was grumpy most of the time, but it was a cute grumpiness, a little like looking at a cute child with a pout on her face. She desperately wanted to preserve that $2,000. Without it she would feel poor, destitute, and afraid. I didn't know what to do. Should I suggest she invest it and try for a 12 percent return, which would be unlikely without some risk? Even though that would give her $25 a month and a shot at paying the heating bill, I knew she would be petrified if there was any downside. If we had a loss, she would not only have no electricity, but, much worse, she would lose her sense of security. She told me in no uncertain terms that I had to keep that $2,000 intact no matter what. She made me aware more than anyone else of how important the goal of *preservation of capital* could be. She was tough. No matter what I suggested, no matter how many times we went over the budget, I knew there was no solution. The $2,000 was sacred.

Then I met Helen! She changed everything. She was upbeat, and you could always hear a smile in her voice. She wasn't beautiful, but there was something about her that made her seem poised and attractive in an odd way. She must have been beautiful when she was young, and she had had money at one time. She was one of those happy, carefree people who probably squandered a lot of money during her life. I guess she was a person who went shopping without a list. Her eyesight was failing, her lipstick was always crooked, and her rouge was always in little red circles in the middle of her face. She reminded me of an aging movie star. Makeup was very important to her. "I hate this cheap makeup," she would say every time she sat in my office looking in the mirror, touching it up.

Poverty to Helen meant not having good lipstick.

Poverty to Emma meant fear of losing her $2,000.

Poverty to Marie meant fear of losing her house and being forced to depend on strangers.

Ironically, in spite of the fact that I had only known these three women for only a few years, they had a big impact on my life and led me to view risk differently. I sat many times with each of them before finally realizing I had a solution for them all: they could live together. They met, they agreed, and things seemed fine the first day. Unfortunately, the very next day Emma called. She hated Marie's cat. Then Helen called. She hated Emma's smoking. Marie called to say she hated these old ladies in her house. Every day I heard about the smelly cat litter, the fur balls in the corner, the meowing in the morning. Every day I heard the complaints about the cigarette smoke, poor table manners, waiting for the bathroom, and the noisy street. But even worse, every day I heard in their voices a pleading, a sense of helplessness, a quest for their independence again. They nagged me because they hated being dependent on someone else. Most of the time, I would laugh with them. I would tease them and joke about their complaints. The cat became the center of most of our jokes. Each one called me separately and spoke in soft whispers, in which there was always fear and anger that they were forced into a situation where they had to depend on others. I thought I was helping. I told them there was no other solution. Either they stopped fighting and got along or they would all be on the street. They stopped calling; they stopped complaining. I thought I had kept them off the street and made their lives a little better financially. But I probably hurt them more than I helped. I was the reminder of their dependence on others, and I made them face the fact that they had lost something valuable in their life. They had each lost the ability to take control of her own life. At one time, each had been in control of her own destiny. They had been independent women, but along the way something went wrong.

Emma died first, less than two years after I met her, of lung cancer. Ironically, by then I realized that the three women had grown close and had actually started to care for and love each other; and they had become grateful I put them together. Helen found Emma's death very hard to take—she loved Emma despite the complaining—and she feared being homeless. She seemed so upbeat when I met her, but somehow life had worn her down. When Emma died, Helen realized her support group was disappearing again, and all her fears resurfaced.

When Helen died, I finally understood why makeup was so important to her. I thought she was in her 80s, but she was almost 89 when I met her and over 90 when she died. She had hidden her age well; the crooked lipstick and rouge circles had done a good job. When she died, only Marie and I were there. Helen did have a good life and lots of friends at one time, but she had outlived those whom she cared about, and the others she claimed deserted her after she lost her money. She also claimed that her husband left money to her in a trust somewhere, but he didn't give her the details, and she never could find it. Even if I found it, it was too late.

Now Marie was alone again, and she refused to take in any more roommates, so each day was a struggle to survive. I wondered for a long time if putting the three women together was the right thing to do. They were happy once, and I think how different things would have been had they sat down at one time and planned their future. A plan would not have solved everything. They would have still lost the people they loved, but they might not have been on the verge of living on the street and might have been able to retain a sense of control over their lives. They might even have seen the warning signs earlier and been more prepared. Emma might have been able to make her little nest egg grow more. Helen might have found her trust (though I doubt it really existed) if she had kept better records. Marie could have been more diversified and might not have had all her money tied up in her house.

Although they were just three of many women in my life at that time, I realize what a big impact they had on my views of risk and saving. They were a scary lesson because none of them became poor as a result of illness or spousal desertion, which are the reasons many middle-class families fall into poverty. Like them, most of the poor I have, met, both men and women, are from good homes, work hard, and are well educated. But because of divorce, death of their spouse, bad luck or poor planning, and lack of insurance, they become impoverished. As the old Irish blessing advises, we have to learn to accept the things we can't change, but we must have the courage to change what can be changed. Much of what ruins our life we can change if we plan properly.

Poverty is fear. Most of the people I have met have done well but some not so well. They taught me that poverty comes in many forms—poverty of spirit as well as financial poverty. My daughter, Allyson, defines poverty as lack of opportunity. Each of us has to know our own meaning of poverty. To some, a lack of independence and sense of security can be more horrible than lack of money itself. Some people can be happy with little money if their goals aren't tied to it. Some must see their money continually grow to feel safe. Others just need to preserve their wealth to feel safe. Ironically, the poor and the wealthy have something in common as often the most important goal for both is the preservation of capital.

Stress that is related to money can ruin the best of lives and the best of relationships. Understanding risk and controlling your investments will give you a sense of security, a peace of mind that allows you to enjoy life every day instead of worrying. I hope that you can live without the stress that many people have experienced, because to me the greatest poverty is the lack of independence and control, and the fear and stress such a lack creates.

Risk Tolerance

Like goals, risk comes in all shapes and sizes in both our financial life and our personal life. It is important to understand risk and the kinds we can tolerate. We need to know how to make risk work for us.

Risk is not all bad; as a matter of fact, risk is what allows us to achieve higher returns.

The many types of risk discussed in this chapter are not meant to frighten you. Every risk offers us an opportunity to achieve and strive for higher returns, but we have to understand the risk and be aware that it exists. I cannot cover all risks, but I do show you ways to minimize the most important ones. Some of the risks discussed here are shown in Figure 2.2.

You will find no hard and fast rules in this book. Not only is everyone different, but usually most investors perceive their needs and risks differently. A 10 percent fall in investments for a young, single person may be tolerable and just part of the game. **Risk means different things to different people.** For a retiree on a fixed income, a 10 percent fall could mean the difference between a comfortable winter or a winter without heat and utilities.

Every person should work to determine his or her own risk levels, and then let a financial advisor be the guide through the investments that will achieve desired goals within the risk parameters. It is your responsibility to set goals and risk parameters. An advisor can only recommend strategies when you are understood.

Risk equals opportunity. There are no perfect solutions. If there were, all of us would be using them, which would dilute or reduce the returns. This is why risk has benefits. Investors who are willing to take a little more risk may be able to improve their returns over risk-free investments. I am not trying to make your investments risk free but merely trying to help you understand risk, minimize it when necessary, and control it so you can achieve higher returns.

Avoiding risk is not playing it safe; controlling risk is playing it safe. So many times investors avoid stocks and go into bonds thinking they are taking the safer route only to find they traded market risk for interest rate risk, credit risk, inflation, and the opportunity risk of bonds. When you think of investing in bonds or other so-called safe investments, remember Harriet's government bond in Chapter 1. **Safety is not avoiding risk— safety is controlling risk.**

FIGURE 2.2 Types of Risk

- Market risk
- Sector or style risk
- Specific risk
- Inflation risk
- Interest rate risk
- Volatility risk
- Event risk
- Opportunity risk

- Target risk
- Forecasting risk
- Credit risk
- Liquidity
- Location or record-keeping risks
- Loyalty
- Currency risk

CHAPTER 3

Risk Trade-Offs

One of the most important statistical tools that professional money managers utilize is correlation, which helps us determine how one investment moves in relation to another investment or in relation to the market. We use correlation to ensure that we have some investments that are moving up while others are going down, or investments that have negative or low correlation. What is correlation?

Think of two small sailboats out on a beautiful afternoon. In the first boat are septuplets, seven identical brothers who have grown up together and always thought and acted in very similar ways. The second boat has seven tourists, some of whom speak English, some of whom don't; some who know a little about sailing, but a few who don't; some who are old, and some who are young.

On boat #1—Someone yells, "Man overboard, starboard side."

All the brothers understood exactly what that meant, and all rushed to the starboard side. Unfortunately, because the brothers moved in the same direction, the boat tipped over and all the brothers ended up in the water.

On boat #2—Someone yells, "Man overboard, starboard side."

A couple of the passengers knew what was meant and went to the starboard side. A couple more didn't know which side starboard was, and they rushed to the other side, keeping the boat in balance. One didn't understand English at all, and when he saw the commotion he rushed to the back to get life jackets. One person stayed at the helm and kept steering the boat. The person overboard was saved, and the boat went on, balanced and steady.

Ironically, even though some of the reactions were not correct and the activity was chaotic, the fact that there was no relationship between the passengers kept the boat in balance. Having investments that move in opposite directions is *negative correlation*. It may not achieve the best returns, but it keeps the boat from tipping over. *Low correlation* is having investments that move in the same direction but not to the same degree. One may move down slowly while others are falling rapidly.

Risk

Risks are associated with investing in equities, bonds, and all other investments, including real estate and collectibles. If we can understand those risks and balance or trade them off, we can build portfolios that allow us to have many different risky investments and reduce the overall risk of our portfolio. For example, oil stocks can be very risky, very volatile, and cyclical. Bonds can be very risky in times of inflation. However, if you combine these two risky investments, you get one safer portfolio. The inflation risk of bonds will be balanced by the inflation protection of oil stocks, and the market risk of oil stocks will be balanced by the maturity guarantees of the bonds. The fact that both had low or negative correlation and move in different directions helps create a safer portfolio.

Stocks versus Bonds . . . Otherwise Known as Equities versus Debt

Equity. Equity is ownership in companies. When you purchase stocks you purchase a piece of the company, and you share in its profits and its failures. You have no guarantees and no contractual agreements on a specific return.

Debt. When you purchase a bond, you are lending money (or an IOU) to some entity. You will not share in any of the issuer's profits, and unless the issuer defaults on the bond, you don't share in its risks. In essence, you have loaned someone money. Your bond is a contractual agreement that states the term of the loan. This is debt. If you think of bonds as loans to a company or government entity, and CDs (certificates of deposit) as loans to a bank, it is easy to understand the risks of bonds and CDs.

Both equity and debt have risks. We will be looking at many of the risks, such as event, credit, loyalty, forecast, target, and liquidity risks, that relate to both.

Event Risk

By now, Y2K is a distant memory for most of us. Yet it unleashed a chain of events that affected all of us, even though the catastrophes, the end of the world, and the big problems that the engineers predicted never materialized. In many ways Y2K is probably the major reason for the volatile market from 1999 through 2001. Remember when everyone was afraid of the lights going out, banks failing, terrorist attacks, businesses going bankrupt, and the world coming to an end. Well, the Federal Reserve Board (the Fed) was watching, aware that it had to keep technology stable, keep tech companies growing, and make sure there was money in the economy to allow businesses and banks to survive in a possible crisis. The Fed especially had to ensure that those software companies monitoring the Y2K problems were viable and that communications and technology companies had the ability to solve the problems, to stay afloat, and to survive. Easy money was needed to ensure that new companies could develop and that investment banking firms could bring them public. When a new company is brought public, it is called an *initial public offering* (IPO). Companies also needed low rates, venture capital, and a lot of support from the investment community. The Federal Reserve accommodated with the necessary low rates and easy money policy. IPOs became the hottest game on Wall Street and everyone was playing along.

However, after January 1, 2000, passed without a whimper, the Fed no longer wanted all that money in the system, and so it started to pull the plug by raising interest rates. The party was over. The days of easy money were gone. The Fed began to turn its attention to inflation, wanting to slow the economy and cure the "irrational exuberance." In hindsight, maybe it eased too much, but with the information at hand and the Y2K scare appearing so real, easing was still probably the best decision that could have been made then. However, although most investors accepted the policy in 1999, there is still a lot of debate about whether the Fed should have ended the party so quickly. Raising rates so fast in 2000 sent the United States and the rest of the world into an economic tailspin that will take years for recovery.

What happened with Y2K and the subsequent Federal Reserve move can be classified mostly as *event risk*. But there is still more to the story. One of the sector rotation strategies discussed later shows how important it is to shift money out of stocks and bonds as interest rates rise. Early in 2000, as rates were rising, if you had gradually hedged your accounts more and shifted to cash as rates increased, then you probably did well. If the event had only been interest rates, we may have come out of 2000 in decent shape, especially as consumer confidence did not seem to suffer early on.

But the business community was another story. Business leaders also noticed what the Federal Reserve was doing, and they didn't like it. Businesses understand, and are aware of, the dangers of monetary policy, and they saw the warning signals early. As rates increase, it is harder and harder for people to spend, for businesses to expand, and for other businesses and consumers to buy their products. These were some early signals. Early in 2000, survey after survey showed that as many as 85 percent of businesses expected a recession. So what do you think they did? They pulled back, stopped hiring, stopped investing, depleted their inventories, and created a tremendous drop in economic growth. It became a self-fulfilling prophecy. If businesses hadn't believed there would be a recession and hadn't responded to those beliefs, the economic fall may not have occurred.

Even worse for the technology companies, most business had upgraded their systems before 2000 to be Y2K compliant, so no large demand was left for big technology items.

The new IPOs were failing in record numbers and selling equipment for pennies on the dollar. Most of the built-in obsolescence in technology and telecommunications equipment would not appear until late 2002, so there was no need to replace all the equipment purchased in 1999. The rest of the world also fell into an economic slump and had no money to buy. There were no buyers and a lot of inventory and supply. Businesses blamed the Federal Reserve Board and increasing interest rates. The Fed blamed "irrational exuberance." Although many of us saw it coming, I think very few expected business to show such a dramatic fall in economic growth. In late 2000, there was still a sense that not only did the Fed not know what it was doing but that its strategies wouldn't work and it had lost control over the economy.

It even surprised the Federal Reserve that its policies slowed down the economy as much as it did. But the Fed kept tightening, claiming that the economy was growing too fast. As the politicians kept talking about the large surplus, most of us started to believe that maybe the economy was so strong that it could survive the Fed's interest rate increases. That was the picture until November 2000!

With the elections, things got worse. Typically, November is the strongest month for the market. There was hope that Alan Greenspan, chairman of the Federal Reserve Board, would soon stop raising rates, that he had inflation under control, and that a drop in rates was likely. But then the elections occurred and *event risk* overtook all technical and seasonal factors. The elections would normally have been a small blip in the market trend because as as soon as most event risks are resolved, the market snaps back. As soon as the Supreme Court ruled that the election went to Bush, the Dow rallied 250 points in less than a half an hour. When the event risk was resolved, we had a V-shaped correction in which the market rallied quickly and dramatically after the big fall. But the story did not end there.

The greater risk. A greater event risk was looming over the market, not just a short-term event risk like the election. Less than an hour after the election dispute was resolved, Alan Greenspan spoke and nothing has been the same since! He told us that our economy had had one of the fastest and most dramatic falls from healthy high growth to an economy nearly on the verge of a recession. Suddenly the Dow fell 250 points—a 500-point swing in less than two hours. Who could have pulled out fast enough to spare themselves losses? The best economic forecasters could not predict the economic trends accurately. The market might have survived the event risk of the Y2K, the Fed's easing policy, then the tightening policy, and even the election stalemate. But the event risk the market could not handle was the loss of faith in the Federal Reserve. This is the worst kind of event risk, one that had no easy and quick resolution.

Event risk is usually completely unforeseen, such as the death of a president, the oil crisis in the early 70s, terrorist activities, and the bombing of Pearl Harbor. Even if we have warning signals, as with many political risks, they are usually too late when we get the first ones. Event risk is even increasing, because all of us get information so quickly and we all react to it at the same time, the swings in the market become more extreme.

The Twin Towers attack was an event risk of the worst kind, but for the market, the loss of faith in the Fed's ability to stop the bleeding in the economy was also an event risk. It led investors to realize that none of us should try to guess what the market is going to do. The best have tried and failed more often than not. Instead, we should have a strategy that helps us whether the market goes up or down and whether there is a recession or just a fast and dramatic fall in the health of the economy. We shouldn't get caught up in the semantics of whether there was actually a recession. The terminology doesn't matter. People were losing jobs in record numbers—the best and highest-paid jobs—businesses were failing, and the whole world's economies were suffering. Can it happen again? Probably, but maybe not as dramatically. Certainly, the volatility in the markets and the economy is getting more and more extreme and more and more difficult to solve with simple monetary tools.

Solutions for Controlling Event Risk

These are a few solutions for controlling event risk:

- Have something to protect yourself in good times and bad.
- Have investments with low or negative correlation and that move in different directions.
- Have market insurance on part of your account for short-term dramatic falls.
- Have some emergency funds set aside, so you are not forced to liquidate.
- Watch interest rates carefully and watch business activity.
- And most important: Don't assume you have a crystal ball.

Inflation Risk

It is almost a certainty that over time prices will continue to go up, and at some point inflation will rear its ugly head again. As technology has improved, we have seen items such as computers, telephones, and the like go down in price, but services, medical care, education, utilities, and most consumer goods tend to go up in price over time. As productivity increases, the likelihood of runaway inflation decreases, but there is always a chance that the economy may be too "exuberant," as Federal Reserve Chairman Greenspan would say. This is *inflation risk*.

Since 1926, inflation has eroded returns by an average of 3.17 percent per year. In the 1970s inflation reached 13.9 percent.* At the 3.17 percent historic rate of inflation, in 22 years you could buy only approximately half of what you can buy today. Can you

---

*The U.S. Department of Labor's Bureau of Labor Statistics shows inflation from 1980 to 2000 at 5.4 percent. Although inflation averaged less than 3 percent in the 1990s, it averaged over 5.4 percent if you include the 1980s.

live in half a house, drive half a car, eat half as much food, take half as much medicine, or use half as much heat or air-conditioning when you retire?

The longer your horizons, the worse inflation can look. What if we went out a little longer to 30 years? The outlook can get even bleaker. A postage stamp, for example, went up from 6 cents in 1971 to 34 cents in 2001. You need nearly six times as much money to mail the same letter. Are you an investor? The *Wall Street Journal* in 1971 cost 15 cents. Now it costs $1. Can you mail one-sixth of a letter or read one-sixth of a newspaper?

Let's assume inflation is 4 percent. How much will your money have to grow in order for you to buy the same amount of groceries that $100 will buy today?

In 5 years	$122
In 10 years	$148
In 15 years	$180
In 20 years	$219
In 25 years	$267

Build Inflation into Your Financial Plans

Inflation can silently destroy a portfolio. Too often when we plan our future, we set goals but forget to add in a cushion for inflation. Don't forget that every future dollar will buy a lot less than it can today. What you could buy today for $80,000 will cost you $175,200 in 20 years at a 4 percent inflation rate. *Planning for inflation is not easy, but it is necessary;* and when you plan your goals, always add in extra for inflation protection.

Solutions for Controlling Inflation Risk

For controlling the risk of inflation, include investments that have historically outperformed inflation, real estate, U.S. inflation-indexed Treasuries,* inflationary assets such as oil and gas, stocks, collectibles, tangible (or hard) assets (things you can touch and feel), participating indexed CDs, and investments that combine stocks and guarantees.

Include inflation rates into your portfolio. When determining needed returns, add a little extra for inflation, usually 2 to 4 percent.

Liquidity Risk

If an emergency occurs, or if the market falls dramatically, or if a great opportunity comes along and you have no money set aside to invest or spend, this is *liquidity risk.* When all

---

*These are U.S. government bonds that are guaranteed by the full faith and credit of the United States. They have semiannual interest payments based on a principal amount that increases as inflation increases.

your money is tied up in illiquid investments, such as pension plans, retirement plans, real estate, collectibles, and annuities, you will have to pay either large penalties or sell at discounted prices. When you are forced to liquidate investments early because of a need to raise cash, you have a liquidity trap. Illiquid investments are dangerous if you don't have some short-term emergency money set aside. Stocks and bonds are usually considered liquid. Although they are easy to sell, they can have liquidity risk if they have fallen in price because you may not want to sell at the bottom. That is why it is so important to have a liquidity map for your investments. Have some that you can get at for short-term goals, such as money market funds, short term Treasuries, and the like. Have others set aside for intermediate goals, such as stocks, short-term bonds, and liquid mutual funds. And have still others for little longer-term needs, such as mutual funds, retirement assets, annuities, and real estate.

Solutions for Controlling Liquidity Risk

Following are suggested solutions for controlling liquidity risk:

- Have two to three months of income in emergency funds.
- Have a plan.
- Have a time (liquidity) map that depicts your cash distribution needs and cash contributions over the years.

Opportunity Risk

When you have invested in CDs all your life and it is time to retire, but you can't because you were too afraid to invest in the stock market—that is *opportunity risk*. When you pass up a great bargain, because you forgot your credit card—that too is opportunity risk. When you can't buy the house of your dreams because you didn't have your credit lined up—that is opportunity risk. When you don't buy a great stock because you don't understand market insurance—that is opportunity risk.

When my husband Paul was a young Navy commander, he was stationed in the Pentagon in a highly secure, vaulted area. Until recently, I didn't know much about his job. He worked from 5 AM until late at night, and soon looked like a ghost because he was so white from lack of sunlight for months at a time. He worked with four other young Navy officers and a few engineers. Their assignment was to help bring to life the missile defense program ("Star Wars") that President Reagan so desperately wanted. Realizing that keeping American security safe from attack then depended on deterring decisions made in the Soviet Union, on which America had no control, President Reagan wanted a military strategy that would "protect Americans, not avenge them." He also felt that such a program was the best hope for bringing the Soviets to the negotiating table to reduce threats to the United States.

When all the admirals and generals briefed the president, they told him it was impossible to field a defense for another 10 to 13 years and that the technological risks were high. Needless to say, the president was not happy, feeling the safety of the free world depended on this program.

Paul came home happy and excited one night. He told me to watch carefully the next week in the *Washington Post*. Despite the risks, President Reagan publicly announced the Strategic Defense Initiative to the world—a dramatic change in American military policy that would "render ballistic missiles impotent and obsolete." Paul said this would change history. And it did.

President Reagan seized an opportunity that would cause the Soviets to believe they could not match U.S. technology, bringing them to adopt *glastnost* (openness), thereby giving the Russians an irreversible taste of freedom, and eventually to bring down the Berlin Wall and end Communism and the Soviet Union. Russia has even helped us in Afghanistan.

What impresses me the most was that if President Reagan had not seized that opportunity, life would be so different for us. He took a great risk in changing the direction of American military policy, but he weighed the risks and the rewards. The rewards outweighed the high technical and diplomatic risks. If he had not taken those risks, all of us would be suffering from opportunity costs and risks today.

In other words, opportunity risk is the failure to seize the moment, allowing great opportunities to slip by because we are afraid of the risk. Every investment has its risks and rewards. Again, I remind you that all risks are not necessarily bad. They give you opportunities to achieve higher goals. However, you want to make sure you determine the risk/reward ratio, and make sure the rewards make it worth taking the risk. Also, make sure that the probability of achieving your rewards is high or at least higher than the

Not ending the cold war because of fear of "stepping on someone's toes" is an opportunity risk.

probability of the risk's occurring. Sometimes the rewards are so high, such as the end of the cold war, and the risks are so low that it becomes obvious the chance is worth taking. Other times, the decision is not as clear-cut, or we may not understand the risks.

Before you invest, you have to think carefully and even write down what the risks and rewards are likely to be. For example, if you have a chance of making 10 percent in the stock market instead of 9 percent in a bond, yet the market has a probability of having a 50 percent fall, then you might want to go for the bond. However, if the market has a chance of returning 15 percent while bonds are returning 5 percent, and the market looks stable, then you might want to go into the market.

Solutions for Controlling Opportunity Risks

Following are suggested solutions for controlling opportunity risks:

- Don't let fear blind you.
- Don't play it safe all the time.

- Be aware that the greater risk may be the opportunities you miss.
- Know the risk and reward of each investment.
- Don't take risks unless the rewards are justified.
- Don't take risks unless there is a good probability that you will succeed.

Target Risk

When you have a specific goal that you need to achieve, you can quantify the goal. Once you have determined how much you need after adjusting for inflation, you can then determine how much you need to save and what returns are necessary. Setting targets helps us define our goals and makes our plans easier to achieve. If we don't achieve our targeted return, we not only would face losses but would also face the fact that our goals may have to be postponed. Missing your target can be disastrous.

In a perfect world, you could set your target, invest in a guaranteed investment like a zero coupon bond or a long-term government bond, and know you'll have all the money you need when you need it. But in the real world *target risk* abounds—that is, the risk of not meeting your goals because your targeted, or needed, returns didn't materialize.

Donna M.

Donna M. is a brilliant and beautiful woman with as generous a heart as anyone I've met. But her husband left her when she was in her 50s. Since then, she has worked for over 20 years but still cannot retire; she has to work even at the age of 72! She is determined not to live on government handouts and welfare. She has courage and accepts her lot in life. She had a goal, a clear idea of what it was, and was willing to save for it and take the necessary risk to try to achieve it. Without her plan and persistence, the best she could have hoped for was to have a decent vacation every few years and the possibility of retiring when she is in her late 80s. She had to sell vegetables from her garden to put food on the table. Without working experience, it is tough to get a good job no matter how bright you are, especially for a 50-year-old woman. When I met Donna in February 1993, she was 63 years old and cleaning hotel rooms. Our target was for her to retire in 15 years, but we realized it might not be possible. Everything had to go perfectly.

How do you build a plan around a targeted goal?

- Step 1: Determine how much income is needed in retirement. We assumed Donna would need $20,000 a year in income to retire.
- Step 2: Determine what kind of rate you feel comfortable relying on in retirement. We determined that 8 percent could be feasible. It may be a little high, but in her situation we did not have much choice.

- Step 3: Determine how much is needed at retirement to generate the income she would need. In order for Donna to generate $20,000 a year in income at 8 percent, our goal was to have a nest egg worth a minimum of $250,000 (if she wanted to keep her principal intact.
- Step 4: Normally, because retirement is such a critical goal, most of us should assume a conservative range of 8 to 10 percent for our expected returns. However, using 8 to 10 percent meant Donna had to save far more than was possible. The most she could save was 15 percent of her income, or $3,600, a year. However, there were no guaranteed safe investments that would turn her $3,600 annual savings safely into $250,000 in time for her to retire. While we were building up her nest egg, we had to strive for 12 percent.

To earn that kind of a return of 12 percent, she could not invest in bonds or CDs but had to be in the stock market, probably in growth stocks. Every little bump or fall in the market could set her back years, but if she took the safer path and earned only 4 percent in CDs, she would not be able to retire until her late 90s. If she took what looked like the safer way, saved $3,600 a year and earned 4 percent after 15 years (age 78), she would have only $107,000, not even close to her $250,000 target. At 4 percent she would have a retirement income of less than $5,000. Can you survive on $5,000 a year in today's economy? At 4 percent she would not have the $250,000 target she needed until age 92. What would you tell a 63-year-old woman who has very little money? What would you do in Donna's situation?

Go for the sure bet and play it safe at a 4 percent rate and be sure of being able to retire at 92? Or take a little more risk by going into the stock market and investing more aggressively with the hope of retiring at or before age 80?

Donna had no choice. She needed to build her account. She saved 15 percent of her income, and we went into the stock market. As bad as the market was in 2000 and in spite of the fact that Donna took more risk than she probably should have, she did not fare that badly. The much greater returns than we had anticipated in the 1990s allowed her to build up over $250,000 by March 2000. Ironically, Donna was still $113,000 better off than if she had played it safe in CDs at 5 percent.

She is still way ahead of target, and if she gets a 10 percent return in 2002, she has a good shot at retiring at the age of 74. If we had lost all that in 2000 and 2001, she would be facing a much bleaker future. But she would have an even bleaker future with the safer CDs. The point is that sometimes what seems like the riskier choice may be necessary, but when you are forced to take more risk than you can handle, try to insure and hedge some of it. And always, always, always **If you have a** have an exit strategy and take some of your profits off the table. **choice, don't**

When you reach your target and have your dreams within **squander it.** reach, think about playing it safe. You may have a choice and if you do—don't squander it or ignore it! Take the risk, but be aware of it, and do whatever you can do to control it so that you can still achieve the targeted returns you need.

After all those years of saving and being so close, Donna almost lost it all. But, fortunately, things have turned out for the best for her. Donna was a skilled investor, did her work, understood her goals, understood her risk tolerance, and worked closely with her financial advisor. She did everything right except perhaps holding on too long when we were at the top.

No one knows what the top is, so we need to remember to protect ourselves, to use stop losses, market insurance, rebalancing, and other strategies discussed in later chapters.

Solutions for Controlling Target Risks

The following are suggested solutions for controlling target risks:

- Quantify your goals, and adjust them for inflation.
- Select reasonable returns after inflation. Base your assumptions on realistic returns for more stable investments.
- Calculate how much you need to save at returns from the appropriate tables in the appendix. Strive for investments with more certainty as you get closer to your goals, such as guaranteed packages or combinations of equities and guarantees.
- Reevaluate goals, target returns, and risks frequently.

Forecast Risk

Look at our example above. Let's say you strived to achieve $65,000, and you reached your target, but then you find you need $80,000, not $65,000. That is *forecast risk.*

An easy solution for most investors saving for their children's school or for retirement is to invest in a zero coupon bond today, so you're certain to have the desired amount. The biggest problem is that although you are certain you may reach your target, your target may have moved. When your target changes, it is not market risk or interest rate risk. It is forecast risk. Usually, we forecast incorrectly because we don't account well enough for inflation and other possible changes that cause our targets to move.

Forecast risk refers to reaching your goals but discovering that you forecasted your needs and goals incorrectly, or you are striving for a moving target.

Solutions for Controlling Forecast Risk

Recommended solutions for controlling forecast risk include the following:

- Reevaluate inflation and other factors that may affect your forecasts.

- If your targets are many years away, save a little more at the early stages.
- Reevaluate your plans and target values frequently. You may find you are on target but that your target has moved up because of inflation or other factors.

Credit Risk

Credit risk is determined by a company's financial strength and its ability to remain solvent, to avoid defaults or bankruptcy, and to pay its debts. Basically, *credit risk* means the ability of a company to survive. We look at credit risk when we deal with bonds, AAA rated being the most solvent. It is also important to know the credit rating for stocks and if the company has the ability to survive. When a company's quality falls and the public no longer perceives that the company has the same degree of solvency as before, then we experience credit risk. Credit risk changes over the years, and even well-known companies can experience credit risk, which may include the risk that they may not only fall in price but may actually face extinction and bankruptcy, such as Enron, Kmart, or Polaroid. To evaluate a company's credit risk, look at the S&P or Moody's ratings.

Solutions for Controlling Credit Risk

Suggested solutions for controlling credit risk include the following:

- Know the rating of your bonds and stocks.
- If you are nervous about the credit risk of bonds, stick with quality: government bonds, insured municipals, high-rated bonds, and bank CDs. Only one ten-thousandth of 1 percent of insured municipals have failed in the United States.
- Diversify through stock and bond funds and trusts.

Loyalty Risk

I am not sure there was any risk more prevalent in 2000 than loyalty risk. I am as guilty of false loyalty to stocks as many of my clients.

Apple Pie and Motherhood

My dad was an army colonel. His whole life was built on loyalty: loyalty to the army, to the U.S. government, to his family, to his friends, and to AT&T. To him, AT&T was as sacred as apple pie and motherhood. Most Americans who owned stocks before the 1990s felt the same way. It was the most widely held stock in the United States and was the first and only stock for many investors.

My grandfather had worked for AT&T and passed the stock on to my mother when he died. My dad felt he could not sell it. Selling it would make him feel disloyal to my mom and to my grandfather. All the little extras that we were able to have in life came from AT&T dividends. AT&T put my dad's five children through college and gave him a sense of security that he would be able to provide for his grandchildren. When I had clients that refused to sell AT&T, or other stocks, I would think of my dad.

However, even AT&T could fall and did—over 80 percent! I had seen clients become so attached to certain stocks, especially when they worked for the companies, that they wouldn't sell no matter how low the stocks went. Usually the worst mistake investors make is to tie up too much of their wealth in their company stocks.

I have seen investors who worked for aggressive growth companies refuse to sell or dollar cost average out of their company stocks. Just as you dollar cost average *into* the market, you should dollar cost average *out*. Owners of AOL, Ciena, and Cisco stood by and watched them fall 30, 40, 60, 90 percent. One client's assets fell from $17 million to less than $2 million and had to change his lifestyle dramatically. I worked with a young mother worth over $2,500,000 in her company stock. She was going to retire at the end of 2000 and stay home with her two young children. Then the market crashed and her $2,500,000 is now less than $450,000. Her dreams of retiring are gone. Employees of Enron never had a chance to retire.

Emotion and loyalty to companies—and not just the high flyers—clouded objectivity and almost wiped out many dreams. I watched clients with value companies also suffer large losses because they held on too long to stocks like Norfolk Southern (NSC) or Waste Management (WMI). One of my brightest clients, a CFO of a Fortune 500 company who deals in finance all the time, still held on to his company stock, no matter how many times we discussed its overvaluation. He knew he was overweighted, and he knew the company did not have the best track record. He understood he was taking not only a large specific risk with the stock, but also sector risk. Even knowing that it was not the best financial decision, he still felt a sense of loyalty to the company.

All of these were people of character who felt they owed the companies loyalty because the companies had given them good income and good jobs for years. No matter how wonderful a company is, no matter how long you have owned its stock, no matter how much loyalty you feel to it when you work for them, don't ever let it take over more than 10 percent of your total wealth. In fact, you should probably never let any sector consume more than 20 percent of your wealth, and you should hold no more than 5 percent of any individual stock (unless required by company restrictions).

As an unknown author admonished: "Never fall in love with a stock. It can't love you back."

Before my dad died and after my nagging and pleading, he agreed to sell his AT&T. I felt so guilty that I was making him give up his "sixth child," so I held on. But finally we did sell it and got out at the high of $60. We also sold Lucent somewhere around $75. At the same time one of my friend's mom died, but because the children were slow in settling the estate, they were forced to sell AT&T at $13 and Lucent at $5. They lost over 60 percent of the value of the estate. Never get attached to a stock!

Solutions for Controlling Loyalty Risk

- Never put more than 20 percent of your money in any one sector.
- Never put more than 5 percent of your money in any one stock or investment.
- Never think a stock cannot fall, and sell when valuations change.
- Never place your loyalty to a company before your responsibility to be rationale.
- Don't fall in love with a stock because it cannot love you back.
- Don't get attached to anything except your family and friends. (They can love you back!)

Volatility Risk

The market goes up and the market goes down which is unlikely ever to change. When market swings to the upside and downside become greater and greater, then we say volatility is getting greater. Most of this book's remainder is dedicated to market risk, which is sometimes considered the same as *volatility risk*. It is basically a matter of semantics. However, sometimes the volatility increases so much that it needs a little more consideration than traditional, or what we consider normal, market risk. When volatility is extreme, you may want to consider more aggressive hedging and exit strategies that I discuss later. When you understand volatility, you can actually use it to increase your returns dramatically.

Solutions for Controlling Volatility Risk

Here are a few suggestions for controlling volatility risk.

- Look for negative or low correlation.
- Look for low beta stocks.
- Watch for funds, stocks, and investments with low standard deviations.
- Use hedging strategies, such as protective puts, covered calls, and collars.
- Use stop losses very carefully, as extreme volatility makes stop losses less attractive.

Recordkeeping Risk

Remember the story about my three older ladies who lived together in one house? One of them kept insisting that her husband set up a trust for her, but we could never find it. Maybe it existed and maybe it didn't, but she was forced to give up her dreams because of poor record keeping.

One of the first women I ever met at my seminars came to me with receipts of stocks and bonds that she found after her husband died. While he was alive, they lived a good life. She could never find the stocks or the bearer bonds they had, but with the receipts I was able to replace her stocks. Even though you can replace your lost stocks, replacement is not free, usually costing about 2 percent. It is almost impossible, however, to replace bearer bonds, which are issued to anyone who "bears" them. (The IRS now requires banks to report the names of individuals who bring the coupons in for redemption, so the income no longer can be hidden.) Because they are like cash, thieves like them, but unfortunately there is no way to replace them. The woman in my seminar died without ever finding those bearer bonds, which were worth over $300,000.

After my brother-in-law's father died, his family was throwing can after can of unwanted items away. They found in the basement lots of tinfoil packages, which they were throwing away. Thinking their dad was saving the foil and putting it in the basement. One day they unwrapped one, expecting to find just more foil inside. But they found hundreds of dollars instead! As they discovered more and more of these foil balls, they found thousands of dollars. They started to look in old books and found dollars there also. They were excited and thrilled to find the money, but they weren't so thrilled when they wondered how much they actually had thrown away.

If the father had shared information on where his valuables were hidden, everyone would have been wealthier. Make sure you let someone know where your checkbooks, tax records, keys, safe deposit boxes, and hundreds of other personal items are. It doesn't do any good if you keep good records but no one can find them.

Solutions for Controlling Recordkeeping Risk

Make a list of all your financial, legal, and medical advisors. **Make an important document locator and make sure a family member or friend knows where it is.**

Market Risk

The risks related to stocks are usually divided into three categories.

1. *Market risk* is the risk related to market movements as a whole.

2. *Sector* or *style risk* is the risk or impact associated with an industry or sector.
3. *Specific risk* is the risk inherent in an individual stock itself, that is, the risk related to earnings, momentum, fundamentals, quantitative factors, and technical data.

Most of us are aware of market risk. When the market goes up we make money, but when it goes down we lose money. By the third quarter of 2001, when 99.3 percent of all mutual funds were down, it was obvious that market risk was the major risk investors had to face. Although debatable, the general consensus is that 20 percent of a stock move is related to the stock itself, 60 percent to the market, and 20 percent to the sector. As you will see, most of the strategies in this book relate to all three of these risks. (When it is important to differentiate them, I will.)

The most important work on risk was done by Nobel Prize winner Dr. Henry Markowitz, who showed through his efficient frontier models the trade-offs between risks and returns. The higher the returns you seek, the higher the risks. His work also showed that diversification was the best way to eliminate specific risk: the more diversification, the less specific risk. Many theories show the ideal number of investments is between 20 and 32 to get the maximum benefits of diversification. Others say you only need 6 or 8 stocks, but the stocks require low correlation and should be in several sectors. For the most part, I assume 20 to 25 stocks will give you the best number to work with for my strategies. More than that does not reduce risk enough to make it worth the extra time, costs, and effort involved.

Many factors will affect a stock's price and moves. Some are unique to the stock and have nothing to do with the market or the sector. These unique moves related to the stock itself are called *specific risks* and can result from such factors as poor earnings, a change in market share, loss of leadership, and write-offs and are easy to find. Other factors, such as betas, correlation with the market, the relationship with other stocks in the sector, support and resistance levels, and so forth, are also important and are available in most research reports.

Past Performance

There is probably no investment that can compete with the stock market over the long run. If you had $10,000 invested in the S&P 500 from 1928 to December 31, 2000, it would be worth over $15,436,011 at the end of 2000. That $10,000 really did grow to *15 million dollars!* Pretty impressive! If you were lucky enough to have gotten into a good fund, you would have realized even more. Pioneer Fund grew to $86,325,013 during the same 72 years. Compare this with a Treasury bill, which grew to only $154,176.

If you took what appeared to be the safer path, you would have thousands of dollars, but if you took what appeared to be the riskier equity path, your estate could be worth 100 times more—over $15 million. Which path you take depends on where you want to go and how much risk you can take.

Although most of us should take the equity path, we need to have the right tools and a road map before we venture into what can truly be a jungle of unexpected risks.

In our example above, the period was 72 years, which is a long time; and not many of us would have that long to save. The traditional view of risk is that it decreases over time, meaning the longer you hold a portfolio, the more likely you will have positive returns. (But some Nobel Prize winners, such as Paul Samuelson, warn that time may not always bring about positive results.)

The market has been great in the past, but nothing is perfect.

Warnings

Did you ever notice that almost every advertisement or prospectus on mutual funds or investments reminds you that *past experience is not a predictor of future performance*? The warning is there to protect authors, companies, and financial advisors. But it is also there to make you aware that you cannot be complacent. The world is changing, and just because the past might have been good, bad, or volatile, it does not mean there will be a repetition of those situations.

Professional investors frequently use probability analysis when they look at the market. They rely on trends, past performance, and historical data to help them determine the future. Although not perfect, it is all we usually have. Although the past cannot predict the future, it is a starting point to help us determine risk. The problem with so many financial and retirement planning programs is that they look at the past performance of various assets, and stop there. They base future retirement estimates on these average returns. However, we cannot just look at the average returns but must look at the probability that those returns will occur. (A popular probability program often used in the financial world is called Monte Carlo.) This complicates our planning, but it is important when you look at those colorful asset allocation charts that you also understand what the probability is that you will get where you want to go.

Solutions for Controlling Market Risks

Because nearly all the strategies in this book address market risk, I am not going to examine carefully the solutions for controlling it here but instead will do so in detail in future chapters. For now, we can look at the following suggestions.

- Learn the risks associated with different investments (bonds, real estate, stocks, etc.) because risks differ from one investment to another.
- Find the opportunities and benefits of risks and exploit them.
- Use risk measurement tools.
- Trade off one risk against another.
- Use some of the 12 strategies to be discussed in later chapters.

- Build diversification into your portfolio by holding at least 20 to 25 stocks or mutual funds, indexes, and trusts.

Interest Rate Risk

Income investments such as bonds, high-dividend-paying stocks, preferred stocks, mortgages, and even bank certificates of deposit have *interest rate risk,* as well as inflation risk, credit risk, and opportunity risk.

The good news: We typically rely on these investments for income, but bonds have an additional value: they offer guarantees. We invest in bonds to give us peace of mind. They provide assurances that we will get all our money back at maturity.

The bad news: No matter which way interest rates go, there is a risk. If they go up, bonds will fall in value. This is *price risk.*

Falling interest rates can also be bad news, as we may have to reinvest our interest returns at lower and lower yields. This is *reinvestment risk.*

Interest Rate Risk: Part 1—Price Risk

We seem to be so aware of and often afraid of market risk and the risk associated with stocks but seldom pay attention to the risks related to other investments. Too often we consider bonds and CDs to be safe investments while forgetting they have risks also, especially interest rate risk, which can be very dangerous.

When Interest Rates Go Up

In the first chapter I told you about Harriet, the poor woman in Norfolk, Virginia, who bought a U.S. Treasury bond thinking it was safe. When interest rates went up, she couldn't sell her bond for the $10,000 that she had paid. If the bonds are for the short term, the price falls will be minimal. If the bonds mature many years away and rates go up, however, then the bonds will fall considerably.

When Interest Rates Go Down

But what if rates were to go down? Harriet would have been a winner. Her long bond would have been worth more money, not less. People would have paid her a premium for a bond paying 7 percent when they could only buy new ones paying 4, 5, or 6 percent.

Interest Rate Risk: Part 2—Reinvestment Risk

Interest rate risk is usually thought of as having two parts. One is the price risk associated with interest rates going up, and the other is reinvestment risk associated with interest rates going down.

When Interest Rates Go Up

When interest rates are increasing, investing in bonds can be risky because you are locking your money up for years. As interest rates went up, the value, or the price, of long-term bonds, such as Harriet's, went down. But what if Harriet hadn't needed the income, and she could have reinvested the interest? That interest would have earned more and more as the rates increased. Even though she would suffer from the price risk of the bond, the reinvestment benefits would work in her favor and she would trade off one risk against another. When investing in bonds, you have to look at how both price and reinvestment risks will have an impact on you. In general, when rates are rising, price risk tends to be threatening, but reinvestment risk tends to be helpful.

When Interest Rates Go Down

Remember Emma, the woman who had a $2,000 CD that she so desperately wanted to keep intact. If rates had fallen, she would be worse off, as was the case with many investors in 2001. These investors found that the high rates of the 1980s and 1990s were gone, and they had to reinvest their maturing CDs and short-term bonds at much lower rates. In this case, there was no price risk, but there was reinvestment risk.

> **Price risk:** When interest rates go up, bond prices go down.
> **Reinvestment risk:** When interest rates go down, reinvestment rates are lower.

Bonds

Bonds represent debt. When you purchase a bond or debt instrument, you share in none of the company's or bank's profits, and unless the issuer defaults on the debt, you do not share in its risk. In essence, you have loaned money. It is like an I.O.U. Your debt comes in the form of CDs when you loan money to a bank and bonds when you loan money to the government or companies. A bond is the contractual agreement that states the terms of the loan. This is debt.

Bonds come in a variety of sizes, types, quality, terms, and features. They range in safety from the most highly guaranteed government bonds to the currently popular, but often extremely risky, junk bonds. Bonds can be offered by corporations, the federal government, government agencies, municipalities (state and local), and banks through certificates of deposit (CDs). These investments have unique hybrids such as zeros, convertibles, annual put bonds, trusts, funds, notes, and adjustable-rate or floating-rate securities. They also have such features as call features and discounts or premium prices. Some stocks also carry interest rate risk, especially such high-dividend-yielding stocks as utilities.

For most of the topics, I use the word *bonds*, though theoretically government bonds have maturities of ten years or more and notes from two to ten years.

Targeted returns. Bonds are particularly attractive for investors seeking specific returns. If you have specific time frames and understand the interest rate risk of bonds, they can give you a sense of certainty about reaching your goals. Bonds come packaged in several shapes: individual bonds, bond trusts, and bond funds.

Why bonds? Why invest in bonds? Bonds offer guarantees. As we saw earlier, the stock market offers much better returns than do bonds over a longer period. If we think of the stock market in terms of the large companies represented by the S&P 500, then returns on stocks were 152 times better than Treasury bills or cash equivalents and 52 times greater than long-term government bonds from 1925 to 2000, according to Ibbotson Associates. Therefore, we certainly should not be rushing to buy bonds for high returns. If you want high returns, then buy antiques, stocks, or venture capital funds. But if you want guaranteed principal, then buy bonds. They give you peace of mind. But bonds have limited growth, inflation risk, credit risk, and opportunity risk.

Pros of buying bonds:

- Guarantee of principal if held to maturity
- Easy to understand
- Provides peace of mind
- Attractive for targeted goals
- Easy steps to eliminate most risks

Cons of buying bonds:

- Inflation risk
- Interest rate risk
- Opportunity risk
- Credit risk
- Difficult to diversify. You usually need to have $100,000 to get effective diversification for credit risk and interest rate risk.

Shapes. For lack of a better word, we can also purchase bonds in various *shapes*. They can come wrapped in trusts or funds as well as through direct purchase by individuals. The risks associated with bond mutual funds and bond trusts differ from the risks of individual bonds, so it is important to look at them separately.

Avoid Bond Mutual Funds

As we will see in later chapters, diversification is one of the best ways to increase safety. I talk a lot about the need to use mutual funds and other vehicles that allow you to diversify your risky stocks and risky investments. Mutual funds give you diversification. However, funds also have high hidden fees and have no guarantees, even bond mutual funds. You use funds for investments that have high risk, investments that need to be traded often, or investments that are difficult to invest in directly. These qualifications do not usually apply to bonds, (except for junk bonds) and, if you have adequate money, it is easy to invest in bonds directly. (Usually you need $100,000 to get adequate diversification in bonds.) Bonds are also relatively simple to understand and to research and have low fees and simple solutions for most of the risk, so there is seldom any need for investing in bond mutual funds. You invest in bonds for the *guarantee,* a guarantee that allows you to sleep at night. But be careful of bond mutual funds. Once you invest in a bond mutual fund, you sacrifice that bond guarantee. Bond mutual funds have no set maturity dates, no guarantees, and higher fees than bonds.

The pros of bond funds:

• Diversification
• Professional management
• Allow investors to participate in higher-returning vehicles used by professionals (junk bonds and lower-quality bonds) with a little more safety.

The cons of bond funds:

• Higher fees
• Professional management not as important with bonds as with small cap stocks or riskier investments
• No guarantees; no assurance of return of all your principal Not useful as a tool for targeted goals

Bond trusts versus funds. Bond trusts are packages of bonds that combine the best of bond funds and bonds. They provide diversification of a bond fund but also give you the guarantees and set maturity dates of bonds. Typically, you would want to diversify your bonds just as you would stocks or any other investment. To attain the proper diversification, you usually need a large sum of money. If you invest less than $100,000 in bonds, it is difficult to get the diversification you need. Bond funds give you diversification but with no guarantees.

Bond trusts are a good alternative for those with smaller amounts of money who want the diversification of a bond fund and the guarantees of bonds. Often these trusts contain 10 to 20 bonds, and, like bonds, they guarantee that you will get all your money back at maturity. (As with bonds, though, there are no guarantees if you sell before maturity dates.) In addition, you can buy in increments as small as $1,000.

The pros of bond trusts:

- Diversification
- Staggered, and sometimes laddered, maturities available
- Guaranteed principal if held to maturity
- Peace of mind

The cons of bond trusts:

- Higher fees than bonds
- Like bonds, have interest rate risk
- Not as liquid or as easy to sell as round lots of bonds
- Like bonds, returns over the long run much lower than stocks

Solutions for Controlling Interest Rate Risk

- Keep the equivalent of three months income in short-term instruments and liquid cash equivalents (money market, Treasury bills, CDs).
- Stagger or ladder maturities (have some principal come due each year).
- Diversify through trusts but avoid bond funds. Funds lack the guarantees of bonds and have higher hidden fees. (However, if you are investing in high-yield or junk bonds, then funds are usually safer than individual bonds because of the high degree of default or credit risk.)
- Use some adjustable rate or variable bonds.

FIGURE 3.1 Watch Interest Rate Risk

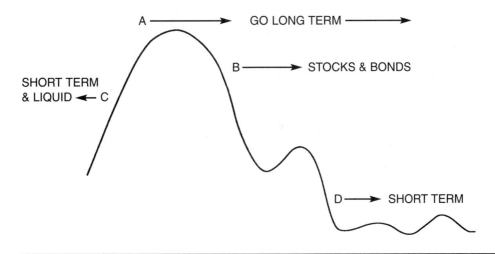

- Consider short-term bonds, short-term government mortgages, and CDs as well as a money market when rates are going up. Avoid long-term bonds when rates are going up, but when interest rates are high and you think they will fall soon, purchase long-term bonds, such as zeros and long-term Treasury bonds.
- Purchase short-term securities when you are not sure which way rates will go.

Summary

Every investment has a risk and a reward. Have a portfolio that trades the risk of every investment with the reward of another. First, list the risks and rewards of each investment you may be considering.

Stocks:

- *Risks:* market, sector, and specific risk, no guarantees, and high volatility (responds poorly to inflation news in short term)
- *Rewards*: Inflation protection over the long term, opportunity to achieve higher returns

Bonds:

- *Risks*: inflation risk, opportunity risk, credit and interest rate risk
- *Rewards*: guarantees and, if laddered or shorter term, relatively low volatility

Real estate:

- *Risks:* liquidity, high fees, and event risks
- *Rewards:* inflation protection

Money market and CDs:

- *Risks:* opportunity risk and inflation risk
- *Rewards:* liquidity

Remember that within each category there are also investments that have additional risks and rewards, such as oil stocks and REITS (real estate investment trusts), which may offer inflation protection but may tend to have cyclical volatility. Preferred stocks may offer some limited guarantees but have little potential for appreciation opportunities. Utilities may offer deflation protection but have less appreciation.

CHAPTER 4

Guaranteeing Your Investments

DEFINITION

Guaranteeing your investments is a strategy that combines insurance, government debt, or other debt with equities to protect principal.

KEY

Safety: ★★★★   Simplicity: ★★★★

High Returns: $$ Tax Consequences: +$–$

SUMMARY

Safety: This first strategy shows you ways to achieve guarantees, control risks, and get high degrees of safety. It gives you a glimpse at some of the prepackaged guaranteed investments and gives you a do-it-yourself formula to create your own guaranteed vehicles.

High Returns: Over the long run, these investments should outperform bonds and CDs because they allow you to participate in the market. During poor markets or large downfalls in the market, these strategies should actually outperform even stocks and allow you to stay in the stock market because of the guarantees. (The operative word here is "should".)

Simplicity: All of these strategies are easy to understand and easy to employ.

Tax Implication: Some of these strategies can have high tax consequences and should generally be used in pensions, IRAs, and low-tax-bracketed accounts. However, the tax consequences can often be reduced by using tax-free bonds instead of taxable bonds. I will note the tax consequences on each of them.

Who Should Consider These Investments?

These simple strategies may make you feel a lot more comfortable investing in volatile times. They are strategies for the *risk-averse* investor. I'll start with some of the simple steps to increase your safety and information such as risk measurements.

Risk Measurements

First we will look at some of the more popular risk measurements: betas, standard deviations, and correlations.

Prepackaged Guarantees

Next we will look at some of the prepackaged vehicles that offer you maturity guarantees and assurances that no matter how bad the market is, you will have all your money back at a predetermined time. Most of the investments I discuss are a combination of equities and some form of market insurance, bonds, or government insurance that I call *combos*. There are no perfect investments, but these provide the risk-averse investor considerable peace of mind. The main flaws with some of the prepackaged investments are the hidden fees and the caps on upside potential. The major benefits are the peace of mind and the assurances of getting back your principal.

There are no perfect investments and all investments have risk. If you cannot find the risk associated with an investment, then you know you are missing something and don't have a clear understanding of the investment.

Do-It-Yourself Guarantees

Finally, I'll show you some of the simple math tricks that allow you to create your own guaranteed vehicles. You can eliminate some of the fees and upside caps by creating your own guaranteed packages.

Building in Safety

If you know how much risk you can handle and where you want to go, you then have to decide which path you want to take: the more conservative, the more aggressive, or the middle of the road. The road with the highest returns has the greatest amount of bumps. Not only are there more bumps, but they are deeper.

Remember that safety is not equivalent to avoiding risk. Safety is understanding and controlling risk.

There are a few simple strategies you can use to make your portfolio safer. The more strategies you use, the more safety you will probably have. Enclosed later in this chapter is an *information scorecard* to help you keep score of your various investments.

Getting Started

Step 1. *Write down the potential rewards that are likely for each investment.* Investors seldom know what kind of returns they should expect from a stock. Don't invest if you do not understand the potential rewards. As you consider each investment, write down potential returns or benefits and the risks. You can get these data from Value Line or S&P Stock Reports.

Step 2. *Look at the economic factors that will have an impact on your investments.* Not only are most investors unlikely to know the potential returns but are often completely unaware of the most likely economic events that will have an impact on their portfolio. Write down the economic events that are likely to influence your investments. Look at your current portfolio. If rates go up, which investments will be hurt? If oil prices fall, which stocks will benefit and which will be hurt? If economic numbers are weak, which stocks will fall? If terrorist attacks continue, how will that influence your stocks?

Looking at economic events is another way for you to view risks. It is easier to understand the risks, if you also look at the impact of economic events on your investments, such as oil shortages, business weakness, drops in consumer confidence, unemployment increases, and so forth. For example, retail stores are very susceptible to low consumer confidence. Technology stocks are more vulnerable to weak business cycles. Real estate and car sales are vulnerable to interest rate moves and unemployment cycles. Airlines are vulnerable to oil price increases, but oil drillers are vulnerable to drops in oil prices. Hotels and travel are vulnerable to terrorist threats.

After you have written down the economic risk factors, it will be easy to understand what economic events will have an impact and the clues you should look for in the economy.

Step 3. *Trade off risks and rewards.* In addition to looking at the economic factors that might impact your investments, you have to look at the risks that are inherent in every investment. (Refer to Chapter 3, which explains many of the risks.) It is your job to find the risks and then make the best of them. Some risks will enhance your ability to achieve higher returns, some will offset other risks, and some will expose you to more downside losses than you can handle. You need to know the "enemy," so you can fend it off. You need to know the risks before you can reduce your exposure to them. For example, if you have invested too much in preferred stocks, utilities, and bonds, you have to know and understand that they will all be hurt when interest rates increase. Knowing that, when you hear the Federal Reserve will increase rates, then you can shift some of your money to less interest-rate-sensitive investments such as a money market fund or indexed CDs.

Look at a typical portfolio, writing down the potential returns, the risks that are inherent in the investments, and the economic events that might influence the risks or potentially influence them. For example:

- An oil stock may decrease your inflation risk, but because much of the return may come from dividends instead of appreciation, it may have greater tax risks.
- A biotech stock may have the greatest opportunity potential, but the greatest specific risk. An economic event that could impact it would be the discovery of a competing drug, changes in medical legislation, and even moral dilemmas.
- A utility stock might diminish market risk but usually has opportunity risk. Increasing interest rates, problems with nuclear power plants, shortages in energy supply, and rising energy costs could all impact it.

Now list the potential risks, rewards, and economic events that will have an impact on a piece of jewelry, an international fund, a new home, or an Oriental rug. There are no right or wrong answers, but thinking about it can be a big help. My answers are.

- A piece of jewelry may offer inflation protection, but the additional carrying costs for insurance and trading it may diminish its appreciation. Changes in the price of gold or gems, as well as increased insurance costs, could impact its value.
- An international fund may have good appreciation but currency risk. Political events and interest rates at home and abroad could have an influence.
- A new home may have inflation protection but have large liquidity risks. Environmental, political, and interest rate factors could impact it.

Every time inflation appeared imminent, I would tease my husband about buying an Oriental rug as a good inflation hedge. He would remind me by the time the kids wore it out, it was unlikely to be worth anything. But I got my Oriental rug anyhow because it gave *my husband peace.* Remember, peace of mind and reduction of stress are also worth something, even if they result in a little lower return. There are no right or wrong answers for each of us is unique and sees things differently, so now try to fill in the information scorecard in a subsequent section of this chapter.

Step 4. *Look at the different measurements of risk.* Now that you have thought through the different economic events and risks that will influence your stock, you need a way to measure those risks. Let's look at three risk measurement tools*: betas, standard deviations, and correlations.*

Betas can be found easily in most stock research reports, such as Zacks, Standard and Poor's, and Value Line. Although standard deviations and correlations can be calculated with math formulas, the actual number is not as important as the concept. If you can think of them intuitively, it will help you understand how to minimize and trade risks in your portfolio. Later chapters also look at support and resistance levels, PEs, PE-growth ratios, and dividend yields.

Before you can understand your investments, you need to list the risks, but you also need measurements that quantify risks in order to compare alternative investments. You should also write down these risk measurements when you are analyzing your investments.

Risk Measurements

Betas

One of the easiest ways to increase your safety in stocks is to know your betas.

Betas measure risk. They measure how sensitive your investment is to the market or how your investment moves relative to the market. For example, if the beta is greater than 1, it means the investment, historically, has moved up faster than the market. If the beta is lower than 1, it means the investment moves less than the market. If the beta is 1, it moves in line with the market.

Beta > 1: moves faster than market (attractive in bull markets)
Beta < 1: moves slower than market (attractive in bear markets)
Beta = 1: moves in line with market (attractive when you're comfortable with index returns)

If you are interested in safer investments, seek those that have lower betas, and if you are interested in achieving higher returns, consider stocks with higher betas. (But be careful when the market sours.)

Watch your betas. When you see the market is going up, you want high beta investments because it would mean your stocks will go up faster than the market. But when the market is falling, you want stocks with lower betas. Watch your betas carefully. The beta of a stock is usually listed in almost all research reports.

Sometimes you may want to shift your investments depending on how much risk you perceive in the market. You may just want to monitor them to assure yourself that your portfolio is made up of correct beta stocks. Have a risk analysis run on your portfolio quarterly, when your life is changing, or when the market is taking dramatic turns.

The Standard Deviation

Looking at a slice of the pie. When you are thinking of adding an individual stock to your portfolio, you should understand if the new stock makes the portfolio safer, riskier, or keeps the risk the same and how sensitive it is to moves in other stocks and the market. Therefore, when we look at well-diversified portfolios and are thinking of adding a stock, we look at the betas of the stock. We may want to reduce risk by striving for a portfolio with stocks of many different betas, some high, some low, and some in line with the market. Or we may want to strive for a portfolio with higher potential so we add stocks with high betas.

Looking at the whole pie. When we want to look at the risk of our whole portfolio, not just the impact of a new addition, we need to look deeper than betas. We want to know how much volatility, or how much the whole portfolio goes up and down, is the *standard deviation*. We tend to use the standard deviation when we are looking at a single stock on its own merit (not how much it adds to a portfolio) or a whole portfolio.

I am not going to discuss the standard deviation in much detail here because for our purposes we don't need to know how to calculate the standard deviation or all its applications. We only need to understand the basics.

What is the standard deviation or variance? You can think of the standard deviation or variance of your portfolio in several ways.

- How much volatility we have in our portfolio
- How much the portfolio goes up and down
- How big the swings are from our targeted or average returns
- How much the returns vary from average returns.

Minimizing the standard deviation. Because our goal is to have a low standard deviation, how can we minimize volatility, or the standard deviation? It is easy to reduce the standard deviation by adding different investments. The more numbers we have or, in our case, the more stocks, the smaller the standard deviation of the total portfolio. In a well-diversified portfolio, we hope to have stocks that move in different directions, and these different movements will decrease the volatility of the whole portfolio. You can eliminate much of the risk associated with individual stocks by diversification or by adding more stocks. Historically, the number most accepted in building a portfolio has ranged anywhere from 20 to 35 stocks. You can reduce the number of required stocks and volatility (standard deviation) even more by diversifying with low-correlation investments, investments in different sectors, or different styles of investment, such as income, growth, value, international, and so on.

Measuring the standard deviation. Watch your investment accounts monthly to see how much they fall and rise, and compare that to a market index that is similar to your portfolio. It will help you understand and become aware of how much volatility you are undertaking compared with the market. For example, if the market is trading each month in ranges from up or down plus or minus 5 percent and your account is making 20 to 30 percent swings, you know you are taking on more risk than the market is. Even if your returns are greater than the market's, you may not want to take the extra risk. If you are striving for higher returns, the extra risk may not bother you, but it is important to know how great the risk is so that you can hedge properly.*

Correlation

Remember the sailboats discussed in the previous chapter, with seven brothers in one boat and seven tourists in another. When someone yelled "man overboard," the seven brothers moved together, thus increasing the risk of the boat's sinking. But the seven tourists moved in different directions, maintaining stability and decreasing the risk of sinking. When you are trying to add safety to a portfolio, diversify with stocks that act differently. Correlation explains how stocks move in relationship with each other. If two stocks move up together, they have positive correlation. If one moves less than the other one, they could have low correlation. If they move in opposite directions—one is moving up while the other is moving down—this would be negative correlation.† One of the best ways to reduce risk in a portfolio is to find investments that move in the opposite direction to each other: when one stocks goes down, the other goes up. In reality it can be difficult to do the math. However, even without numbers, understanding the concept can be a tremendous help when building a portfolio.

Are there any investments with negative correlations? We used to think that gold moved in a different direction than bonds, that utilities moved in a different direction than oil, or that growth stocks moved in a different direction than value stocks, or bonds in a different direction than stocks. But over the years, these investments have tended to move together. In Chapter 5, I discuss an artificially created investment—market insurance— that truly has a negative correlation to the underlying securities. Strategies that exploit the idea of negative correlation.

Diversifying with similar investments does not decrease risk as much as does investing in stocks that move in different directions.

For now, if you can just think about the direction of your stocks and how they move under different situations, you will understand correlation. For example, if the price of oil went up, that might be good for the oil sector, but what would it do to the airline sector? These two sectors probably have a very low or negative correlation (i.e., oil stocks go up,

---

*It is important to compare to the correct indexes; that is, if you have mostly Nasdaq 100 or small cap stocks, don't expect to have the same volatility as the Dow. Compare instead to the Nasdaq 100 or the Russell small cap index.

†In reality, a correlation is a comparison of how stocks move around their averages, but for our purposes we can simply think of it in the terms stated above.

but airline stocks go down). Or if oil prices go up, what happens to oil drillers? Because oil drilling stocks would probably go up, they would have a positive correlation with oil stocks.

Information Score Card

When you are reviewing your investments, you should look at Standard and Poor's Stock Reports or the Value Line Investment Survey or check with your broker for risk measurements.

On the information scorecard, fill in all the relevant data for each of your investments: the *expected returns or rewards,* the *inherent risks,* and the *economic events* that may have an impact on your investment. Find the *betas and risk measurements* of stocks.

FIGURE 4.1 Information Scorecard

NAME _____   Symbol _____

Expected return _____   Your target return _____

Expected risk _____   The maximum downside _____

Beta_____   Standard deviation _____

Inherent risks of investment

ENTRANCE STRATEGIES (Where do you want to buy?):

PE _____   PEG _____

Support_____

EXIT STRATEGIES (Where do you want to sell?):

Current price_____   Target price_____

Resistance _____

What strategies do you want to use?

Selected strategy: Stop losses _____

                    Puts _____

                    Calls _____

Time frame:_____

Tax consequences: Long term _____

Where to Go from Here

As I mentioned above, investors often have no idea what to expect from a stock. If you found out that your expected return would only be 3 percent, would it be worth taking a lot of risk? On the other hand, if you found an investment that had a very high return, a very high probability that it would succeed, and very low risk, you might be willing to take the risk. Think of your investments in terms of reward/risk ratios. Without having some kind of sense of what you can expect from a stock, why would you want to invest in it? The next section walks you through ideas that may help you think of the rewards (the expected returns) as they relate to the amount of risk you are willing to take.

What Kinds of Returns Can You Expect?

There are trade-offs in any investment scenario, especially between returns and risk. Theoretically, the more risk you take, the higher the returns you can expect. I'll take the license to adapt one of the most famous formulas in the financial world that was created by Nobel Prize winner Harry Markowitz. The premise of the formula is that the more risk you are willing to take, the greater your returns will be (this is still debatable).

First, we'll look at two of the ideas discussed above: the potential return of your investment and its risk. I then examine them to see how they have an impact on each other mathematically. Don't worry, this is a cinch, even for those who flunked fifth grade math.

Risk Premium

First think about the fact that over the long run Ibbotson Associates has shown that large cap stocks have averaged a return of about 11 percent, but Treasury bills have earned only 3.8 percent. The person who takes the risk of going into the large company stocks earns over 7 percent more than the person who invests in Treasuries. This is called the *risk premium,* or the excess return. It is the extra return that you are rewarded with for taking risk. Had you invested in small company stocks, which have averaged returns of about 12.4 percent, according to Ibbotson, your risk premium would be 8.6 percent. The risk premium therefore is the difference between the stock market and the risk-free investment.

Expected Returns

Your expected return, or how much you can expect to make on your investment, will equal the risk-free return such as that on Treasury bills plus the amount of risk you are willing to take (measured by betas) times the risk premium of your portfolio.

Sounds like a mouthful, but all you simply need to know is what the Treasury's and stock market's historic rates have been and the risk of your stock. I'm going to use beta as our risk measurement, which you can find in almost all research reports.

Expected returns = Treasury returns + Risk (Market returns – Treasury returns)

Sometimes you will see the term *risk premium* used in the formula. Just remember that the risk premium is simply the difference between market returns and Treasury bill rates. To make the examples easier to work with, I'll round the market returns to 12 percent and the Treasury's to 4 percent. Therefore, you were paid 8 percent to take the risk to go into the stock market. Your risk premium was 8 percent. Or simply put:

Expected returns = Treasury returns + Beta (risk premium)

Example 1. Assume your stock has a beta of 1, or the same risk as the market. Logically, if it has the same risk as the market, you should expect to get the same returns as the market.

Expected return = Risk-free Treasury rate + Beta (market rate – Treasury rate)

Expected return = 4% + 1 (12 – 4%) = 4% + 1 (8%) = 12%

Your stock has a 12 percent expected rate of return, which is the same as the stock market. This is logical because they both have a beta of one.

Example 2. Now let's assume your stock has 20 percent more risk than the market, or a 1.2 beta. What is your expected return?

Your expected return = 4% Treasury rate + 1.20 (the beta)
multiplied by the risk premium of 8%

Expected return = 4 + 1.20 (12–4) = 4 + 1.20 (8) = 4 + 9.6 = 13.6%

Your expected return is 13.6 percent. Simply put, if you were willing to take 20 percent more risk than the market, you could expect to have a return higher than the market return of 12 percent. You would thus need to be rewarded for the extra risk. If your stock has a beta of higher than one but returns less than the market, then you have a poor risk/reward ratio.

Example 3. Perhaps you want to take less risk than the market. How much would taking less risk reduce your return? Let's assume you want to be 20 percent safer than the market, which is the same as taking 80 percent of the market risk.

Expected return = Treasury rate + Risk multiplied by the Risk premium

Expected return = 4% + .80 (8%) = 10.4%

Would you be happy with a 10.4 percent return if you were 20 percent safer than the market?

The point of these exercises is to show you there is a relationship between risk and reward and to give you tools to help you think through that relationship. Debate still exists about whether taking more risk actually results in longer-term higher rewards. There are also ways to decrease risk without impacting returns as dramatically, and those are the strategies that we will explore, ways of reducing the risk while still achieving returns in line with or above the market. But this chapter concentrates on lowering the risk and protecting your principal. When we do lower the risk, it will in most cases lower our returns versus what we could expect from the market. However, if you were nervous and didn't have some way to protect your portfolio, you might never go into the market. These strategies at least give you an opportunity to perform better than bonds, CDs, or savings accounts.

Guaranteeing Your Principal: The Rip Van Winkle Approach

After the extreme volatility of the last few years, you may have a low risk tolerance for large downside swings. You might be able to tolerate some risk and sleep at night if you knew that in ten years you would have all your money back, no matter how poorly the market did. Or instead, let's say you could invest in the stock market and still know that in ten years you could be guaranteed that you did at least as well as having your money in a savings account at 3 percent or 5 percent. Would that make you more comfortable about investing in stocks? If you want that peace of mind, it *is* available.

If you want to share in a large portion of the stock market's gains but still want guarantees that you'll have all your money back and earn returns at least equal to a savings account, then this strategy is for you!

How to Guarantee Your Investments

Guaranteeing your investments relies on a simple, not very exciting, math strategy, but it can make us feel more comfortable if we have longer-term horizons and can park our money for 5, 10, 20, 30, 40, or any other number of years.

To guarantee your investments, simply match government bonds, CDs, annuities, zeros, and municipals to offset the risks of your stock portfolio. You may be wondering how we are combining two risky investments—bonds and stocks—to get safer investments. As discussed previously, there are trade-offs in risks. The market risk of stocks is balanced against the guarantees of bonds. The inflation and opportunity risk of bonds is a trade-off for the appreciation potential of stocks.

I'll be using the guarantees of bonds frequently to offset some of the market's risk and using the potential of stocks to outperform inflation and offer opportunities for achieving higher returns to offset the historically lower returns of bonds.

Using Combos

This section concentrates on prepackaged investments, which are usually combinations of stocks and bonds. Let's call these guaranteed investments *combos,* a combination of equities and guarantees. (In the last section of this chapter, you'll learn how to create these investments yourself.)

Prepackaged guaranteed investments include the following:

- Indexed CDs
- Pathfinders and Government Securities Equity Trusts (G/SETs)
- Principal protected notes
- Annuities and protector insurance for mutual funds

Indexed CDs

One of the simplest and most straightforward of these prepackaged combos are indexed CDs, technically called *participating* or *equity-linked callable certificates of deposit.*

What is a CD? CDs or certificates of deposit are loans from banks. A bank is borrowing money from you with the guarantee that at a certain maturity date it will pay you back. The nice part about CDs is that most Americans find the federal insurance very attractive. The Federal Deposit Insurance Corporation (FDIC), an agency of the federal government, guarantees up to $100,000 of your money back in case of a bank's default. (You would spread the money around to several banks if you have more than $100,000.) The FDIC guarantees the return of your principal only if the bank defaults, not if you cash your CD in early. If you cash it in early, you take the same interest rate risk described above or you pay the bank a penalty.

CDs give you government guarantees but no inflation protection. CDs provide government guarantees, but remember that the biggest drawback of bonds and CDs is not keeping up with inflation, nor do they offer us the high returns associated with the stock market. However, if instead of paying you a fixed interest, a CD offered to give you the returns of the market, then you would have the best of both worlds.

On the surface this is what participating indexed CDs do: they combine government guarantees with stock market returns. They can be tied to the S&P 500, the Dow, or even the Nasdaq 100, so you can easily build a well-diversified portfolio with bonds and stock market returns. You can get coverage in hundreds of sectors. The pros are extremely attractive: government guarantees, participation in stock market returns, and simplicity. *The pros, however, are only in theory; the real world works differently.*

Sounds too good to be true. There seems to be almost nothing negative about these investments. However, there is no perfect investment, so what you will usually find in the fine print is that the CDs are *callable,* which means that the bank can call back your loan before maturity—pay back your money before the loan is due. Why would the bank want to do that? If the market is doing really well, the bank wants the ability to pay you back before the interest it owes you gets too high. This is to protect the bank if the market runs up very high.

So the major flaw of these investments is that they have a cap on the upside appreciation you can achieve. Although they do let you share in a large part of the market's upside, it is seldom all of it.

> **The major flaw of indexed CDs is limited upside because they are callable.**

As examples, let's look at two different participating indexed CDs that were trading in June 2001. The first will be linked to the S&P 500 and the second to the Nasdaq 100.

S&P 500–Linked CD. Assume you purchase a $10,000 CD in June 2000. You know in 2007 you will have all your money back, and you know if the market does well, you have earned a variable interest rate that is tied to the S&P 500, or what we refer to as the stock market. You do not know the final amount because your return is tied to the stock market and the bank may call or pay back early on your CD, but what you do know is that you will get all your money back at maturity.

If you want to know what the limits to your returns are, you would look at the call features, or at what prices the bank can call your certificate back from you. On a typical CD in 2001 that was linked to the S&P, you could expect to receive a maximum of 9 percent simple interest annually, no matter how high the market went. That's not as great as the average 12 percent historical market return . . . but on the other hand the market has also fallen two out of every five years, and knowing that you will have no downside may make it worth giving up 3 percent on the upside. Your risk here is giving up a 3 percent return on average per year for the reward of having no downside.

S&P 500–linked CD

Callable June 2003 @ 118; the most you can make if called in two years is
18 percent.

Callable June 2004 @ 127; the most you can make if called in three years is
27 percent.

Callable June 2005 @ 136; the most you can make if called in four years is
36 percent.

Callable June 2006 @ 145; the most you can make if called in five years is
45 percent.

If held to maturity, the highest returns you would likely get are 9 percent annual returns (not compounded). Of course, over the years the rates will change, and in the future you could get much higher or lower rates. I used this as an example of what was typically offered in June 2001 so you could work with a real example. Although your returns are tied to the S&P, you really only earn up to 9 percent and do not share in all the upside potential. That would be too good to be true. The nice part, though, is if the market went down 50 percent, you would not want market returns; and with the index CDs, you don't share in any of that downside. You still get all your money back. Although the odds are very unlikely that the market would go down that much over a six-year period, no one knows.

Nasdaq 100–Linked CD. In 2001, you fared a little better with the Nasdaq 100 Index–Linked CDs because of the potential to earn up to a simple interest rate of 10 percent per year (versus the S&P-linked returns of 9 percent). However, the Nasdaq historically has done even better than the S&P 500 so there is an even larger trade-off in returns for safety.

Pros:

- FDIC insurance: same guarantees as any other certificates of deposit.
- Peace of mind.
- Ability to participate in some of the upside of the market without any downside.
- Part of your return is taxed at capital gains rates.

Cons:

- Although these often appear to offer the same upside potential as the market, the fact that the banks can call them before maturity limits your upside.
- Part of your return is taxable as ordinary income.

Guaranteed Investment Trusts

Many prepackaged zero and equity packages are offered by brokerage firms. Each firm has its unique twists and uses different names, but basically they offer you the same peace of mind and ability to strive for some of the stock market's outstanding returns. PaineWebber calls theirs Pathfinders, Prudential Securities calls them G/SET, and Merrill Lynch has a variety of RUMS, MITTS, and the like. Although each varies slightly, all are packages of equities and guaranteed vehicles. They tend to have an advantage over indexed CDs discussed earlier because they have no upside caps. However, they also pose the likelihood in good markets of underperforming the underlying stocks or funds.

I start with PaineWebber's Pathfinders and Prudential Securities' G/SET because they demonstrate a simple and straightforward concept. PaineWebber's Pathfinders is a combination of U.S. Treasury zero-coupon bonds and a fixed package of stocks (trusts). Prudential Securities' G/SET is a combination of U.S. Treasury zero-coupon bonds and a mutual fund.

The basic difference is that PaineWebber's stocks remain the same or are "passive" packages of stocks, but Prudential's are combined with a fund that allows active management of the stocks. Neither is necessarily better. (The pros and cons of active versus passive management are discussed in later chapters.) Certain tax advantages accrue to passive trusts and there are opportunity advantages of active management of the funds in the G/SET. A few differences in the termination value exist also; PaineWebber offers guarantees of principal only, but the G/SET guarantees a return of principal *plus* a minimum return. If you are interested in these, you should call the firms for more information and a prospectus.

Guaranteed Investment Trusts

Although I describe the G/SET only, you can get information easily from PaineWebber about the Pathfinder. The differences between the two do not significantly influence our rationale.

The G/Sets are simply a combination of U.S. Treasury zero-coupon bonds and mutual funds. In 2000, it was priced at $12.50 a unit. The trusts invest enough in the zero-coupon bonds so that they can guarantee you that at maturity (usually 14 years) you will get back $15.00. Thus, you are assured of not only getting all your funds back but also a small return. But the best part is if the funds go up, you get all that appreciation in addition to the minimum returns on the zeros.

There are several different G/SETs, some combined with aggressive funds, some with more conservative, and so forth. It is unlikely that over a long period of time the market will fall dramatically, but if it did you know you will have your money back.

It seems so simple that it doesn't seem worth discussing further, but there are a couple of things to keep in mind.

Look for bargains and sales. Before maturity, G/SETs will move up or down with the market. If they are down, you may be able to buy them at a discount. For example, if you can purchase a two-year-old G/SET for $9.00 (the price in 2001), you will have an even better guarantee and built-in return. You know it will mature at $15.00, so you have a much larger guaranteed return than the person who bought it new at $12.50. Your guarantee is that you will make at least $6.00 on your $9.00 investment over only 12 years, or 66 percent over 12 years for a simple annual return of 5.5 percent plus the full return on the mutual fund portion. The person who paid $12.50 and has to wait 14 years will only be guaranteed $15.00, or a 20 percent return for 14 years, that is, less than 2 percent a year. A great way to buy a G/SET is on the secondary market when it has fallen in value, because you have a much higher guaranteed annual return than the investor who pur-

---

FIGURE 4.2 What Happens If Funds Returns Equal 10 Percent Per Year?

$12,500

$6,250 Fund $6.250 U.S. Treasury zero coupon
↓   ↓
14 years later $23,734   + $15,000

= total return = $23,734 from the mutual fund @ 10 percent and $15,000 from zero Treasury (@ approx. 6.40 percent) = $38,734 or more than triple.

---

chased on initial price. And the maturity dates will be shorter! If you do see the market falling, ask your broker to check the secondary market for G/SETs.

The best move is to buy an older G/SET at a discount—the guarantee is higher and the wait shorter.

Avoid paying a premium. If you invest when the market is up and you pay $15 or more, the guaranteed price is still only $15, even if you pay more. If you want assurance of a certain return, then you want to make sure you do not pay a premium or more than the guarantees. It is not necessarily bad to pay a premium (more than par), but it does reduce your guarantee, even though it still allows you to share in the appreciation of the fund.

Also remember to look at the funds that are combined with zeros. I like to use them for my risky funds, as those are the ones that I want the most insurance for and the ones least likely to give me peace of mind. You should insure items and things in life that have the greatest risk, so I tend not to insure my safer investments. But you would have to decide what is the best for you based on *your* risk tolerance (not mine). Some of these funds are very aggressive, some more conservative.

The pros of guaranteed investment trusts:

- Simplicity
- Peace of mind
- In the above example, if the underlying mutual fund grows by only 5 percent, you will double your money by maturity. At 10 percent you would triple your money, and if the fund grows 15 percent annually, you would quadruple your money.
- Assurances that if you hold until maturity you get all your money back
- Stocks offer you appreciation.
- Usually can use for target investing
- Makes attractive additions for "safe money" or for safer ways to get into risky investments, such as emerging market funds.
- Can be more attractive than indexed CDs because there are no call features that cap the upside.

The cons of guaranteed securities equity trusts:

- The odds are that over a long period of time the protection may be unnecessary.
- The odds are that if you invested in the stock market or good funds over a 14-year to 15-year period, you would do a lot better than with the trusts.
- There are hidden fees in these trusts that are much higher than if you created your own combos, sometimes as high as 4 percent.
- The full guarantee exists only if you buy at par or less and hold until maturity.
- Zeros have tax consequences so these are usually more appropriate for tax-deferred accounts.
- If interest rates go up, both the zeros and bonds as well as the stocks are likely to fall, so the volatility before maturity can be very extreme—it is only at the maturity date that you have the guarantees.
- Although liquid, they can only trade at the end of the day and do not trade on the exchanges.

Now after looking at the pros and cons, would you want to put all your money in these trusts? Probably not all of it, but wouldn't it be nice if on your time map you had some guarantees along the way at different points that you would not have to worry about. Look at your time map to see where it is critical that you have the certainty that all your money will be returned to you.

Principal Protected and Equity-Linked Notes (ELNs): MITTS, RUMS, and a Whole Pile of Other Good Things

Principal protected equity-linked notes, are much like the equity-linked CDs, except that instead of being linked to FDIC-insured CDs, these equities are linked to a bond or a note. These are debt instruments that are generally designed to return 100 percent of the original investment at maturity, but they differ from standard bonds in that the returns are determined by the appreciation of an underlying equity, and therefore we get the term *equity-linked*. The underlying equity may be a single stock, a basket of stocks, options on stocks, or an equity index. As with CDs, your principal is guaranteed, but you forego the guaranteed income in return for an opportunity to participate in the appreciation of the underlying stocks or equities.

Merrill Lynch, Lehman Brothers, and hundreds of other banks and brokerage firms have similar products that offer investors certain underlying guarantees and participation in the market's appreciation. I can only touch on some of them here, so make sure you ask your financial advisor for more information before you invest in them.

MITTS. The Market Index Target-Term Securities, or MITTS, theoretically allow you to participate in the upside of the underlying basket with 100 percent principal protection. The principal indeed is protected if you buy at par and hold to maturity, but as with the indexed CDs, MITTS have call features and expenses that in fact limit some of the upside (remember I said there was nothing perfect).

The MITTS cover a wide range of sectors and allow you to diversify with considerable peace of mind. However, as with some guaranteed trusts and packages, you have to be aware that the guarantees apply only to the issue price, so you need to know the issue price and the current price as well as the maturity dates when you are looking at these. Examples of MITTS, which can be purchased through any broker (your financial advisor will have all the necessary information) are shown below:

Principal protected	symbol	index	issue price	maturity date
Energy	ESM	XLE	$10	Feb/2/06
Consumer staples	CSM	XLP	$10	Apr/19/06
Spiders growth	GWM	GWI	$10	May/25/06

Many more are offered with varying underlying baskets of stocks or indexes. Some of the popular ones indexed to the Standard and Poor's 500 are:

- Morgan Stanley S&P 500 PEEQS—(MPQ) due in 5/0/01
- Morgan Stanley S&P 500 (bridges)—(BGS)—due 12/31/03
- Salmon Spins—S&P 500 (XNPA A)
- Smith Barney S&P 500–linked notes (XSB) due 8/13/01
- Smith Barney S&P 500–linked notes (YSB) due 3/11/02
- Smith Barney S&P 500–linked notes (ZSB) due 10/03/03

Some of the principal-protected notes are linked to the Dow, which is often considered a more value-oriented index. They are:

- Merrill Lynch Dow Jones Average Index (DJM)—due 1/14/03
- Morgan Stanley Dow Jones Bridges—(BDJ)—due 4/30/04
- Salomon Smith Barney DJIA (DSB)—9/6/05

There are others tied to the Nasdaq 100 (MNM) and yet others to the Russell 2000 (RUM), the Japanese Nikkei 225 index (Niki), the Major 8 European Index (EMX), or the Major International 11 Index (EEM). Lehman Brothers' Prudents or equity-linked notes (ELNs), are a combination of bonds and an underlying basket of 20 stocks covering 8 sectors. I could write a book on these notes alone. There are also health care, oils, dot-coms, and other sector-protected notes as well as some tied to individual stocks, such as Oracle and Sun Microsystems. If that is not enough, there are many more, too many to include here!

If you want to look at ways to get in the market with downside protection, there are plenty of alternatives.

Mutual fund insurance. In addition to the guaranteed products described above, annuities carry guarantees at death. Now many mutual funds can have the same guarantees, however. These guarantees are usually available only at death. For those concerned about their estate, these may be worth investigating. However, the fact that they usually offer a death benefit only makes this insurance more appropriate for estate planning rather than for retirement or financial planning. In general, they all work the same. There are insurance policies for mutual funds, just as there are for mortgages. Often it may be less expensive to purchase a cheap term insurance policy because it would work the same way. Mutual fund insurance is not my favorite approach to guaranteeing your portfolio.

Summary

I would love to tell you I've just found the perfect investments for everyone, investments that give you peace of mind, good returns, and tax efficiency, and that are simple to employ. For many investors who are comfortable with good returns or returns that are better than bond returns, these investments discussed in this chapter can be close to perfect, especially for older clients in pension accounts. The main flaw is that they often cap the upside, and in good markets underperform stocks. The tax implications often make it necessary to be careful where you place them. In addition, the guarantees exist only if you hold them to maturity. They can have hidden fees as high as 5 percent. If you try to sell early, you may be penalized by exit fees, by interest rate moves, and by the volatility of the underlying baskets of securities.

Guaranteeing Your Principal

Building your own guaranteed portfolios. If you are willing to take the time to do some simple math, you can use some of the math tricks and investments that the pros use to create the prepackaged vehicles explained above.

Chapter 6 explores market insurance (protective puts). Using the insurance can give you packages similar to MITTS, RUMS, and so on. Using zero-coupon Treasury bonds can give you packages similar to the G/SETs and other trusts that are prepackaged by brokerage firms. You could just buy bonds directly if all you wanted was a guarantee, but they offer little appreciation protection. By combining bonds with stocks, you can not only improve the safety of the stocks but also increase the returns on the bonds.

Safety and returns increase when you add stocks to your bond portfolio.

A portfolio with 20 percent stocks and 80 percent bonds not only performs better than bonds but historically has been much safer, according to Harry Markowitz (*Portfolio Selection: Efficient Diversification of Investments*, Yale University Press, 1959). By building in your own guarantees, you can save on fees and get a better handle on the mix and underlying equity positions.

Step by Step

I'll use the same concept as above, splitting our dollars between equity and bonds or zeros.

First we need to determine how much we want to put in both the funds and the zero to give us all our money back at maturity. The math is relatively simple, but we need to gather information first.

Step 1. Call your broker or banker, or look in the *Wall Street Journal* or *Investor's Business Daily* or any other financial publications, and find the rates on U.S. Treasuries, zero-coupon bonds, GICs (guaranteed insurance contracts), preferreds, GNMAs, CDs, and other fixed income investments.

Step 2. Look at the Saving for Future Goals table in the appendix. Determine what you have to put aside today in a guaranteed investment to get your entire principal back. For example, if you have $10,000 to invest for ten years and you found you can get 10 percent, go to the table and look down the 10 percent column until you come to the ten-year row. You will find that you need $386 for each $1,000 you want in ten years. If you want $10,000, you need to invest $3,860 at the guaranteed rate of 10 percent. To make our task easier, the tables are rounded, leading to close approximations but not exact numbers

Where do you put the rest of the money? Because in this example we are assuming that all you need for comfort is the assurance that you will have all your money back in ten years, you can put the rest of the money in the stock market.

Even if the stock market falls to zero (an unlikely scenario), you know your money will be returned. Remember, the reason for creating this package is to give you peace of mind.

Let's assume that you get 12 percent on the mutual fund; over a ten-year period that is a relatively good estimate based on historic returns. How much would you have then? You will be investing $3,860 at 10 percent and $6,140 at 12 percent.

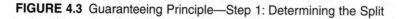

FIGURE 4.3 Guaranteeing Principle—Step 1: Determining the Split

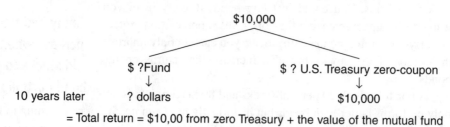

$10,000

$?Fund $? U.S. Treasury zero-coupon
↓   ↓
10 years later   ? dollars $10,000

= Total return = $10,00 from zero Treasury + the value of the mutual fund

FIGURE 4.4 Split between Zero at 10 Percent and Fund: The Worst Scenario Is All Your Money Back

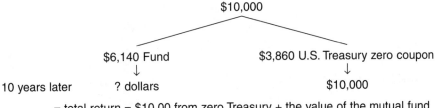

$10,000

$6,140 Fund $3,860 U.S. Treasury zero coupon
     ↓   ↓
10 years later   ? dollars $10,000

= total return = $10,00 from zero Treasury + the value of the mutual fund

FIGURE 4.5 Split between Zero at 10 Percent and Fund at 12 Percent

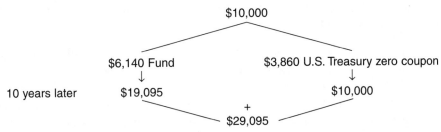

$10,000

$6,140 Fund $3,860 U.S. Treasury zero coupon
     ↓   ↓
10 years later $19,095 $10,000
                            +
                        $29,095

= total return = $10,00 from zero Treasury + $19,095, the value of the mutual fund = $29,095

Compare this to the $16,288 that your $10,000 would have earned in a 5 percent money market account or savings account. A $12,807 difference—a little math and a willingness to hold for awhile went a long way! What if your mutual fund returned 20 percent? a little unrealistic, but worth considering. You would have almost *a $32,000 difference over a savings account at 5 percent.*

The risks were limited and the reward potential was high. You can see that your risk/reward scenario is attractive if you can let your investments sit for a while. Of course, you might have done better if you had all equities, but would you have taken the risk?

Guaranteeing a Minimal Return

Let's us assume now that you are not content with just having your $10,000 back and you want to do at least as well as if you had placed your funds in a money market account or bonds paying 5 percent. We know then that you must have approximately $16,000 in ten

FIGURE 4.6 Guaranteeing a 5 Percent Return

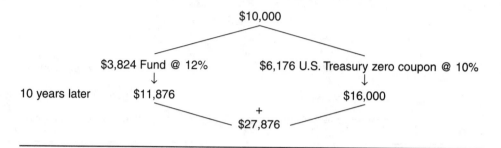

years, because $10,000 at 5 percent will be worth $16,288 in ten years (find on future value table).

How much do you have to set aside in a 10 percent zero to have $16,000 in ten years? To find out, do the following:

- Go to the "Saving for Future Goals" table. Find the intersection of the ten-year row and the 10 percent column. You will find that you need to save $386 for each $1,000 you want in ten years.
- Multiply the $386 by 16 (16 is the number of thousands that you want in ten years; i.e., $16,000). Multiplying 386 by 16 = $6,176, which is what you need to invest today at 10 percent to be sure of having your $10,000 back plus $6,000 in interest, or to have the same result as putting your money in a 5 percent money market account today.

Therefore, you would invest 61 percent of your money in the zero at 10 percent and 39 percent in the fund.

If the mutual fund achieved just a 12 percent return, you would have $11,876 more than if you had kept it in a money market account, in return for liquidity risk. If you were fortunate enough to earn 20 percent on your mutual fund, you would have over twice what you would have had in the savings account. If you were planning on setting aside your money for ten years and did not need to dip into it for emergencies, there is little rationale for not building a guaranteed trust instead, because for a little liquidity risk you get two to three times the reward.

Before you stash money in savings accounts or money market accounts, look at these examples. With little or no additional risk, you could possibly have twice as much money.

Pros:

- High degree of safety: guaranteed not to lose principal
- Allows you to participate in stock market with peace of mind

- Can be less expensive than participating in market prepackaged trusts
- Offers inflation protection from the stock portion
- Over the long run, probably much better returns than bonds
- Better returns than stocks in bad markets
- Attractive for buy-and-hold strategy

Cons:

- Tax consequences need to be considered
- Usually underperform stock market returns over the long run in good markets
- Takes a little work

FIGURE 4.7 Guaranteeing Your Principal Worksheet

1.) List the amount you have to invest and divide by 1,000.

1.) _____

2.) List the number of years you have to invest:

2.) _____

3.) Select a guaranteed investment that you feel comfortable with and find it's current yield. (Call your broker, or banker or look in the financial sections of newspapers and magazines for these guaranteed yields.

3.) _____

4.) Refer to the "Savings for Future Goals: Lump Sum Required" in Appendix B.

Find the intersection of the number of years you can invest (line 2) and the guaranteed yield listed on line 3.

4.) _____

5.) Multiply the dollar value on line 4 by the number of thousands you have to invest (line 1). For example, if you have $16,400 multiply by 16.4, if you have $10,000 multiply by 10.

5.) _____

This amount on line 5 is what you have to invest in guaranteed investments to assure you of having all your principal returned in the number of years you selected. The remainder you can invest in more aggressive investments and still be assured that you will have the same principal that you started with. To see the difference fill in the chart below. Find the "value expected" by using the "Future Value."

GUARANTEED INVESTMENT	GROWTH INVESTMENT
@ _____ %	@ _____ %
Amount invested or Value Expected _____ (from line 5)	_____ (Total to invest minus line 5)

FIGURE 4.8 Guaranteeing Your Investment—A Minimal Return Worksheet

1.) Select a yield your investments must achieve for you not to worry. Usually this is the return you can achieve in a savings account or cash value in insurance policies.
List that % here
1.) _____

2.) List the number of years you have to invest your funds.
2.) _____

3.) List the amount of money you have to invest here.
3.) _____

4.) Refer to the "Future Value Table" in Appendix A and find the intersection for the number of years listed on line 2 and the % listed on line 1. This is the amount $1.00 will grow to at the minimum yields you listed above.
4.) _____

5.) Multiply the number on line 4 by the number on line 3.
5.) _____

6.) Select a guaranteed investment such as a zero coupon bond or a C.D. and find the current yield. (If this yield is less or the same as the yield you have listed in number 1, it means you are not willing to take any further risks; therefore do not continue.)
6.) _____

7.) Now look at the "Savings for the Future" Table in Appendix B. Find the intersection of the yield listed on line 6 and the number of years listed on line 2. This is the amount you need to invest for each $1,000 you wish to acquire.
7.) _____

8.) Multiply the amount in number 7 by the number of thousands on line 5, i.e., if you have $19,600 then multiply by 19.6. This is the amount you must invest in guaranteed income investments to assure you of achieving your minimum standards. The rest you can invest in growth or more risk-oriented investments.
8.) _____

GUARANTEED INVESTMENT @ _____%	**GROWTH INVESTMENT** @ _____%
Amount invested _____ (from line 8)	_____ (line 3 minus line 8)

CHAPTER 5

Stopping Losses and Exiting Gracefully

DEFINITION

Stop loss orders are orders to sell a stock at the market price if the stock falls to the stop price. They are basically orders that yell "**Stop,** we want to get out now."

KEY

Safety: ★★★★   Simplicity: ★★★

Returns: $$$$ Tax efficiency: –$$

SUMMARY

Safety: Although stop loss orders do not add as much safety as buying market insurance on falling stocks, they can often eliminate the emotion in sell decisions and get you out of falling stocks before it is too late.

Returns: Stop loss orders can improve returns by limiting your losses.

Simplicity: This strategy is simple to understand but it does have to be monitored.

Tax efficiency: Stop loss orders can trigger capital gains on the underlying stocks, so they should be carefully monitored and are better used on long-term capital gains positions. They can be used, however, in all tax-sheltered accounts, where it is critical to minimize losses.

What, Who, Why, Where, and When

What are stop loss orders? Stop loss orders are simply orders you place to sell your stock below the current price. If the stock falls to your specified price, called the *stop price,* the order will be activated and become a market order.

> **Stop loss orders are a way to exit gracefully from your stocks.**

Your stock does not automatically get sold at the stop price. However, once your stock hits the stop price, it is then sent to the floor of the exchange, becomes a market order, and is then sold at the current price. There is no guarantee that you will get out at the stop price because there may be many more market orders that are ahead of yours. In fast-moving markets, when everyone is trying to exit at once, you may get out at a much lower price. That may not be bad if the stock keeps falling after you sell, but you might be disappointed if your stocks rally quickly after the sale. Stop loss orders are not perfect, but they are free, and they have the potential to avoid a lot of the downside risk in a stock if you use them carefully.

> **When everyone is rushing to the exit at once, yelling "stop" might not work well.**

Stop Loss Orders versus Market Insurance

The next chapter shows you how to insure your portfolio. You buy insurance to guarantee that you can exit on your own terms and sell your stock at a certain price, the *strike price.* Stops provide you possibilities, not guarantees. But stops are free and can help you get out before small losses turn into large losses; and they help you develop an exit strategy. Both market insurance and stop loss orders have flaws, but you will see later that combining them can be a very effective way to limit your losses and exit on your own terms.

Where should you set your stop loss orders? In most situations you want to limit your losses to 10 percent or less. It is extremely difficult even in good markets to make up falls of more than 10 percent. If the stops were guaranteed, you could set your stop price at 10 percent under the price of the stock. However, stop loss orders don't get you out at exactly the stop price, so if you want to protect yourself against 10 percent falls, the usual rule of thumb is to place your stop at 7 to 8 percent under your current stock price. There is no perfect number. As you will see later, I set my stops near what is called the *support level.* If you use 7 to 8 percent and the market is moving slowly, you may get stopped out at a price higher than you want. If you use 10 percent and the stock is falling fast, you may get out at a price lower than you want. However, even if you get stopped out a little lower than your stop loss order, the likelihood of limiting losses to 10 percent is reasonable.

Stop loss orders are used to help you take small losses instead of large losses.

Assume you own stock XYZ that you purchased at $25 a share. You may be willing to tolerate a 10 percent loss, so instead of placing your stop at $22.50, you may wish to place a stop loss around $23 a share. If your stock falls to $23, your order will then become a market order. You may be sold out at a little lower price— let's say $22.50—but you are in the 10 percent range. If you know that you absolutely cannot let the price fall lower than $22½, you may want to buy the insurance instead.

The stop loss is a maybe. You may get out at 22½ or lower. Insurance is a sure deal!

Who Should Use Stop Loss Orders?

Stopping losses is a strategy for risk-averse investors looking for ways to avoid large downside risks. Investors often know when to buy stocks, and they tend to do a pretty good job of it. However, they seldom seem to know when to sell or exit gracefully. If you are an investor who wants reasonable protection and wants to limit the downside risk, consider stop loss orders. If you need certainty, then insurance is more viable.

Why Use Stop Loss Orders?

Most of us need strategies that take the emotional roller coasters out of investing. We need rules and guidelines that get us out when we think stocks are overvalued or have lost their momentum. Stop loss orders are a way to put your account on autopilot. Although they are not perfect and don't work all the time, the added benefit of removing emotion and second-guessing will help you build a more rational portfolio. Most of us can't watch stocks all day, but stop loss orders allow us to go on with our life knowing that if something drastic occurs, our stop orders will work for us.

Where Do I Use Stop Loss Orders?

Traditionally, investors have been hesitant to use stops in taxable accounts because if stocks are at a profit, they are afraid to pay the capital gains. However, with the new long-term capital gains rates at 18 percent for stock purchased after 2001 and for investments held more than five years, it is better to have 82 percent of something instead of 100 percent of nothing.

If you have a loss in a taxable account, the Federal government subsidizes your loss through tax savings. If, for example,
you are in the 33 percent federal and state tax bracket and have
a loss in your stocks, you can write that off against other gains
and $3,000 in losses against ordinary income and save $1,000 in
taxes. The government shares your loss; it absorbs $1,000 and you absorb $2,000.

Whether you have a profit or loss, still consider stops.

If stocks are no longer attractive, it may be better to pay the taxes, especially if they
are long-term capital gains, and if you have losses, take them and let the government
share your pain. You can always buy the stocks back, sometimes at much lower prices.

IRAs and other retirement accounts. No one shares your loss in tax-deferred accounts so be very careful and use stop loss orders often in these accounts. If you have a
loss in your pension account or IRAs, you cannot write it off and no one shares your loss.
Instead, not only do you absorb the whole loss, but you also probably risk your most
valuable asset: your retirement funds. If there is ever a place to minimize losses, it should
be in retirement accounts.

When Do I Use Stop Loss Orders?

These are the top ten times to consider selling and using stop loss orders.

1. You're overweighted in stock. When you have more than 5 percent in any one
stock, you should gradually reduce your position. Instead of selling, you can set stop loss
orders to cover part of your position. If the stock goes up, you will not be hurt by overweighting, but if it falls, your position will be reduced to a safer amount.

2. Stocks you own are riskier than you wish they were. You need to look at risk
measurements for your stocks. Keep track of the betas. If you feel uncomfortable about
the market and your stocks' betas are high, you may want to switch to lower-beta stocks
by using stop loss orders as your exit strategy.

3. Your stocks are overvalued. In addition to risk, you need to monitor the valuations of your stocks to determine whether it is wise for you to hold or sell. If you had
been monitoring the valuation of the Nasdaq as it approached 5000 in 1999 and had
started to use stops before it fell 70 percent, you would have appreciated how important
valuation and exit strategies are. Some of the easiest valuation measures to find and use
are PEs, PEGs, and yields. I spend a lot of time with these in future chapters, but a brief
comment on them now will help you understand the overall picture.

- *Price-earnings ratios (PEs) get too high.* There are no hard-and-fast rules; I have
  seen stocks with PEs in the hundreds do well. A good starting point however, is to
  watch your PEs when they start to get 30 percent above the average PEs for their

sector or the market, or if the PE is much higher than it was when you purchased a stock. You may want to even become cautious when your PEs move up against their own average. PEs are usually best used as a relative tool and used in comparison with a benchmark; however, in the absence of a benchmark, you may want to look for stocks with PEs lower than 20 if you are looking for a safer portfolio. As your PEs move up, consider moving stop loss orders up to 5 percent under the current price.

- *PEGs get too high:* A later chapter is devoted to PE/growth ratios, but for now a simple rule of thumb is that when PEGs get higher than 3, move stop loss orders up to 5 percent below price. As you will see later, when PEGs are less than 1, you have the potential for large returns, but once PEGs are more than 2, the potential for high returns drops dramatically. You want to get out before the potential for positive returns disappears and ends up negative.

4. You have a large profit. If you have earned more than a 20 percent return on a stock in less than six months, place a stop loss 5 percent below price.

5. Interest rates increase. Interest rate increases are likely to create falls in the market. Place stop loss orders 5 percent away under stocks that are interest rate sensitive.

6. The fundamentals have changed. Consider stop loss orders if a company has lost its competitive edge, its markets have dried up, foreign competition is likely to eliminate profits, or its market share has fallen.

7. The market or sector looks weak. Remember that 80 percent of a stock's move is related to its sector or the market.* Only 20 percent is usually related to the stock itself. If you see trends in the market or the sector that look disappointing, then use stop loss orders even if your stock seems fine.

8. When you've made a new purchase. When you first buy a stock and have little or no profit, you can expose yourself to the greatest risk. I often use market insurance when I first buy, but stop loss orders can work well also. You need to admit you made a mistake and move on, so consider stop loss orders, usually around 8 to 10 percent below the purchase price.

9. When stocks approach their resistance levels. Stocks often trade in ranges. They have a floor or support level that they will fall to; then they become undervalued, and investors purchase them until they get to a price where they are overvalued and can-

---

* These numbers are commonly used and are often credited to Dorsey Wright & Associates, Richmond, or the Lathan Group.

not seem to go above that. This is their resistance level. At that time, when a stock starts meeting resistance, it can either break out and trade in a whole new range or fall back. Placing stop loss orders 5 percent away when a stock approaches resistance can help get you out at or near the top. If the stock goes above the resistance level, you still own it, but even if it starts to fall, you may be able to get out before it gets back to the support level.

10. All the time. Although I think you have to be selective and use stop loss orders on part of your portfolio, many advisors suggest using them all the time. Because the market flips back so fast or because of taxes, I prefer using stops for only part of an account. I hope getting stopped out will prompt you to reevaluate the rest of the account.

The Top Ten Reasons (or Excuses) for Not Selling

Why Can't We Sell?

There are legitimate reasons why we shouldn't sell, but there are also some very irrational reasons why investors don't sell.

1. We have been brought up to believe buy and hold is the best strategy. Buy and hold is a wonderful strategy and often works perfectly, but it is not usually a legitimate reason not to sell. There are major drawbacks to the buy-and-hold strategy. The biggest is that it makes us comfortable with the notion that if we just sit tight, everything will be fine and the market will come back to where it was. It may be true that the market will come back, but in the meantime your portfolio and stocks could have been decimated, and it could be decades, not years, before you'll see your accounts back to where they started. Granted you don't want to sell at the bottom—panic, depression selling—but you do want to have stops and other strategies to dollar cost average you out of the market.

2. We believe stocks always come back. Another reason for buying and holding is the eternal optimism of investors, which is not a legitimate reason to avoid selling. It is difficult to sell. Investors have great faith that stocks will always come back. It is just a matter of time. Time is what is important. If they come back in weeks, months or even a couple of years, you will usually be fine. But what if it is ten years?

Money rotates from sector to sector, style to style, and stock to stock. Many stocks will fall and come back, and sometimes it is worth waiting if there is no better place to put your money. But was it really worth waiting ten years for IBM to come back after the 1987 crash? Actually, IBM traded around $40 before the crash and took until 1997 to get back. Even though it was trading over $100 in July 2001, IBM's return for almost 14 years was 150 percent, which sounds great. But that is about 11 percent or a little less than the S&P 500. We can use IBM as an argument to hold on and wait patiently for 14 years and your stocks might come back. We can also use it to argue that if you had sold IBM in 1987 before the crash, invested in 8 percent bonds until 1998 and then bought IBM back, you would have had twice the amount of money today, or a return of over 22 percent annually.

If IBM didn't sound so bad to you because eventually, after ten years, it worked out, then let's look at the Xerox (XRX) story. If you had bought Xerox in the 1970s at about $14, you were still down in July 2001 over 40 percent when Xerox traded at about $8 after 30 years! It was even worse in June 2001, when it traded at $5 and you were down over 64 percent after 30 years! Time does not resolve all problems in the market. Buy and hold is a great strategy, but only if you are holding great stocks. Investors had hundreds of opportunities over the years to get out of XRX above $14, but because we have been trained to think that all stocks go up over the long run, we may often hold too long.

3. Loyalty risk. As I noted earlier, seldom is loyalty a good reason not to sell. Sometimes we don't sell because we feel a strong sense of loyalty to a stock, such as my dad with his AT&T. Loyalty risk is a major problem for most investors, especially when it comes to the stock of companies where we work.

4 & 5. Fear and greed. The two emotions that drive the market are fear and greed. Neither is bad, but neither should be a reason not to sell. You need to have a little fear and greed to invest, but you need them at the right time.

Most of us are afraid at the bottom of the market, and fear forces us to sell—just at the wrong time. Most of us are excited and greedy at the top of the market, and we want to be part of the big home runs, so we buy. Again at the wrong time. Obviously, I don't want you to sell at the bottom, but after being burned so many times, investors tend to react to emotions—fear and greed—instead of thinking through their decision to sell. A legitimate reason for not selling is that investors almost always sell at the wrong time.

Don't sell when stocks have already bottomed. A study done about Fidelity Magellan, which has been one of the best long-term mutual funds, showed that even though it had beaten the market for most of the 1980s, more than 70 percent of the people who invested in Magellan lost money. How could they have lost money if they were in the best-performing fund? Because of fear and greed: fear when the market was down and they sold, and greed when the market was up and they bought.

6. Our stocks are too low. I have a great client, Georgia, who will never sell a stock at a loss. She says that it is not a loss until she sells and if it's only a paper loss, it's not a real loss; and her stock will come back and, of course, then she will sell. Like most investors, she is right to think that until you sell, your paper losses are not realized. However, they are still real whether you sell or not. I begged her to sell her AT&T in 1999, then again in 2000, then in 2001, and always with the same response of "They are too low."

At 50 AT&T was too low, maybe, but then when it reached 40, it was lower, and she responded, "I just hate to take losses." When it got to $15, I gave up because by then she was right—it was too low. The point is not whether you take losses but whether you take big or small losses. There are always going to be losses in your portfolio, but the question is do you take big losses or small losses? Unless there are fundamental reasons to believe a stock will come back, sell even if it is too low. Ask yourself, would you buy it today? Do you think it is going to go up faster and better than some other stocks, or would you prefer to own something else instead? Don't look at what you paid for it. Look at what you think it is worth. If you don't think it will come back soon, sell before it falls dramatically and then buy it back at lower prices.

7. We're not paying attention. One of the main, and the most inexcusable, reasons not to sell is that we weren't paying attention. We got comfortable or lazy or just didn't bother to monitor the risks, the valuations, or the fundamentals, and we let it slip by. If those are the reasons why you hold, then you should definitely consider stop loss orders. Sometimes we make mistakes, but the worst mistake usually is doing nothing, not paying attention and letting losses run.

> **"I forgot" is not a legitimate reason for not selling.**

8. A stock is too high. Sometimes it's hard to let go of a dream. Often investors hope all their financial problems will be solved if they get into the one hot stock that is going to make them millionaires. As I mentioned earlier, Qualcomm was one of those dream stocks. The stories of the expected wealth that would be experienced by investors if they got into Qualcomm were everywhere, from CNBC to the local newspapers. I had sold calls on Qualcomm in 1999 for a $120 strike price. When it was called away, some of my clients were very disappointed because it kept going higher and higher. However, when it fell to $20, they were thrilled they had sold.

> **Don't get emotional over a stock and don't build your dreams around it.**

9. Taxes. This is one of the most popular excuses for not selling and may even be legitimate. But when a stock is no longer attractive and it is time to sell, don't let taxes stand in the way. Too many times investors will hold mutual funds or taxable bonds and CDs and not think anything of taxes in the 28 percent or even 39.6 percent tax bracket. But they become stressed over selling at an 18 percent or 20 percent capital gains tax. If you are nervous about taxes, look at family members or charities to whom you can gift your stock. If you have a child in a 10 or zero percent tax bracket, instead of paying school or medical bills, gift them your appreciated stock and have them sell it in their low tax bracket. Or if you are gifting regularly to a charity, gift your appreciated security instead of cash. Everyone will end up with more money if you avoid the taxes and you can reinvest the cash that you were gifting into a better stock.

Sometimes it really is better to pay taxes and keep 82 percent of your profits than to have 100 percent of nothing.

10. *Your stock has great fundamentals.* The most legitimate reason not to sell is that the stock is fundamentally sound and still has strong appreciation potential. In these cases, selling is not the best solution. After you have large profits, however, stop loss orders and insurance on your stock is a good idea.

Moving On Up

Using stops can be an effective way to help us eliminate a lot of the decisions and emotions that often prevent us from selling. Although stops are easy to understand, they must be monitored monthly. If your stock has moved up and your goal was to have your stop loss at 10 percent away, then you have to physically move your stop loss up. You need to call your broker to change the stop loss.

Stocks aren't static, so your stops shouldn't be either. Remember to move them up as your stock prices increase in value.

Once your stock has reached your targeted price, don't be greedy; move your stop orders up very close to the current price. If you have decided you would be willing to sell your stock but want to hold off for a higher price, then move your stop loss order to 5 percent away.

Stop Loss Orders Don't Always Work

One of the dangers of stop loss orders is getting stopped out much lower than you wanted if the market is falling fast or your stock is falling fast. What if your stop loss order was at $50, the stock fell over 20 percent in a day, and you could be sold out instead at $40, or at whatever the lowest price the stock traded on that day? Your stop loss order at $50 was not guaranteed. Instead, your order goes to the floor of the exchange and becomes a market order. If the stock is falling fast, it will trade like other stocks and get caught up in the free fall. If the stock keeps falling later, that might not be bad; but what if suddenly the next day the Federal Reserve dropped interest rates by one-half point and the market rallies strongly, bringing XYZ back to $52? How would you feel? Stops are not perfect as I said, but even in fast falling markets they work if the market goes still lower.

Increased Volatility Limits Stop Loss Orders

The recent volatility in the market makes it more difficult to use stop loss orders. If stop loss orders are used and your stock is stopped out, the price can snap back quickly in volatile markets. From 1945 to 2000 there were moves of 1 percent or more approximately 16 percent of the time. In 2000, however, moves of 1 percent or more occurred more than 44 percent of the time, or 110 out of 252 days. Nasdaq swings were even more violent. From 1971 to 2000, according to the Leuthold Group, there were moves of 3 percent or more less than 1 percent of the time, but in 2000, 76 out of 252 trading days, or over 30 percent of trading days, the Nasdaq moved more than 3 percent!

Stop Loss Limits

Stop loss orders are sent to the exchange where the stock trades to be executed when a stock hits its stop price. There may be thousands, even millions, of other orders in front of yours when it gets to the exchange. Your order will be placed in a queue, and although it may be only seconds before it is filled, it could be filled at a much lower price. Because investors would often be willing to sell at the stop price but don't want to be caught in a free fall, they use stop loss limits. If your stop loss limit was $45, your order would be executed if the stock was trading at $45. However, if the price had already fallen below $45, your order would not be executed, and you would hold your stock. You only sell at the limit price that you designated, which protects you from selling your stock at a much lower price than you had planned. But if your stock price keeps falling day after day, you may have been better off getting out on the first day, even at a lower price. Stop loss limits are a good alternative but not the best. In the next chapter I show you how to insure your stock. By combining stop loss limits with insurance, you can place your limit at a reasonable price but be insured at a lower price, so you have an alternative exit strategy if the stock falls dramatically.

Investor's Business Daily

Most advisors suggest that you limit your losses to 10 percent, but William O'Neil, the publisher of *Investor's Business Daily,* believes in limiting losses to 7 or 8 percent. I agree with O'Neil, but it is usually very difficult to get out with limited losses if the market is falling fast. Even if you use stop loss orders and set your stop prices at 7 to 8 percent below the current stock price, expect the worse. It's hoped you'll average out at a 10 percent loss.

The problem. As noted above, stop loss orders have a problem. If the stock is falling fast, you may be stopped out at a much lower price than you expected. However, if an individual stock is falling because the whole market is weak, there are additional problems. Usually when you sell a stock, you want to use the proceeds to invest in other stocks. But if the market is weak, be careful before you reinvest. Even if you had gotten out at your stop price, you could still face problems if you then reinvest in other stocks. Let's look at our previous example.

You invest in XYZ; it falls from $50 to $45—10 percent—and you are stopped out at $45. Assume you feel the problem is your stock and not the market, so you take your $45 and invest in ZYX, which now falls to $40—you're out at $40.

Now you take your $40 and reinvest into YZX, which falls to $36 and you are stopped out again. We obviously can go on and on until there is no money left. The point is that it does no more good to move out of one stock and go into other stocks that are equally vulnerable to falls. Although stop loss orders are a great place to start building exit strategies, at some point you may need to look at other hedges and exit strategies.

Use stops and take 7 to 8 percent losses, but don't take losses over and over in bad markets.

You Need to Know When to Hold and When to Fold

Although stop loss orders are automatic and an excellent strategy for many situations, they are not something to use without thinking. You have to constantly evaluate when to hold and when to fold. Stop losses take the emotion out of selling but not the need to plan. You can't merely guess, but rather you have to look at the criteria I mentioned above: PEs, PEGs, fundamentals, the market, the sectors, risk factors, profit, taxes, and the potential to move higher.

Reverting to the Mean

In later chapters I discuss probabilities and other statistical tools, but for now it is worth mentioning that one of the most accurate truisms is that the market reverts to its mean, or average. That means when the valuation of the market based on PEs, PEGs, and so on is too high, the market will fall until it comes back into a normal range. When the market is too low, it will rise to those averages. Knowing this, it seems plausible then that when the market gets overvalued, we can expect it to fall back to a normal level, take a breather until things settle, and then start off again. We know the market will fall and rise, but what we don't know is how quickly these things will occur. If the market falls abruptly but comes back quickly, we call it a *V-shaped correction.* The solutions for that type of correction are much different from the solutions for a market that falls and stays down for years, as it did in the '70s, or the *U-shaped correction* of 2000 and 2001.

1987 versus 1997. Because stop loss orders saved me from large losses in 1987, as I explained in an earlier chapter, it's hard to believe I can find something wrong with them. The Friday before Black Monday in 1987, when I landed from Puerto Rico to find the market was down 108 points, I had been stopped out of nearly all my stocks at about 5 percent under Thursday's price. Instead of being thrilled, I was nervous that my automatic strategy, which was supposed to make my clients feel better while I was traveling, had just created a nightmare of tax problems and commission readjustments. In addition, the stops had just gotten me out of the best market I had ever seen. As I called my clients in panic, promising I would wave the commissions and get them back in on Monday, I was heartbroken. But on Monday October 19, the market fell 508 more points, and I was not only able to get back in at lower prices but looked like a hero. Having a plan, sticking to it, and taking the emotion out of investing helped a lot. Stop loss orders helped tremendously.

V-shaped corrections. When the market falls and stays down for a while, stop loss orders are a great benefit. The greatest problem with stop loss orders occurs in a V-shaped market correction.

On October 28, 1997, the Dow had the largest fall ever, down 554 points in one day. If you had stops, they would have worked and done their job. The next day was one of the greatest moves up, and the market recovered over 380 points. Fortunately for most investors, if you had held tight because of the rally the next day, the fall would have had little or no impact on your investments. This was one time it did not pay to be nimble; it was obviously better to hold. In a quick V-shaped correction, market insurance is better.

Even though stop loss orders can help you go on autopilot, you need to monitor monthly. Nothing works all the time, but I also have decided it is much nicer to be safe than sorry, so I recommend stop loss orders and hedges nearly all the time.

> **Stop loss orders do not work well in V-shaped corrections, but they can prevent a lot of damage in U-shaped corrections.**

> **The moral is "Some things work most of the time, and most things work some of the time, but nothing works all of the time," so keep several strategies in your portfolio.**

The Pros and Cons of Stop Loss Orders

Pros of stop loss orders:

- They remove emotion.
- They help put your account on autopilot.
- They force you to reevaluate and monitor your portfolio.
- They can often spare you from letting small losses turn into large losses.
- They offer a disciplined way to take profits and exit gracefully.

Cons of stop loss orders:

- You have to be careful about tax ramifications and commissions.
- There is no guarantee of a set price when you're stopped out.
- Stocks may rebound quickly (V-shape), making sales unnecessary.
- Commissions can be a problem and need to be evaluated carefully.

CHAPTER 6

Insuring Your Portfolio with Protective Puts

DEFINITION

Protective put options are contracts that give the holder the right to sell his or her stock at a predetermined price. Insuring the market and your stocks with puts is a conservative strategy for risk-averse investors.

KEY

Safety: ★★★★★   Simplicity: ★★★

Returns: $$$ Tax consequences: $$

SUMMARY

Safety: The third strategy, buying *market insurance,* is for the risk-averse investor seeking high degrees of safety and protection when the market falls.

Returns: Buying insurance in and of itself usually lowers returns by virtue of the cost of the insurance. However, by giving investors peace of mind and the ability to stay in the market, insurance may offer an opportunity to increase returns over bond or risk-free portfolios.

Simplicity: Insuring your portfolio can be a simple strategy similar to other insurance once you understand the costs and how much you need.

Tax implications: Market insurance has no significant tax consequences, but it can often be used to minimize capital gains by allowing investors to postpone the sale of stocks yet lock in profits.

What This Chapter Is About

This chapter discusses how you can share in the historically long-term high returns of the stock market without fear or panic. It shows you how to add safety yet still improve your returns over risk-free cash or bond portfolios by utilizing insurance on individual stocks and markets.

Insurance

Most of us have a clear understanding of insurance and own life, disability, health, auto, or even long-term care insurance. We know that the more coverage we need, the higher the cost or premiums we have to pay. The healthier we are, the less costly the insurance is, but the costs can be prohibitive for the sick and elderly. There are three important elements to insurance: how much, what type, and when to buy.

How Much Insurance Do You Really Need?

Assess risks. Do you think of insurance as a lottery? Are you hoping when you die that your heirs will have a windfall? Do you think of insurance as a way to help them maintain their lifestyle? Before you can discuss insurance, you have to understand your attitudes toward it. Do you usually regard it as a waste of money or as an important risk management tool?

How much to buy. Before we buy any type of insurance, we need to assess our risk levels to determine how much loss we can sustain and then buy insurance to protect us from the losses that we can't handle. We need to know how much insurance will let us be comfortable with market risks and also how to keep the costs down so that the benefits outweigh the costs. One of the first rules of financial planning is to plan for emergencies and set aside emergency funds for market falls, disability, unforeseen events, and accidents. Usually the recommended amount is the equivalent of two to three months of income. Continually evaluate how much risk you can sustain yourself as insurance can get expensive, and we should only buy as much as we really need.

What type to buy. A retiree with a house, no debt, and sufficient assets to generate good income doesn't need disability insurance, but may need market insurance to protect investment income. A single person with no heirs may not need life insurance but will probably need disability insurance. Why waste money on life insurance if we have no heirs, or disability insurance when we are not working, or household insurance when we have nothing of value?

When to buy. We need to buy insurance when we are young and healthy and before an accident occurs. After we have a couple of accidents or after we get older, insurance will get more and more expensive. We cannot wait till we are in our 80s and in poor health to buy health and life insurance. We want to buy auto insurance when our car is new and worth insuring and not wait to buy when it is old and after several accidents. We insure things that have high value. We don't insure an old car because it has little or no value. We also usually do not need to insure investments of little value or that are unlikely to fall further. We don't want to overinsure investments, because it will be too expensive and the costs will outweigh the benefits. We need to find a happy medium that allows us to buy when insurance is at a reasonable cost and yet before an accident or market crash.

Insurance for Investments

The same reasoning holds true for insurance on our investments. We must first assess how much risk we can handle and then buy the right kind of insurance when it is inexpensive. Insurance is cheapest when the market is high. We can't wait until the market becomes "sick" or starts to fall to buy insurance because then the costs become high. When the market falls, it is a good time to invest and buy stocks, but usually it is a bad time to buy insurance on stocks that have already fallen and experienced large losses. Just as it is silly to buy car insurance after your car is totaled, it is usually not worth buying market insurance after the crash has occurred (unless of course you think it might fall more).

Assessing risk. How much risk can you really handle? Can you afford to lose 10 percent or 20 percent of your money and ride through market fluctuations? Can you postpone important events like retirement, your children's education, and home purchases until the market rallies again? Do you want to avoid time worrying, rethinking, and trying to forecast the market? These are important questions that we need to ask ourselves to understand how much risk we can handle. After setting goals, understanding risk tolerance is probably the most important step in creating your financial plan.

In considering life insurance, we can assess our risk levels by considering our mortgage, debts, and the replacement income needed for our family. In considering disability insurance, usually the rule of thumb is to replace 60 percent of your pretax income. But with our investments we usually don't consider how much risk we can afford until things go badly. Investors often wait until the market has fallen before they realize they have little risk tolerance. We tend to let emotion determine our market insurance needs, not rational risk assessment.

Emotional Cycles

Janus Funds has a thought-provoking chart it uses to describe investors' moods—it shows how happy investors are at the top of the market, but how despondent they are at the bottom. It is difficult to see the pain investors feel when market volatility is extreme and how market moves can dramatically affect so many lives. It is not just financial cycles but emotional cycles as well that affect investors along with the sense of helplessness and lack of control that investors feel. Investors do let the market control their emotions, being euphoric when the market is high and depressed when it is low. Not only do investors think they are brilliant at the top, but they credit themselves with the success. They think that investing is easy, that it is merely a matter of stock selection. As the market starts to fall, investors go through stages of anxiety, denial, fear, desperation, and panic until they finally become despondent and depressed. It is at that moment of depression that they are finally ready to give up, but this in fact is the time to buy. Often it is at the very moment investors are thinking of selling their stocks or buying insurance and regretting all the times they didn't take their profits off the table that it is the time to buy. But instead, they too often let emotions take over and they sell. As the market starts to rally, those who sold will become more despondent, lose more of their confidence, and become even more depressed. Those who held will feel a sense of vindication, hope, and relief, but they will still have suffered unnecessary financial losses.

The psychology of the market and seeing the stress it creates for investors is the main reason I am writing this book. It is why I emphasize over and over that it is crucial to have a plan, to have a strategy, and to understand the total picture, not just pick stocks. It is critical to have an exit strategy at the top and an entering strategy at the bottom. The problem is that most of us have a tendency to let emotions and market cycles control us. Instead, we need to take control; we need to be able to think rationally. The losses are too great in these volatile times to merely buy and hold without protection. We can have buy-and-hold strategies if we have something that is doing well for us through both up and down cycles. Market insurance can do that for you. It can let you hold because as the market is falling, you will be offsetting losses in your stock position with gains in your insurance. You will be in control and feel good at any point in the market cycle. The fact that the market has highs and lows doesn't mean that you must experience the same ups and downs. There are risks associated with insurance costs, but the peace of mind and sense of control over our own life and destiny make the costs worthwhile in most cases.

The market is always going to go up and down. Since 1900, the Dow has been up at the end of the year 69 times and down 32 times. It has been down more than 20 percent at the end of the year 8 times. Three years out of ten it has been down at the end of the year. The Nasdaq has been even more volatile. We need to plan for the down markets as well as the good markets.

What Can You Do to Protect Yourself?

If you were nervous during the millennium crash and 2001, and you feel you cannot sustain a lot of downside risk, consider downside protection and insurance on stocks and the market. It is especially important for those investors who are seeking returns higher than bonds but cannot afford the downside risk of stocks.

Minimize cost. As with any insurance, market insurance has a cost, and because we want maximum protection for minimum cost, we need to buy insurance when the market or our stock is high. You may want to purchase short-term insurance just to get through those first few uncertain months and then discontinue the insurance when a certain level of appreciation or return has been achieved. Or you may want to switch to stop loss orders. Or you may want to continue the insurance over a longer period, but as with other insurance, you will have to continue to pay the premiums for your market insurance if you want to stay insured. Once you stop paying, your insurance will expire on a specified date (the expiration date). You may want to consider insurance only for events that have a higher probability of occurring and possibly even go without insurance for times or events that are less likely to occur. Often it may not be worth insuring very low-risk investments or investments that have a low risk compared with the market (beta).

It is important to insure the risky portion of your portfolio but not investments that offer low potential returns. If it costs you 2 percent to insure a stock that historically has only returned 5 percent, you would probably be better off to switch to a money market account or skip the insurance altogether. However, if you want to purchase a stock that has the potential of doubling (which probably means it has a high degree of risk), then you may want to buy insurance and the stock.

Disability Insurance for Our Investment Income

Most individuals know they have to protect their sources of income. Most workers purchase disability insurance to protect the flow of income during their work years. Too often, however, people neglect to protect the income that comes from their investments. Investment income insurance is especially important for retirees. If that income is lost, it could jeopardize our ability to retire with a decent standard of living and the ability to keep our home, help our family, or educate our children. Yet too often we overlook insurance for our investments.

A few key concepts are similar for nearly all insurance produc
insurance: coverage, or face value; premiums, or cost; maturity, or
payoffs.

Market insurance. Market insurance is a contract called a *pr*
the owner of the put the right to sell a stock at a predetermined price, .
There is a cost, or premiums, for this protection from losses.

Investment coverage. As with any insurance, you need to determine how much coverage you want to protect yourself from financial losses. With market insurance, or puts,
I refer to the face value or the coverage amount as the *strike price*.

Let's assume you are investing in a stock—I'll use Cisco for our example—that is
trading at $62 a share. You found from your risk analysis that you are a person who can only
handle a 5 to 10 percent loss. You could sell the stock when it starts to fall, but then if it
rallied you might feel bad. You think this is a good stock over the long run, so instead of selling you could buy enough insurance to protect yourself for all losses under $60. To do this
you would buy a put with a $60 strike price. No matter how low Cisco falls, you can always
sell it at $60. Think of it as buying $60 worth of coverage. If Cisco falls below $60, you
collect on your insurance, or put contract, by selling your stock (exercising your put) to
the insurer. (The insurer is the seller of the put. You are the buyer.) You could also sell your
put for a profit and keep the stock. In either situation you would avoid any losses under $60.

Premiums. You have to pay premiums to keep your insurance intact. If your stock is
trading at $62, let's assume you have to pay a premium of $2 to buy a put at the strike
price of $60.

Expiration date. Insurance has expiration dates and renewal periods. To keep insurance in force, you have to pay premiums at regular intervals. Your auto insurance might
have premiums payable every six months; your house insurance is perhaps paid monthly;
and your life insurance annually. But if the premiums aren't paid, the insurance will be
canceled or will expire. It works the same with puts, or market insurance. Puts too have
expiration dates, dates when new premiums have to be paid or the insurance expires.

Payoffs. Life insurance pays off only when the insured dies. Disability/accident only
pays off if we get sick, and puts pay off only if the stock falls. The put will expire with
no value (i.e., worthless) if the stock never falls to the strike price or if the insurance expires before it falls.

The insurance, or puts, offer a high degree of safety* for those afraid of stock market risk and event risk. This is one strategy that is very attractive for risk-averse investors
who feel panicky when the market falls.

---

*It doesn't offer 100 percent protection because the cost of the put has to be subtracted.

derstanding Market Insurance and Puts

As we saw above, puts are insurance. They are also a type of *option,* which is a contract between two parties. I did not use the word *options* because most people are intimidated by options, thinking them risky and dangerous. For sure, there are option strategies that are extremely risky but not all options or puts are alike. Buying protective puts adds safety and hedges your portfolio. Although some option strategies are risky and compli- cated, buying puts is simple, especially if you think of them as insurance. When we buy a put option, our option contract states that we have the right to sell our stock at a pre- determined price in return for the premium we paid.

Because most options can be confusing and risky for investors, I urge you to contact the Chicago Board Options Exchange (CBOE) (400 S. LaSalle Street, Chicago, IL 60605. 800-678-4667) for free educational material and an in-depth booklet, "Characteristics and Risks of Standardized Options," for a look at the tax ramifications, strategies, risks, and rewards of options. The book is intended to walk you through general concepts so you can better work with your investment advisor.

What's Wrong with Puts as Market Insurance?

There are negatives to every investment and every investment strategy, including the mar- ket insurance strategy here. The fact that you are paying a premium for puts is the biggest negative because the cost of the premium reduces your return if the market or your stock goes up. If it costs you 2 percent a year and the market is up 20 percent, it may not be that bad to pay for the insurance. If the market is down badly, the cost will certainly be justified. But if the market is up 6, 7, or even 8 percent and you are giving up 2 percent a year, then you may not even beat a bond portfolio. Because of the cost, you have to as- sess your own risk tolerance so you know how much insurance you really need. Over- insuring is a risk that can dramatically reduce overall returns to levels of bonds or certificates of deposit, thus negating the benefits of being in the stock market. It is im- portant when you work with a financial advisor to keep him or her informed about your risk tolerance, so your advisor can recommend the most appropriate strategies and in- vestments. If you handle your own investments, it is even more important that you quan- tify the risks and losses you can tolerate.

Is Buying Insurance Worth It?

Why waste money buying insurance knowing that historically over the long run the market goes up? The best reason is that the insurance allows you to stay in the market without panic and to avoid selling at the bottom and buying back at the top.

The market is typically down one of every three years. If that holds true, having insurance may be worth it.

Insurance allows you to reap most of the benefits if the market goes up. If the market falls, it negates most of your downside exposure. If the put is worthless at expiration, that's OK. It means you have a good market and you never needed to use the insurance. You got less overall return because of the cost of the put, but the benefits often outweigh the cost. Most of us hope we will never use our disability insurance, our health insurance, or prematurely need our life insurance. We hope the same for the market, but be prepared for the worst.

Some of us may be able to tolerate a few short-term losses, feeling insurance isn't needed. When we are looking at the whole market, that is probably true. However, individual stocks and sectors tend to be even more volatile, and although the market tends to come back relatively quickly, not all stocks and sectors do. What if you had had Phillip Morris in 1991, Xerox over the last 30 years, AT&T in 2000, Enron in 2001, or, even worse, one of the hot Internet stocks in 2000? Remember the Nasdaq! It fell more than 70 percent in 2000 and 2001. If the risks were that high all the time, I probably would avoid the market altogether, but fortunately market corrections like that do not happen often. Before 2000 the worst Nasdaq falls were down 35.1 percent in 1974, down 31.1 percent in 1973, and down 17.8 percent in 1990.

What if you had insurance that cost you 2 percent of your portfolio and bought you protection or a guarantee that the most you could lose was 5 percent?

Assume the market falls 50 percent and your 10,000 investment has a 5% loss; account falls to $9,500. Without the put, your investment would be worth $5,000.

Was the $200 insurance worth it? Without it you ended up with a $5,000 loss. With it you lose $500 plus $200 for the put, or $700. I can't tell you if the market will go up or down, but if it does fall dramatically, I can tell you that the insurance will give you a sense of control and peace of mind.

If the market had gone straight up, you would have wasted a lot of return—2 percent a year. But because the market on average closes down once every three years, it may be worth it to have insurance. It's nice to know that you were insured for some of that downside. Try to force yourself to buy insurance when the market is high rather than wait until things have collapsed.

Options

Now that we've acknowledged that not all options are risky, it may be time to look at options in financial terms. A put option, as noted earlier, is a contract that conveys to the buyer the right to sell shares at a specified price at a given date.

In our examples, we are the buyer of puts. The specified price is the strike or exercise price; and the maturity date or date the insurance expires is the expiration date. We use the term *strike* or *exercise price* because at that specified price we can exercise (or enforce) our contract. We would probably only want to exercise the contract if the stock were trading below the exercise or strike price. It would be silly to exercise our Cisco 60 put if Cisco was trading at $70. But if Cisco fell as it did in 2001 to $13 a share, we could enforce our contract and sell it at $60, avoiding a catastrophic loss and grateful for the insurance. Remember though that the puts, or insurance, last only until the expiration date. If we bought insurance on Cisco at $60 for June expiration but didn't renew it and Cisco fell in August, we would have had no insurance.

To review: don't make puts more complicated than they are. They are simply insurance that gives you the right to sell the stock at the exercise or strike price. This right is granted to you by the seller of the put. Think of the seller as the insurer or the insurance company. Also remember that the CBOE has an enormous amount of information about options that you can get free of charge.

When Do You Want to Buy Insurance, or Puts?

In general, you should consider insurance, or puts, in most of the same situations in which you would sell or use stop losses, when you are nervous or overweighted.

1. As an alternative to selling. If your stock or portfolio has reached a level where you are comfortable selling but you think it might go higher and you want to capture more upside potential, then you may want to wait before you sell. You can buy insurance as an alternative to selling while still locking in your profits. In case you are wrong, the puts help you exit gracefully and guarantee that you lock in your price.

2. To enter the market. You may want to get into the market but aren't sure if the market has bottomed. Buying a put provides protection until you have enough profits to ease a potentially painful market drop. You don't want to get wiped out as soon as you enter the market and then have nothing to invest later.

3. To lock in your profit. If you have an established profitable stock position and are aware that stocks don't go up forever, you can buy puts to protect your profits and still hold onto the stock. You could also use stop loss orders, but remember they don't offer any guarantees.

4. To postpone taxes. At some point you may feel you have a stock that is ready to fall, but you don't want to sell now because of tax concerns. You may want to move your taxes to following years, in which case you can use puts to lock in your profits without selling the stock. (I discuss some of the tax ramifications later.)

5. An overvalued market. When the market is overvalued or very high, you may not want to take the chance that a correction will occur, so consider insurance.

6. *Always.* Yes, always. For many of us the answer is to always have a little insurance. For those of you who cannot afford risk and are very dependent on stability and income, insurance may be the answer. When the market goes up, you have stocks that will do well, and when the market falls, you will still have something (your puts) that does well. You may only need to insure a small portion of your portfolio—the portion that is in the stock market and you depend on for income or the portion that is very risky. When stability is a concern, safety strategies are crucial.

7. *When stocks meet some resistance.* If you think your stock may meet resistance, that is a good time to buy a put because usually at that level the stock will fall back to its old support levels or break out to new levels. There are no hard-and-fast rules, but this is something to consider for those who follow the technical elements of stocks.

8. *As an alternative to stop loss orders.* Puts are similar to stop losses as both set floors for our stocks. At certain prices we want to sell or limit our losses. With stop losses there are no guarantees, however, that the stop will get us out at the exact stop price. But puts guarantee that we will be out at the exact strike price. Stop losses have the advantage of being free, but we have to pay for the insurance of puts. A combination of stop loss limits and puts can be an alternate, less expensive strategy.

9. *When PEs and PEGs are high.* If stocks have high betas, high PEs, or high PEGs, then you should consider insurance on these stocks. Usually stocks with high PEs and PEGs tend to be viewed as overvalued and fall dramatically when they meet their resistance levels.

10. *When crystal balls don't work.* Did you guess right about the Fed's cuts or the 2001 terrorist attacks? Do you notice how often the government is revising statistics? It takes the National Bureau of Economic Research six months to tell us what happened in the past! Do you really think anyone knows what will happen in the future? If your answer is no, you're in good company. Even the Federal Reserve with its wealth of data could not have predicted the dismal economy. We all work with probabilities and past performance to help us predict market moves, but with the increased volatility in the market, do you really want to depend on this information? Probably the dumbest thing I have done in my career was to stop buying puts in November 2000 for my growth accounts. I think how different things would have been for those clients if I had done the same for them as I had for my hedge, balanced, conservative, and value accounts. I stopped insuring then because November is typically a very strong month, especially in election years where six of the previous seven election Novembers were up 16 percent for that one month alone! However, there is always the possibility of event risk in the market. I don't think any of us were prepared for the election debacle in November 2000 or September 2001.

When we stick with automatic strategies, when we take the guesswork out, when we avoid emotion and try to be rational, we have the best chance for success. But whenever we think we are smarter than the market, we expose ourselves to a lot of risk. Whenever I get too smug and think I know what is happening, I remind myself of November 2000 or September 2001. I also remind myself of the times that puts worked—when I was nervous and a little more cautious. Probably the smartest decisions I have made in my career revolved around the stop losses I used in 1987, the large number of bonds I bought in the 1980s, and the puts I bought for many accounts in the early months of 2000 and 2001. When we are nervous and base our decisions on reality rather than guesses on the direction of the market, we can make good decisions. But when we are overly confident and excited, we often don't look at the risks as well as the rewards. When you don't think you can read into the future, be careful. The dumbest mistakes involve thinking we have a crystal ball and forgetting how volatile the market is. It is when we think the market is rationale and moves within certain risk parameters that we get burned.

How Puts Work

How Do You Make Money on Puts?

If the price of the underlying stock goes up after you purchase your put, you will have a loss. In taxable accounts you can usually write off the cost of the put, and the tax saving helps reduce the actual cost of the put.* If the stock price falls more than the cost of your put, the put will usually be profitable.† If the stock is down in price at expiration date, you have two choices. One, you can sell the put, which will have gone up in price and be profitable; the profit on the put offsets the loss in the stock. Two, you can "put" the stock to the insurer, which means you are exercising your right to sell the stock at the strike price. No matter how low the stock goes, you can still sell at the strike price. For example, no matter how low Cisco fell, you would sell at $60 if you had the $60 put, even if Cisco fell to zero.

Comparing Our Puts to the Stop Losses

As with puts, stop losses set exit prices for us. We pay the premiums for puts because stops don't always get us out in fast-falling markets.

To reduce the cost of puts, you may want to consider using a stop loss limit with a put at a lower price. The puts are less expensive as you can place them under the limit order.

---

*For example, if you paid $2 for the Cisco put and Cisco went up but you were in the 28 percent federal tax bracket and 5 percent state, then you would save 66 cents in taxes and your net loss on the put would be only $1.33 instead of $2.

†Depending on whether the put is in, out, or on the money, and because of time premiums, puts may not always be profitable. I'll go over the math in Chapter 4.

FIGURE 6.1 Stop Loss versus Put

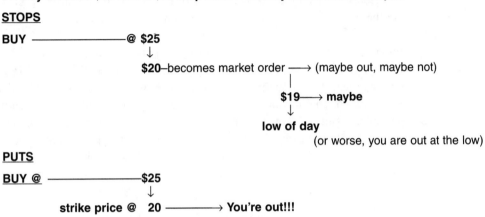

#1. Buy stock at $25 with a $20 stop loss.   #2. Buy stock with a $20 put.

STOPS

BUY ————————@ **$25**
                                 ↓
         $20–becomes market order ———→ (maybe out, maybe not)
                                            |
                                   $19——→ **maybe**
                                              ↓
                                   low of day
                                              (or worse, you are out at the low)

PUTS

BUY @ ————————**$25**
                           ↓
     strike price @   20 ———————→ **You're out!!!**

The Mechanics

> Remember, the stop loss is a maybe, the put a sure deal!

Let's look at Cisco again. Assume you bought ten shares at $62 per share and at the same time purchased the $60 put, which cost you $1.50 per share. (One put protects 100 shares, so the total you need to spend is $150 for 100 shares.) In order to make a profit in the stock, it has to rally above $63.50 as you paid $62 plus the cost of the put for $1.50. If Cisco goes up to $80, you would have a $16.50 profit. Of course, you have $150 less profit than the person who did not buy the put because the profit on the stock position would be reduced by the cost of the put insurance. Now assume Cisco fell as it did in 2001 to $13 a share.

Without the put:

Sales price	$1,300
Cost	–6,200
Loss	**–$4,900**

With the put:

Assume you purchase 100 shares of Cisco at $62

Stock cost = $62.00 per share or a cost of	$6,200
Put cost = $1.50 per share or a cost of	150
Total cost	$6,350
Sales price	$6,000
Cost of stock plus cost of put	–6,350
Loss	**– $350**

As you can see, when the stock was profitable you made $150 less, resulting in a net profit of $1,650. However, when the stock fell to $13, your loss was only $350 versus the person without the insurance who lost $4,900!

The question you should ask yourself here is: Would you be more upset if you did not make the best return, or would you be more nervous if you thought you might have a loss?

There is another way you can make money on puts. You don't have to sell the stock. Alternatively, you could sell the profitable put and come out with exactly the same dollars. For example, if you thought the worst was over with Cisco and it had fallen as low as it was going, you might want to keep the stock and sell the put instead. You would realize the same loss of $350 even though the stock fell from $62 to $13. The put has become worth $4,550. For example, the difference between the $13 and $60 was over $47. However, you paid $1.50 so your profit per share is $45.50, or on a hundred shares it is $4,550!

$$\begin{array}{r}
\text{Profit on Put } \$4,550 \\
\underline{\text{minus Stock loss} = \$4,900} \\
\text{Total loss} = \$350
\end{array}$$

The put became worth a lot more money. Your $150 investment grew to $4,550 and so the large fall in Cisco was offset by the put's appreciation. You can close out or sell your put, make a large profit on the put, or hold Cisco and hope it comes back in price. No matter which exit strategy you use, you have saved yourself over $4,550 of downside risk.

Know When to Hold; Know When to Fold

The difference between a successful investor and a long-term investor is knowing when to get out of the market and take some profits. Often when an investor watches stocks go up and then fall, he or she will feel like a long-term investor. When trades go sour or we let profits disappear, we need to justify our inactivity as a result of being in the market for the long term. But even if the market comes back, it does not necessarily mean an individual stock will come back. Remember that if you invested in Lucent and rode it down 80 percent, it will take a 400 percent return to get you back. It takes a long time even in the best of markets for stocks to come back 400 percent.

Investors often think that buying insurance is a waste of money, but because none of us has a crystal ball and we all learned that even what we consider the bluest of the blue chips had the potential to fall over 70 percent, 80 percent or even more, a little insurance may give us a lot of peace of mind and let us stay in the market without emotion and panic. Those who sell into bad markets usually regret it. Those who ride through the ups and downs seldom find that the market does not come back. However, it is stressful to stick in there when your stocks have fallen badly. When the risks in the market seemed to be 20 to 30 percent and the rewards, especially in growth stocks, seemed to be almost the same, the reward/risk ratio seemed reasonable. But now with 2000 and 2001 behind us, there is an awareness that things may never be the same. The risks now often outweigh the rewards. Great stocks can and do fall, often by never-before-seen amounts. Examples of those who sat too long and soured are:

- AT&T fell over 73 percent from a high of $61 in 1999 to a low of $16.50 in December 2000.
- Lucent fell over 90 percent from a high of $84 in December 1999 to a low of $6.95 in April 2001.
- Cisco fell over 83 percent from a high of $82 in March 2000 to a low of $13.60 in April 2001.
- Intel fell over 70 percent from a high of $75 in 1999 to $22.25 in April 2001.

Remember too that even though 2000 and 2001 saw one of the worst market corrections ever, there is no reason that it cannot happen again. Do you really have the patience to wait for a recovery? It is important that you have a strategy to deal with investments when they are falling or just sitting for years. Risks will always be here:

- The risk a stock will not make its numbers.
- Some conflict or tragedy will occur someplace in the world.
- Allan Greenspan might see inflation again.
- The Fed might raise rates too fast again, consumer confidence might wane, or monetary fine-tuning may be overdone.
- Fiscal policy may be determined by political biases instead of concerns for the well-being of our citizens. (Do you think politicians would ever put themselves ahead of the country?)
- A well-respected analyst might change his or her opinion.
- Maybe CNBC will air a negative statement and viewers will overreact.

Lately, the market has a tendency to snowball and to avoid the avalanche, maybe the cost of a put is not all that bad. In reviewing puts and their uses, remember I am not saying they are perfect investments; as a matter of fact, most of the time the market goes up and you will probably lose money on most puts. Additionally, 100 percent of the put premium is at risk if the stock price goes up.

As you start to use market insurance, you will need to make many decisions similar to those you make when you buy other insurance. You must decide whether you want

- coverage for your whole account or just for selected stocks;
- long-term or short-term insurance; or
- protection for all possible events and risks or just the most likely.

Do You Want to Protect the Whole Pie or Just a Slice?

Insuring the Whole Package

The first thing you need to determine when choosing personal property insurance is the value of your assets. If you are just starting out and have only a few valuable items, it may be worthwhile to buy insurance on just those few items rather than purchasing a policy to cover all your household items. As you accumulate furniture, computers, a home, appliances, and so on, you may also want to buy insurance to cover the whole package. It is important to determine if you should insure just those items that are especially valuable or insure everything with extra insurance or riders on the valuable items. With stocks you need to make the same decision. Do you have the bulk of your wealth in just one or two stocks that need to be insured or do you need to insure the whole package, or do both?

In 1978, the navy hired a moving company to move our furniture from Boston to Virginia Beach. During the trip the truck ran a red light and hit a building, tearing off the door of the truck. The truck fell into a river in Salsbury, Maryland. Everything we owned was on that truck, including my most prized possessions. My mother's mementos and all the things my dad gave me of hers were lost forever. The love letters from my husband, our photos, our children's favorite toys, everything ended up in the river. Also what would end up being our two most valuable material items, two Picasso vases that we purchased in Europe for a couple of hundred dollars, and were valued years later at over $350,000 were lost.

We thought we had one of the best insurance companies, USAA, but it denied our claim, at first saying it was an act of God. Finally, it denied our claim because the drivers were underage and the movers not technically licensed. Even if it had agreed to pay, it would have never paid for the few high-value items, such as the vases, because we did not have special riders on them. We learned that we had to learn to read the fine print and evaluate carefully the right type of insurance for the market and other personal financial contracts.

Have the right contracts. We should have had riders on our most valuable items, just as you should probably have more protection on those investments that make up a large part of your personal wealth.

The divers we hired found a few items and placed them in our garage. As we waited for the insurance claim to be settled, the mold and mildew from these items filtered through our air-conditioning system, causing my daughter to become extremely ill. Suddenly, we discovered our military health insurance was not adequate either.

I am telling you this story for several reasons. First, I think we sometimes don't plan carefully enough before changes occur. Second, even if you think you are savvy in financial matters as I thought we were, you might want to think twice.

The accident changed my life. It made me realize that what mattered most were my family and our health. Nothing we lost compared to my daughter's illness. We vowed we would make health insurance the highest priority in our financial plan. The accident also taught us that the right kind of insurance is critical and that as boring as it is, we had to spend more time researching and understanding exactly what we needed and how much risk we could afford. I had to give up teaching and consulting to pay the hundreds of thousands of dollars in bills we incurred: medical, scuba diving, furniture, and clean-up.

Things eventually turned out fine for us, but there is another side to this story. People would scavenge through our belongings that were either too wet or too filthy to bring into the garage. A young woman came by early one morning, pleading with me to give her the mattresses. Even after I showed her they were filled with bugs, worms, oil, and sewage from the river, she still begged for them. She said her husband had left her and her three children with nothing, not even beds to sleep on. I promised her I would buy her mattresses as soon as our insurance company paid. Little did I know then it would never pay, but maybe she did because she was so desperate that the next morning I saw that the mattress had been dragged off. That incident made me aware of how important it is for all of us to be in control and to protect ourselves from as many threats to our financial security as possible.

The accident changed how I did business. It made me pay close attention to the risks and losses that my clients could afford and the need to have protection on all assets. I became a lot more aware and interested in hedging strategies and safety nets for investing. It made me focus much more on target returns instead of market returns.

After the accident I was able to put information together for Congressman Whitehurst from Virginia to change the law on military moves. I set up seminars for women and for military families to show them how to protect their financial future. If we had had extra health insurance instead of relying on the navy's medical system, we would have been spared eight years of work pulling ourselves out of what could have been financial ruin. If we had had insurance riders on our few valuable items, USAA would have been forced to honor the policy we paid it to provide. A few riders would have dramatically minimized our financial loss. Remember to insure separately the valuable stocks—those that have a large impact on your future financial health. Especially insure stocks that are over 10 percent of your portfolio.

We all assume that small losses are likely, but catastrophic losses occur so rarely that we don't prepare for them. Think of AT&T and Lucent. How many of us thought they would have catastrophic falls? I think most would have guessed the worst to be 20 percent . . . but never 70 or 80 percent falls. Those are catastrophic, not just part of the acceptable ups and downs in the market. When there are changes in your life, consider insurance. When there are changes in the market—in a company's earnings, in market share, in competitive abilities, or in PEs—take a second look and see if insurance is needed. Look at your own situation every few years, especially when you retire, get married, have children, or get divorced. Maybe for years you could handle market risk, but there may be a time when you have to cash in some of

Make a list of the things in life and in the financial markets that are the most important to you and make sure they are protected.

your savings to pay for college, a new home, or retirement. Don't let one dramatic move in the market—like the millennium crash or a terrible accident—change your life and wipe out your dreams. When you can't afford to lose money, when you have large profits, or when you are at the top of a bull market, either pull out or consider a little insurance. Don't wait until you've lost everything to try to change the rules as I did. Insure yourself before the accidents happen.

At turning points in your life or with big changes (or moves), you need to reevaluate your risk tolerance and market insurance. In our example above, if you had had only a few stocks, such as Cisco, it would probably have been worthwhile buying a put on individual stocks, especially if these few stocks are a large part of your overall wealth. However, if you had a well-diversified portfolio with lots of mutual funds and stocks in many different sectors, you would probably benefit more from the purchase of an index put option. If you are invested in many sectors, such as health care, oils, food, technology, biotechs, telecommunications, and the like, your portfolio will probably move up and down closer to the market than if you had a few stocks that were in only one or two sectors. If you have lots of positions, it can be burdensome and very time consuming to shop for puts on each stock. If you have one piece of art that makes up 90 percent of your wealth, a rider might be feasible; but if you have many items in your home of equal worth, it may be more economical to purchase insurance on the whole house.

Insuring the Whole Pie

If your portfolio is well diversified, consider puts on the whole market or an index, such as the Dow, the Nasdaq, or the S&P 500. Buying an index put is similar to buying insurance on your whole house and its belongings instead of insuring just a few items. For example, you could purchase Standard & Poor's 500 Index options (SPX), which trade on the Chicago Board Options Exchange (CBOE). You purchase a stock put to protect an individual stock position, and you purchase an index put to protect or hedge a diversified portfolio of stocks and mutual funds. A decline in the market could cause your portfolio to fall, but your put or insurance would become worth more, and the put's appreciation could offset a substantial part of the loss.

Again Think about How Long and How Much

Long-term versus Short-term Insurance

You can buy most insurance for short periods to cover special situations, such as life insurance when you are young to cover children's education, or you can buy insurance to cover you for many years. The same is true for insurance on your investments. We need to think of how long and how much. We can think of puts as long-term or short-term disability. Although many stocks actually died in 2000 and 2001 and will never come back, most of the time stocks just become sick for a while, so sick that they can no longer work for us. That is why we need disability insurance for them. The decision often boils down to short-term or long-term insurance. Long-term put insurance, or Long-term Equity Anticipation Securities (LEAPs), is available for some stocks and stock indexes for as long as three years.

How Nervous Are You Really?

In, on, or out of the Money

As with any insurance we need to decide how much coverage we want. Do we want to be protected from all downside risk? Do we want to be protected from falls greater than 5 percent, 10 percent, or another percentage? Let's look at Cisco again. If we assume it is trading at $60 and we want no downside risk (except the cost of the put), we want to buy a put at a strike price of $60. This is an *on-the-money put.* (Options usually trade in $5.00 increments, but for some stocks they trade in $2.50 increments.) If we wanted no downside and even wanted some assurance that we could get out at a higher price than $60, we might have to buy a $65 option. No matter how low Cisco falls, we could sell it at $65 even though it currently trades at $60. This is an *in-the-money put,* as the strike price is higher than the current market price. If you were willing to take a little risk, you could buy the $55 put, which would be *out-of-the-money,* as the strike price is less than the current price. This is similar to a copayment on health insurance. Obviously, the higher the strike price, the more the protection and the more the cost, so the in-the-money $65 will cost more than the $60 on-the-money or still more than the $55 out-of-the-money.

LEAPs on Indexes

If your fears are longer term, you could purchase longer-term insurance, or LEAPs, on indexes just as you can with individual stocks.

Buying options, or puts, on individual stocks is easy, but it gets a little more confusing on market indexes. (The differences are summarized at the end of this chapter.) Let's look at a well-diversified portfolio you want to protect for the long term. You can buy puts on the S&P 500 if your portfolio is balanced between growth and value. If your portfolio is overweighted in technology, Internet, and biotech stocks, and looks more like the Nasdaq, then you can purchase puts on the Nasdaq (QQQ puts known as the Q). If you have a few old-line value stocks that look more like the 30 stocks in the Dow, then you can buy an index put on the Dow.

Most portfolios should include some value stocks, which tend to be more stable; some growth stocks, which tend to offer higher returns; some stocks that are inflation hedges; and some stocks that can protect you from deflation. Achieving that kind of diversification can be daunting for most of us. That's where indexes come in. One that is probably the best to start with is the S&P 500. The Standard & Poor's 500-Stock Composite Index, or S&P 500 for short, is an unmanaged, weighted index of 500 stocks that represent many different industry groups. It is designed to provide investors with a tool to measure overall stock market performance. The S&P 500 index is made up of 500 companies in over 80 different industries, something nearly impossible for individual investors to duplicate. You can see why this is a good measure of overall stock market activity. It is probably a lot better than the Dow, which represents only 30 companies. Investors trying to get a well-rounded portfolio may want to start first by purchasing something that looks like the S&P 500 index.

If you want a well-balanced account, you could buy an index mutual fund geared to the S&P, or you could purchase a trust that duplicates the S&P 500 directly. The unit trusts that are modeled after the S&P 500 are called Standard and Poor's depositary receipts, SPDRs or Spiders for short. (SPDRs trade under the symbol SPY.) To keep it simple, when you purchase Spiders, think of it in terms of buying one-tenth of the S&P 500 index. Because Spiders represent one-tenth of the value of the S&P, if the S&P 500 is trading at 1,000, then Spiders will be trading at about $100 per share. They provide considerable diversification and representation in many sectors and usually much more safety than a single stock.

Times for Passive and Times for Active Management

Most readers are probably familiar with mutual funds designed to track the performance of the S&P, such as the Vanguard 500. SPDRs, or Spiders, seem to be similar to index mutual funds, but there is an important difference. SPDRs are exchange-traded funds (ETFs), listed securities that can be bought and sold during the trading day unlike an index mutual fund, which can only be bought or sold at its net asset value (NAV) based on the closing prices of the representative stocks at the end of the day.

Not only can you trade SPDRs, but you can use stop losses under them; and although you can insure index funds with puts, it is more difficult to match up the amounts. Also, because the S&P 500 is unmanaged, it often doesn't make sense to pay a fee to a mutual fund company to manage something that doesn't need to be managed. I am a big believer in using funds and paying fees for professional money managers to manage small cap stocks, hedge portfolios, risky stocks, and sector funds. However, I find it hard to recommend funds for nonmanaged indexes or for most bond portfolios.

Spiders versus funds:

- Spiders have minimal management fees.
- You can trade Spiders any time during the day; they trade on the American Exchange under the symbol SPY.
- You can use stop losses.
- You can hedge Spiders more efficiently with protective puts.

In this chapter I use the S&P depositary receipts, or Spiders, in our example instead of index funds. There are also exchange-traded unit trusts that mirror other indexes; for example, the Diamonds (symbol DIA), which represent the Dow indexes, and QQQ, which represents the Nasdaq index.

The Spider and Put Combo . . . one of the best on Wall Street

Add a LEAP for Safety

One of my favorite strategies for those looking to share in market returns while retaining a high degree of safety is the combination of the S&P 500 index trust and insurance. This Spider and put combo is one of the best combinations on Wall Street.

Because SPDRs represent the market, they can be protected or hedged by using the long-term put options, or LEAPs, as discussed earlier. If the S&P 500 is at 1,000 (representing an aggregate market value of $100,000), the LEAP index will be at 100 (representing an aggregate market value of $10,000). For each 100 SPDRs held, one S&P 500 LEAP put could be purchased to protect the investment in the SPDRs from a market fall.

It's easier to understand if you look at a hypothetical example. The market moves so much that it is difficult to pick any exact trade. I am going to use Spiders priced at $100 to make the example simple to follow and will exclude commissions and trading costs. Remember the puts protect 100 shares, so you can only protect in increments of 100 shares.

Assume you were to purchase 1,000 SPDRs at $100 each for a total cost of $100,000. Now assume you are nervous about the long term and you purchase 10 three-year LEAPs on the S&P 500 index with a strike price of $100 and a premium (cost) of $5 each, or a total cost (without commissions) of $5,000. The total investment is $105,000: $100,000 for the SPDRs and $5,000 for the put insurance.

What happens if the market falls? What if we have another correction as we did from March 2000 to March 2001? What if the S&P 500 falls 40 percent? That would put the S&P 500 in our example at 600, or a 40 percent fall from our assumed level of 1,000.

Because the SPDRs are one-tenth the value of the S&P, the $100,000 investment is now worth only $60,000. The LEAPs that you purchased at $5 each would have an intrinsic value of $40 ($100 strike price minus $60 current price). Even though you would have lost $40,000 in the market, the LEAPs would be worth $40,000, thus offsetting your loss. The only loss you incur is the $5,000 cost of the put insurance.

S&P falls 40%:

    Your SPDRS fall from $100,0000————→$60,000 =   **–$40,000 loss**

S&P falls 40%:

    The put insurance increases from $5,000 to $40,000 =   +$35,000 profit

Net loss suffered in a 40% market correction is cost of put,

    or 5% =   **–$ 5,000 net loss**

Not too bad! Does it make you wish you had some insurance in 2001?

What happens if the market goes up? The problem with insurance is that it can be costly if done on entire portfolios all the time. As volatile as recent market corrections have been, types of falls are infrequent, so we need to use care with insurance as with any other investment.

    If the market goes up, you have just paid for insurance that is never going to pay off. However, having that insurance probably gave you peace of mind and allowed you to stay in the market until it rebounded. Consider your risk tolerance. Would you have sold in a panic if you hadn't had the insurance and had actually taken a large loss? If the answer is yes, then the insurance was worth it. If you would have ridden the market down and waited for the rebound without worrying, then the insurance is probably not for you. If the market had gone up 40 percent instead, your $100,000 investment would be worth $140,000, but you would have cut off about 5 percent of your appreciation potential as you spent $5,000 on unnecessary insurance. Your profit is 35 percent instead of 40 percent. A poorer scenario is if the market had only gone up 10 percent over those three years. Your 10 percent return would be only 5 percent, and you would have been better off in money market funds or bonds. But wait! There are some offsets to your costs. If you are investing in a taxable account, you may be able to take a loss for the put cost and also offset your cost with some of the dividends on the S&P.

Dividends and Taxes May Pay for the Insurance

When you buy insurance, it often accrues dividends that you can reinvest in the policy to pay for some of the premiums. The same is true with the S&P 500—a hidden surprise. The S&P pays dividends, so let's assume the dividends average about $1.25 per share or $1,250 a year. If you paid $5,000 for the put insurance, you would have $3,750 worth of dividends over the three years that could offset the $5,000 cost; so in our example the cost could be as little as $1,250 depending on the dividend yield on the S&P. If you add in tax savings (assuming you are investing in a taxable account) of $1,000 (assume a 20 percent capital loss), your out-of-pocket expense is only $250. So for $250 you bought yourself much peace of mind and the ability to stay in the market through good and bad times.

What's Wrong with This Picture?

Is your out-of-pocket expense really only $250? In reality, you gave up the $3,750 in dividends as you used them to pay for the insurance. Theoretically, the loss of dividends is part of your loss. However, if you compare this to investments that have no dividends, this package looks very attractive. I like to think of this as an insurance policy that reinvests the dividends to pay off the premiums.

However, there are no perfect investments. If there were, all of us would be invested in them, and there would be no need for money mangers like myself or for books like this.

Options have risk, so you should have a clear understanding of your risk tolerance. Consider the tax consequences of your strategies and determine if they are more suitable for IRAs and tax-sheltered accounts or for individual taxable accounts. Also don't forget to read the CBOE booklet.

LIFE and DISABILITY INSURANCE	MARKET INSURANCE
*Pay someone to guarantee you a certain $ amount	*Pay someone to guarantee you a certain $ amount
*The greater amount insured, the higher the premium	*The greater amount insured, the higher the premium
*Pays when you die, are disabled, or have an accident	*Pays when stocks falls below certain price
*Insurance stops when you cease paying premiums	*Insurance stops when you cease to buy puts and pay premiums
*You buy insurance to protect you from financial ruin	*You buy insurance to protect you from financial ruin

The Pros and Cons of Puts

Pros:

- Peace of mind
- Allow you to hold your positions through good times and bad
- If position trades below strike price, you can sell at strike price no matter how low it goes—even to zero.
- Can participate in upside appreciation
- Can keep voting rights, dividends, and any other distributions and splits
- Can be used to manage accounts with tax efficiency

Cons:

- Cost of premiums
- If the market goes up, the puts expire and are worthless.
- Premiums have to be paid up front.
- Tax straddle rules apply on index puts.

- Can be complex, so for most investors hedged accounts are better handled by professionals.

Summary

Over a three-year period in the past, it was much more likely that the S&P would return over 10 percent annually so we might not need the insurance. If you have five-year or six-year horizons in the market, there is no need for insurance on most of your portfolio. You may occasionally want to consider short-term LEAP puts when the market looks as though it has topped or is overvalued. We never know if we need insurance until something happens. I didn't plan on my truck's falling in the river or the 2000 elections stalling so long or Alan Greenspan having such poor data on which to base interest rate hikes in 2000 or the world being turned upside down by terrorists in 2001. The good part is if we do have insurance, it can save us financially. With the extreme volatility in the market and with almost 70 percent falls in the Nasdaq from March 2000 to March 2001, I would prefer to opt for a little less appreciation and a little more peace of mind. I tend to prefer shorter-term puts, one year at a time. They provide more flexibility and can be renewed each year to lock in higher and higher profit levels. Remember though, as with any insurance, the shorter the term, the lower the cost, but when you may have to renew it year after year, the costs can go up.

Index Options versus Stock Options

The three major differences between index options and stock options that you should consider revolve around the exercise date, the valuation of the puts at the end of the year, and tax consequences.

The exercise date. Exercise dates on index options work a little differently than those on individual stocks. For example, on an individual stock put, you have two ways to take your profit. You can elect to put the stock, or "exercise" it, any day up till the expiration date. With both you can sell the put and take your profit. However, on index options you can exercise the option only on the expiration date.

Mark to the market. Index options are also "marked to the market" at the end of the year. That means your brokerage firm will value these options at the end of the year, and you will be liable for the profit or loss up to that time even if you have not sold them.

60/40 rule. Index options also have a slightly different tax treatment. They follow what is called a 60/40 rule, which simply means that the index is subject to 60 percent long-term and 40 percent short-term rates. Although these options have a tax treatment that is more confusing than that for stock options, it is still something for investors who have a well-rounded portfolio and a good accountant to consider.

CHAPTER 7

Writing Covered Calls
Generating Income and Getting Paid to Sell

DEFINITION

Writing covered calls is a strategy of selling call options to increase the safety of stocks and to generate income while you are waiting to sell. Through *covered-call writing,* the owner of a stock enters into a call option contract promising to sell the stock at a specified price. In return, the owner receives income, or premium payments. Like puts, covered calls are used in this strategy to decrease risk.

KEY

Safety: ★★★★   Simplicity: ★★★

Returns: $$$$ Tax efficiency: –$$

SUMMARY

Safety: Writing covered calls adds safety to investing and can often decrease risk by 10 to 20 percent, although it doesn't offer the safety and guarantees of puts.

Returns: Writing covered calls can increase returns dramatically in flat markets and help minimize loss in bad markets. However, covered calls can cap the appreciation in strong rallies.

Simplicity: Although this strategy takes time to understand, it is relatively simple to employ.

Tax efficiency: Calls often generate short-term income. They can trigger capital gains on the underlying stocks and are usually used for low-income investors and in tax-sheltered accounts, such as pensions and IRAs. However, careful evaluation of underlying stocks and using out-of-the money calls* and long-term calls (LEAPs) can make this strategy suitable for taxable accounts as well.

What This Chapter Is About

This chapter walks you through the covered-call strategies that are used most often to reduce risk. There are many other strategies in which call options are used, but I concentrate on covered-call strategies. Before you can decide on a strategy, you have to determine how you feel about the market and your stock's potential appreciation.

When the market is falling, use puts. When the market is flat or in a trading range, use covered calls. When the market is rising use buy and hold.

- *Covered calls* work best when the market is flat, or in a trading range (rallies and falls ±10%).
- *Puts* work better when the market is falling.
- *Buy and hold* works best when the market is rallying.

Who Should Use Covered Calls?

Covered-call writing is a strategy for risk-averse investors looking for income, consistency of returns, stability, and, in addition, a 10 to 20 percent reduction in risk. Historically, professional money managers used options to reduce the risk in portfolios. With the increased volatility in the market, individual investors are now taking a much more active interest in defensive options as well. Covered-call writing is used most often by the following:

- Disciplined investors who are either neutral or slightly pessimistic about the market.
- Investors seeking better returns with minimal increases in risk.
- Investors who believe that the market will trade in narrow ranges, up and down by 10 percent, or that the market will be flat for a while.
- Investors who don't want to sell their stocks at current prices but would be willing to sell 10 to 20 percent higher.
- Investors who want to generate income from their stocks.
- Investors seeking 10 to 20 percent downside protection.

---

*Out-of-the-money means selling above the current price of the stock.

- Institutions and pensions that have fiduciary responsibilities requiring th
  several risk-reduction strategies.

Before you decide whether you want to use covered calls, you have to understand your goals, your targeted returns, and your risk tolerance.

Who should not use covered-calls? Investors who think the market or their stocks have bottomed and don't wish to cap any upside potential should not use covered calls. Those who are optimistic and think the market might rally more than 20 to 30 percent and seek home runs also should not use covered calls. In addition, investors usually should not use covered calls in taxable accounts.

What Are Covered Calls and Covered Writes?

Options go back to the 1600s when flower merchants in Europe tried to protect themselves from the dangers of price falls and damaged crops. In the United States, options started to be actively traded in 1973 on the Chicago Board Options Exchange and now trade on more than 2,000 securities. They can be used by aggressive traders to maximize returns or by conservative investors to reduce risk. The terminology, more than the concepts, often confuses investors, so let's review the terminology.

Calls. *Calls* are option contracts. If you are a call buyer, you have the right to buy the stock at a specified price. If you buy a call, you usually are optimistic and expect the price of the stock to increase. If you are a call seller (writer), you are obligated to sell the stock if it reaches the strike price. Call sellers are either neutral or slightly pessimistic or have a target price.* This chapter focuses on selling calls, not buying them.[†]

Strike price. The *strike price* is a specified price, or exercise price, at which an investor agrees to buy or sell a stock. *Assume we sell a call option on XYZ, promising to sell our stock at $50 in May in return for a payment of $5.* For XYZ the strike price would be $50.

Premium. The *premium* is the payment that an investor pays or receives for the option contract; the premium for the May $50 call in our example was $5.

Covered Calls. With all options you have the ability to either buy or sell. With the puts, we bought protection; but to use calls to give us safety, we sell the calls. Writing *covered calls* involves selling call options against stocks that we own. If you did not own the stock and sold a call, that would be a *naked call* as there would be no underlying stock to cover.

---

*A pessimistic investor would buy a put or sell a call. The put would give the investor the right to sell the stock at a specified strike price. An optimistic investor would sell a put and buy a call.

[†] I talk only about buying puts and selling calls. Of course, you can do the opposite—sell puts and buy calls—as discussed in the final chapters. Usually, those strategies are used to increase returns, not safety.

Write. *Covered call* and *call write* are synonymous terms. We frequently use the word *write* instead of sell. Writing a call means selling a call. A covered write program is a program of selling covered calls. I will be using the term *covered calls* for most of this text.

Covered writes = Covered calls   Writing calls = Selling calls

Total return. If you own the shares of a stock, you can add the premium that you receive for selling the call and the dividend on the underlying stock to the stock's appreciation and thus possibly increase your returns.

Total return = Appreciation + Dividends + Call premiums − Taxes

It is important to think in terms of total return for all your investments, not just covered calls. When taxes are a concern, you should compare investments based on the returns after taxes and commissions. For example, if you own real estate, you shouldn't consider just the appreciation but also the cash flow (negative or positive) and the tax savings. Looking at total after-tax returns allows you to compare investments and strategies more accurately.

Covering. There are many variations of call strategies for traders and those looking for maximum return, but I discuss only selling calls on stocks that we own, and I always refer to covered calls instead of naked calls.

Exercise date or strike date. The date by which you are obligated to sell or buy (exercise) your stock. An American-style option is one that you can exercise any day up to the exercise date. European-style options allow you to exercise only on the exercise date. In our example above, the May $50 call, the strike price is $50 and the strike date is the Saturday after the third Friday in May. If it is an American-style option, you can exercise or sell any time up to the exercise date. We are covering them, putting a cap on them, thus limiting the upside appreciation.

Why Sell Calls?

To generate Income. You sell a call option on your stock to generate extra income and provide protection if the market falls. You are basically selling someone the right to call your stock away from you if it goes up in price. In our XYZ example, you would increase your income by $1,000 if you sold two $5 calls per year.

To add safety. Calls don't give you the guarantees of limited downside losses as puts do. However, calls do give you some downside protection as the call premium reduces your cost and therefore gives you downside protection. The amount of protection you receive is equal to the call premium. For example: Let's assume you have a $50 stock and you are paid $5 for a call premium to promise to sell your stock at $55. You get $5 downside protection because it has reduced your cost from $50 to $45; and because your net cost is only $45, you can lose only $45 versus $50.

The trade-off, or what you are giving up to get that money, is any appreciation over $55 (you are capping or limiting your returns to 22 percent).* You have capped your upside at $55 in return for $5 worth of protection on the downside, or $5 worth of income.

If the stock is not called away from you, you could then sell another call for a $5 premium, and your cost basis would then be $40. If you still are not called away and are able to sell another call for another $5 premium, your cost basis is reduced to $35. Theoretically, if the stock is not called away, you could sell calls over and over for years, constantly reducing your cost basis. In the real world it is unlikely that at some point the stock would not get called away. Even worse, the stock could fall so dramatically that the call wouldn't protect you enough on the downside.

Looking at the Top and the Bottom: The Covered Call Protects You Down to the Net Cost, or $45, but Caps You on the Top to $55.

Strike price $55————→ $55 - cap
　　　　　　↑
　　　$50 Current price
　　　　↓
　　　↓ } $5 downside protection
　　　　↓
Net cost = $45 ($50 current price minus $5 call premium)

Important Features

In Chapter 6, I explained protective puts as option contracts that give you the right to sell your stock at a predetermined price no matter how low it fell.

The three main features of your put include:

1. The premium you paid someone.
2. The strike or agreed-on price at which you can sell your stock (protects you on the downside).
3. The maturity, or exercise, date.

---

*The most you can make is $10 for your $45 investment ($50 price–call premium of $5 = $45) $10/$45=22.2%.

Covered calls have the same three features, but they don't provide you as much downside protection. Their main features are:

1. The premiums someone pays you. You can find these premiums with any financial quotation service or in the options tables in most newspapers.
2. The strike, or agreed-on, price at which you have to sell your stock.
3. The maturity, or exercise, date.

With protective puts, you were the buyer but with the covered calls, you are the seller. What you are being paid to sell is the appreciation of your stock over the strike price.

The trade-off with covered calls is more safety and income for less appreciation.

In addition to income and safety, covered calls also offer an automatic and disciplined system of taking profits off the table.

What is wrong with covered calls?

- When prices increase, you are forced to sell your stock to the call buyer who paid you the premium, no matter how high the price goes.
- Tax ramifications
- Costs

Covered calls limit your upside—you can't climb all the way to the top.

Why Should You Use Covered Calls?

Because the market is likely to be up two of every three years, you may not feel you need any protection over the long run. However, just because the market is up doesn't mean your portfolio will follow along. In addition to going up, the market also falls—and falls a lot. It has fallen 10 percent or more over 110 times in the last 100 years. Those 10 percent dips and rallies are what make covered calls attractive.

Confused? Don't worry; once we get to examples, it becomes very easy to see.

When you sell your calls, set targets that you are comfortable with. If you know you would be happy to sell if your stock went up 10 percent to $55, there should be no reason why you would be upset if it sold. You not only get your target of $55 but also an additional $5 call premium. Let someone pay you to sell and move on. But human nature makes us a little greedy. When you feel sad that you sold at a good profit, remind yourself that it is likely that someday that stock will fall again and you can buy it back at a cheaper price. (Or even better, you can use the put-selling strategy explained in Chapter 9 that lets someone pay you to buy your stock back.) The person who is not sure at what price to sell might regret getting out at $60 ($55 + $5 call premium), but if you have set a target to get out, you shouldn't look back.

Sometimes it is easier to think of adding the call premium to your stock price when you sell. If the stock price goes to $55, you are in fact actually out at a price equivalent to the stock's trading at $60. (The $55 strike price + $5 call.) Or you can think of the call as decreasing your cost or increasing your sale price, whichever is easier for you to understand, but to be more accurate mathematically, think of it in terms of a decreasing cost basis.

Let's look at the math.

- XYZ ↓ —If the stock falls $5, you have lost nothing.
- XYZ ↑ — If it goes up to $55, you sell it as you planned and receive $5 appreciation and $5 for the call premium, or $10 for a return over 20 percent (It is actually 22.2 percent—I'll explain the math later.).
- XYZ →goes nowhere. If the stock just sits there and does nothing, you still made $5 per share, or $500 for the total trade, and the best part is you can sell another call and do the whole thing all over again.

Call premiums reduce your cost basis.

What's Wrong with This Picture?

The only thing wrong with this picture is the rearview window. If you are a person who will feel worse if you didn't get the best return and will regret selling if the stock goes higher, then this is not a strategy for you. If you are a person who sets targets or goals and is happy when they are achieved, then covered calls are for you.

The Problems

Personally, I think covered calls are a great strategy in flat or trading markets. However, in good markets or when the market has bottomed, I think they should be used sparingly. But different situations, as we will see, require different strategies.

Sometimes critics say that you sell your winners and hold your losers. First, you want to sell at least part of your winners. That is the purpose of the covered calls: to help you formulate a disciplined approach to taking reasonable profits. Second, there is no reason to hold your losers. If the price falls, close or buy back your call. The call will usually be at a profit and then sell your stock. The call premium will offset some of your loss.

Comparing Buy and Hold with Covered Calls on XYZ

Scenario 1—Buy and hold the stock
Scenario 2—Sell a call for $5 at a strike price of $55

	Scenario 1— buy and hold	Scenario 2— covered call	And the winner is!
XYZ stays even	Earn $0	Earn $5	Covered call
XYZ ↑ $5 ($50 to $55)	Earn $5	Earn $10	Covered Call
XYZ ↑$10	Earn $10	Earn $10	Covered Call*
XYZ ↑ >$10	Unlimited	Earn $10	*Buy and Hold*

---

*Covered calls are the winner because you earn $10 on a $45 investment ($50 minus a call premium), or 22 percent, versus $10 on a $50 investment, or 20 percent, without the covered call.

XYZ↓ $5	Lose $5	Lose 0	Covered Call
XYZ↓ $10	Lose $10	Lose $5	Covered Call
XYZ↓100%	Lose $50	Lose $45	Covered Call

As you can see, the only case where you were better off without the call was when the stock price went above $60. Of course, that one time can be very important if the stock rallies strongly.

And the winner is

- You can see that if XYZ stays even, you are better off with the call.
- If XYZ goes up $5, you are better off with the call (you made $10 versus $5).
- If XYZ goes up $10, you are in better shape with the covered call because although you only made the same $10, you made $10 on a $45 investment versus a $50 investment.
- If XYZ goes above $61, you are better off without the call.
- If XYZ falls $5, you still don't lose anything if you have the call.
- If XYZ falls $10, you lose only $5 versus losing $10 without the call.
- If XYZ falls more than $10, you are in bad shape no matter what you did, but at least with the call you lost $5 less.

> **Don't get greedy—you may not survive to tell about it. If the stock price goes up, you cap your upside, but if the price stays even or falls, covered calls help increase your returns or minimize your losses.**

None of us has a crystal ball, but if we assume the stock in this case has a 50-50 chance of going up, you can see why calls are attractive for part of your portfolio.

Because the calls win in more cases, they increase the probability of having a better return. Don't be greedy and try to hit the big home runs; be smart and increase the probability of making good, steady returns.

Qualcomm

I can tell you hundreds of horror stories about stocks that crashed in 2000 and 2001—Enron and Ciena falling more than 90 percent, Intel and Qualcomm over 75 percent. Qualcomm, which fell from $200 on December 27, 1999, to a low of $42.75 on April 2, 2001, was one of the more interesting as well as more devastating.

Martha's love affair with Qualcomm. In 1998, I met Martha, whose husband had died in a car accident shortly after my husband and I were in a car accident, so I empathized strongly with her. Martha was extremely bright and had a high-paying, powerful job, but she was so depressed after the accident that she couldn't work and went on disability. Martha had enough money, but she fretted about not making more, so she threw herself into stock selections. She watched and listened to every financial talk show, became an expert on stocks, and almost daily would call me about some hot new stock.

My life experiences had made me much more conservative and careful about losing my clients' money, whereas Martha's experiences had made her much more daring. I wanted safety for her as an unemployed widow and constantly encouraged her to consider safer positions and taking profits off the table. But she wanted to be in there for the full ride. Every time I covered a stock with a call, if it rallied and we made our targeted 20 percent, Martha was disappointed. To me, having the stocks called away and making the 20 percent was great. But to her, trying for the best return was more important. Risk is different for everyone: *For me it was having a loss; for Martha it was not making as much money as possible.*

I wanted consistency, downside protection, and to take profits for her. Martha wanted the excitement, the possibility of home runs. We were two people, neither right nor wrong, who could not come to an agreement. We each had different risk tolerances. The final straw was when I sold calls on Qualcomm at $120, after making two 20 percent hits, a total of 40 percent. But Qualcomm went all the way up to $200 in 1999, so Martha would have been better off holding that one particular stock. In 1999 she certainly was right not to want to cut off the upside. But most of her stocks and most stocks in 1999 had PEs and PEGs that could not be sustained for any length of time. Nothing goes up that fast forever. The historical returns for the market are closer to a 12 to 15 percent range, so at some point the market would revert to its mean, or average. My risk tolerance was low then, Martha's high. There is no right or wrong answer. I was trying to fit Martha into my mold. She didn't need peace of mind; she wanted the thrill of the market, to be part of something she thought was exciting. As it turned out, Qualcomm fell to $16, making it seem I might have been right. Just because it fell didn't make me more right than had it gone up to $300 and made Martha look right.

The fact is that our financial decisions have nothing to do with a stock; it has to do with understanding at what point you want safety. In 1999, calls worked wonderfully in getting us out of an overvalued market. With Y2K approaching, covered calls by mid-1999 became a great exiting strategy. It didn't get you out at the top, but close to it, and it would have spared you a lot of the pain in 2000. By mid-2000, protective puts and collars would have worked better. The higher the market gets, the more defensive I like to be. But that's my attitude, not yours. You need to discover who you are. You'll find that some strategies may not be appropriate for you now but may work when the market changes or when your goals change. You may want to be more conservative when you get closer to retirement or when you need more stability and income. Even if your situation doesn't change and you don't want covered calls now, you may want them when the market is high or when you have lots of profits to protect or when you need to take some money out to spend. Consistency may be better than trying to shoot for one or two home runs.

Ideally, you want to hedge at the top of the market instead of at the bottom. When the market looks as though it has bottomed and is ready to turn is not the time to sell calls.

Investing Is Not Gambling

If you are very wealthy and can afford to lose a lot of money, or if you like to gamble, then take some risk but only on a portion of your portfolio. If you want the excitement of a strong bull market, then take 2 to 4 percent of your portfolio and go for the home runs. However, for the other 96 percent, build in some balance and safety and have exit strategies. You may want to hedge only 20 percent with covered calls and puts and use other exit strategies as well as stop losses for another 20 percent. Consider investing a portion of your portfolio in guaranteed packages, maybe some in bonds and the rest in asset allocation or sector rotation strategies. There is no perfect mix, so you need to think about many different strategies instead of randomly selecting stocks. *Investing is about disciplined and thoughtful analysis of risks and rewards.*

Even if you feel good about the overall market and the economy but you're not sure of an individual stock, you may want to consider protection on that stock.

Before you continue, ask yourself some simple questions:

What returns do you feel over the long run are right for you?	_____%
How much risk do you feel you can handle? 10% downside, 20%?	_____%
What is your tax situation? (Do you have carryover losses; can you invest in tax-sheltered accounts?)	_____%
Do you believe in taking some profits?	_____
Do you believe there are certain stocks that will never fall and you feel comfortable holding on to them forever? If so, what stocks are they?	_____
How long would you be willing to wait for a stock to recover?	_____
If your stocks fell 20%, would you sell, buy more, or hold?	_____
If you were invested in the market in 1999 and 2001, did you spend time worrying about your future? Did you postpone some dreams?	_____

After you answer those questions think about how it took IBM ten years to recover from its fall in 1987. It's hoped your answers will help you determine if you would like a few exit strategies.

Covered Calls versus Puts

As good as covered calls can be, they don't offer the downside protection of puts. In late 1999, selling covered calls worked well by getting a lot of investors out at the top of the market. In 2000 and 2001 they gave some protection but in most cases not enough to offset the dramatic falls in many stocks. In those years, buying protective puts would have been better.

If you feel over the long run that you would be happy with 12 percent returns and that 10 percent downside protection is reasonable, then selling covered calls could work for you. If you think that the market will rally strongly, then balanced, or buy-and-hold, strategies will be better.

If you feel you can't handle more than 10 percent on the downside or that the market will fall more than 10 percent, then use protective puts, sector rotation strategies, or collars (discussed in the next chapter).

Be careful about commissions and taxes when you use covered calls. Instead of one commission, you could have several if you keep rolling calls over and over. Consider "wrap," or flat-fee, accounts for your trading accounts. In taxable accounts, buy-and-hold strategies are usually better than trading. Often, strategies like covered calls give you better returns, help you take profits, offer discipline and structure to portfolios, lower risks, and provide the chance for less volatility, but they have terrible tax consequences! Therefore, you should usually consider a well-balanced account built on diversification, solid companies, and a negative correlation between investments when taxes are a concern. Consider covered calls mainly if you are in a low tax bracket, have large carryover losses, or are in pensions, IRAs, and the like.

kid's trusts ?

Charitable? fund !

Alternatives

You have alternatives when the market is on a roller-coaster ride as it was in 2000 and 2001. You can sit there—grin and bear it, pray, and hope that the market will come back over 30 percent for each of the next four years. Or you can be proactive and take control. You can't look back though. You have to look forward and determine what you want in the future. Assume you are starting today. You can set 20 percent targets, sell some calls, and get income and downside protection while you are hoping. If the market goes up 30 percent, you can think of it as a mistake. But if it goes up 20 percent or less, you have made the right decision. It is unlikely that we will have 20 percent returns over the long run, but you have to be judicious when using calls after a crash, because it's after large crashes that the market usually comes back the strongest. Realistically, there is a good chance that we may see only 9 to 12 percent returns for the next few years,* and if that is so, calls should work really well.

How Safe Do You Want to Be?

You can sell different types of calls depending on how much safety you want. Think of a box with a cover. You can place the cover in the box or on the box, or you can hold it over the box. There are degrees of the depth to which you can push the cover into the box. There are also degrees of the height over the box. The deeper into the box, the more protection, but holding the cover too far above the box provides less protection.

---

*Professor Jeffrey Jaffrey, Wharton School of Finance, CIMA, London, Ontario, June 26, 2001. Using a forward-looking economic model, Professor Jaffrey anticipates market returns of 9 percent over the next few years, basing his estimates on dividend yield, inflation, and expected earnings.

FIGURE 7.1 Boxes with Covers

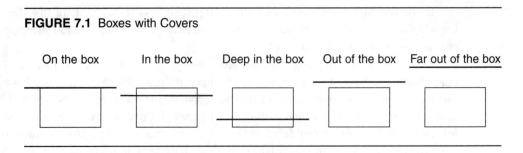

Now think of the cover as covered calls and the box as your stock.

- You can sell covered calls that are *at* the price of the stock—*on-the-money* calls.
- You can sell calls that are *below* the price of the stock—*in-the-money* calls.
- You can sell calls that are *above* the price of the stock—*out-of-the money* calls.

On-the-Money Calls

There are many reasons why you may want to sell an on-the-money call. You may be a little nervous and not mind promising to sell your stock at the current price knowing you would get a relatively large premium for your willingness to sell. You may want to sell your stock but would like to wait for tax purposes until the following year, and until then you want protection and extra income.

Assume XYZ is selling today at $52.50, and you think the market will be flat. If you wouldn't mind selling the stock at 52.50, you would sell a call with a strike price of $52.50 and receive a premium of $1.50.* You may get only $1.50, but if the stock stays flat you keep the $1.50; if it rallies, you're out at 52.50 + $1.50 premium or $54.

In-the-Money Calls

You can select various call strategies depending on how nervous or conservative you are. If you are nervous, you'll want the maximum protection and highest premiums, so you'll want to sell in-the-money calls. You need to be careful about these calls because the IRS looks at them as though you were selling the stock as of the date you write/sell the call.

For example, if you have a stock priced at $52.50, you can promise to sell it at a lower price, or $50. You will get a lot of safety and will be paid a higher premium than if you sold on-the-money or out-of-the money calls. Let's say your premium is $4. You have capped your upside to $54—the $50 strike price plus the $4 premium. Because your stock is at $52.50, you would have to assume that it will not go much higher or is likely

---

*Strike prices, as noted earlier, usually come only in increments of $2.50 and $5.

to fall a little. Your stock is protected for a fall all the way down to $48.50 ($52.50 minus the $4 premium). Notice that you receive much more than when you sold the on-the-money call.

Deep-In-the-Money Calls

You may be very nervous and think your stock's price might fall, so you want more income and higher premiums. In that case you sell a call for a strike price of $45 and you get a $9 premium—a lot of downside protection.

Out-of-the Money Calls

If you feel the stock might rally but you want only a little protection and some income, then you may want to sell a $55 call and get just $1. In this case, you are promising to sell your stock if it goes up to a higher price. You usually do this if you just want a little downside protection or to generate income, but you would probably be inclined to believe your stock has more upside than the person selling on-the-money or in-the-money calls. The closer or tighter in the calls, the more premium you receive.

Far-Out-of-the Money Calls

You could sell a call far out of the box and get only 50 cents for a $60 call. If you think your stock is unlikely to ever get to $60, you may think of it as a gift, especially if you have thousands of shares of the stock.

No Calls—Buy and Hold

Then there is just the box. You think the stock will go up or you are in a buy-and-hold account, so you want no caps. But you have no protection so you suffer the entire downside if the price falls.

Some Alternatives

Assume you are unhappy with covered calls but aren't sure what your other alternatives are. As I said earlier, covered calls work better or worse depending on the market scenario. They worked very well in 2001; and puts also worked well in 2000 and most of 2001. But if the market rallies for the next few years, then stop losses may be more appropriate. You can no longer pick just one strategy just as you can no longer pick one stock and assume it will work well in all situations. You need to assess the risks and rewards, use common sense, and again have an understanding of the market risk and your risk tolerance.

You use covered calls when you are nervous about falls in the market, when the market is very overvalued and you are protecting your downside, or when an account is in transition. When the market looks as though it is at a bottom, it's not worth buying insurance then. You buy insurance on a car before the accident, not after it's totaled.

How to Use Calls

Strategies like covered calls are often better left to the professional money managers. If you like the idea, you should seek a manager who specializes in loss reduction. But whether you work with a financial advisor or you are a hands-on person, you'll need to determine where you want to get out and then look at the financial journals for quotations on the call premiums.

In general, I use a rule of thumb that I don't do calls unless I can get a 10 percent total return, including the appreciation, dividends, and the call premium for nine months or less. If I had a $53 stock, for example, I would want to make on the call and the appreciation at least $5. If I thought there was approximately $2 for the appreciation, then I would want to sell a call that gave me $3 in premiums. Therefore, I would want approximately $3 for the $55 call.

Let's go through some specific examples. The following cover-write worksheets make it easier to work with calls.

STOCK PRICE minus CALL PREMIUM = NET COST

_____ – _____ = _____

WHAT IF STOCK CALLED AWAY AND YOU HAVE TO SELL?

PROFIT (strike price – net price)

STRIKE PRICE minus NET COST = NET POTENTIAL PROFIT IF CALLED AWAY

_____ – _____ = _____

NET POTENTIAL RETURN IN % = PROFIT/NET COST = _____

WHAT IF STOCK SITS THERE AND DOES NOTHING?

PROFIT = CALL PREMIUM   = _____

WHAT IF STOCK PRICE FALLS ?

DOWNSIDE PROTECTION = CALL PREMIUM = _____

Let's use some actual trades. Although I'm using real trades for 2001, don't read too much into these numbers as the prices and premiums will change dramatically in the future.

Some Examples

If you don't understand calls and have never done them, I suggest you walk through the first example with me, but then try the rest by yourself. I'll give you the answers and do the worksheets for you, but try to use the covered call worksheet. You will find when you do them yourself you catch on a lot faster than just by following along with me. Let's start with AMDOX and an out-of-the-money call.

Purchase price in March 2001= $41.65

Price as of June 2001 = $61

Call :

Strike price: $50

Strike date: July

Premium = $4

STOCK PRICE MINUS CALL PREMIUM = NET COST

$41.65   – $4.00   = $37.65

WHAT IF STOCK CALLED AWAY AND YOU HAVE TO SELL?

PROFIT = STRIKE PRICE – NET PRICE

STRIKE PRICE minus NET COST = NET POTENTIAL PROFIT IF CALLED AWAY

$50.00   – $37.65   = $12.35

Instead of looking at your profit in actual dollars you may want to look at percentage returns.

NET POTENTIAL RETURN IN % = PROFIT/NET COST = $12.35/$37.65 = 32.8%

A return of 32.8 percent is a great return, but if we hadn't covered and the stock was trading at $61, your profit would be almost 49 percent. How would you feel in this situation? Would you be happy that you made 30 percent or regret that you didn't hold off for the bigger return? Before you answer, look at what would have happened if the stock had stayed even or had fallen.

What if stocks sits there and does nothing? Even if DOX never moved, never went up a penny for the three months, you would have still gotten 10.62 percent for just three months because you get to keep the $4 call premium that was paid to you.

What if it had fallen? Calls do not protect you as well as puts, but at least you would have some downside protection that would be equal to the premium you received.

DOWNSIDE PROTECTION = CALL PREMIUM = $4

Now you try one. Assume you want to buy AOL and want to try for at least a 20 percent return but would like a little downside protection. You could sell an out-of-the-money call.

Let's look at AOL—Out-of-the-money

Purchase Price = $43 in March 2001
Call: July $50.00 with a call premium of $2.05
What is your profit if the stock goes up? What is your profit if it stays even? How much downside protection do you get?

1. **Find your net cost**
   STOCK PRICE minus CALL PREMIUM = NET COST
   $43.00   – $2.05   = $40.95

2. **Find your profit**
   What if stock called away and you have to sell @ $50?
   Profit (strike price – net price) = $50.00 – $40.95
   NET POTENTIAL PROFIT IF CALLED AWAY @$50 = $9.05 ($50.00 – $40.95)
   NET POTENTIAL RETURN IN % = PROFIT/NET COST = 22% ($9.50/40.95)

3. **Now find return if stock sits there and does nothing**
   PROFIT WILL BE CALL PREMIUM = $2.05
   That is 5 percent for less than four months (we sold a July call on March 26)
   If the stock sat all year and did nothing, every four months we had the potential to make almost 5 percent, or 20 percent per year.

4. **Find what downside protection it offers**
   DOWNSIDE PROTECTION = CALL PREMIUM = $2.05

Why would we do an out-of-the-money call? At the time we did this trade, we would be relatively optimistic about AOL, only shooting for a little downside protection and trying to give ourselves a lot of upside. If we were nervous about the downside, we would have done an on-the-money or in-the-money call, done a collar, or bought a put.

Of course, there is a chance that in three months, the price will go up more than 20 percent, but there is a greater probability that 20 percent runs every three months are unlikely.

FNM with an In-the-money call

Let's do one more where your target is still a 20 percent annual return with FNM (Fannie Mae).

Purchase Price = $80.15 on 5/24/01

EXAMPLE
FNM purchased 5/24/01 at $80.15. Call = A September 80 in-the-money call with a $5.27 premium.

STOCK PRICE minus CALL PREMIUM = NET COST (stock price minus call premium)

$80.15   minus $5.27   = $74.88

What if stock called away and you have to sell?
PROFIT (strike price – net price) = $80.00 – $74.88 = net potential profit if called = $5.12

NET POTENTIAL RETURN IN % = PROFIT/NET COST = 6.8% ($5.12/$74.88)

What if stocks sits there and does nothing?
PROFIT WILL BE CALL PREMIUM/ NET COST = $5.27

What if stock falls?
DOWNSIDE PROTECTION = CALL PREMIUM = $5.27

We sold an in-the-money call. Why would you sell an in-the-money call on a conservative stock?

Economic or fundamental changes may cause us to want to sell. As a result of economic events, I think there will be some change in sectors. We may love the stock and have a large profit in it, so we may want to protect part of the profit when we think the Fed rate cuts are over for a while, causing financials to fall. You may want to sell for technical reasons, as I explore in later chapters, or for tax reasons. Perhaps you may simply want to sell calls to add stability and consistency to your portfolio.

Don't be tempted by call premiums. Don't select stocks because of the premiums that the calls offer. Select your asset allocation first, and then select the stocks and sectors you want. Look at the call premiums after that. Once you have picked your investments, determine what return you expect from them and what amount of risk they have demonstrated in the past. Usually, the higher the premium, the riskier the stock. First pick your stocks and then look for the premiums. That will keep you focused on good companies, not rich premiums. As my husband and one of our coworkers, Bill Woodhull, used to warn clients: if the calls are too rich, it probably means the stock is too volatile. I agree.

Summary

With protective puts, you are paying someone; but with covered calls, someone is paying you. With protective puts, you are in control and it is your choice whether to sell. With covered calls, because you are now the one receiving the premium and getting paid, you give up some control. If the stock goes up, someone can force you to sell at the strike price. Therefore, covered calls cap the upside, that is, limit your ability to climb all the way to the top. The trade-off here is that you are being paid and get extra income and safety in return for less appreciation.

CHAPTER 8

Wearing Collars for Maximum Protection

DEFINITION

Collars are a combination of *protective puts* and *covered calls.* They are a two-way trade offering limited appreciation and income as well as downside protection.

KEY

Safety: ★★★★★   Simplicity: ★★

Returns: $$$ Tax efficiency: –$

SUMMARY

Safety: Collars often offer the maximum protection and are for risk-averse investors looking for income, consistency, or returns and stability.

Returns: Because collars are a combination of protective puts and covered calls, they can increase returns dramatically in flat markets and minimize or prevent losses in bad markets, but in strong markets the calls can cap a certain amount of upside potential.

Simplicity: If you understand protective puts and covered calls, then collars will be simple. They merely combine the two strategies into one, which requires a little more work than either one separately as you need two trades instead of one. The concept is easy for most investors and, once understood, relatively simple to employ.

Tax efficiency: Taxes can get complicated and have to be monitored with collars. Although this strategy is more suitable for tax-sheltered accounts, as you'll see, there are ways to offset some of the tax consequences.

Collars

In Chapter 1, I described collaring as the strategy that would keep you out of a straight jacket in such crashes as the Nasdaq falls in 2000 and 2001. This strategy provides the downside insurance of protective puts and pays for the protection with the premiums from the calls. It is like an insurance policy with dividends that pay the premiums.

The easiest way to think of collaring is as a strategy that covers you on both sides—somewhat like a collar on your shirt. It wraps around your neck and covers you on all sides and is definitely part of the wardrobe for bears. Another term for collars is *hedge-wrapper,* an apt term because it tells us exactly what collars do. They wrap your investments with hedges (or protection). When we hedge a portfolio, we protect it.

Who Should Use Collars?

Collars are easy to understand but require a lot of attention, so I usually recommend you seek a manager who is experienced in hedge strategies instead of using these strategies yourself. Always insist that the strategies be used in flat-fee wrap accounts, which eliminate commissions per trade, because each collar requires three trades.

Collars are attractive for many investors and in many situations—in particular for bears and others afraid the market may fall. They are also attractive for these investors.

- Those who have large profits that they want or need to protect.
- Those who are planning to sell their stocks but want to hold a little longer and try for a higher price.
- Those who want a lot of downside protection but don't want to pay for it.
- Those who want to borrow money and make the collateral more secure.

What Are Collars?

Earlier, we discussed participating indexed CDs, which limit the upside with a cap as a result of their call features, but also have a floor that provides guarantees on the downside. Collars are like do-it-yourself participating indexed CDs. They combine similar downside guarantees as the CDs but also have the limited upside as a result of the call features, or caps.

Indexed CDs	Collars
• Share in part of upside	• Share in part of upside
• FDIC protection on downside	• Put option protection on downside
• One transaction	• Can be multiple transactions
• Simple	• More complicated
• Good returns	• Better returns
• Limited flexibility	• Flexible
• Have a floor and cap	• Have a floor and cap

Collars simply combine buying protective puts with selling calls. Remember that the major flaw with buying insurance in the form of puts was the cost. By combining the puts with the covered calls, we minimize or eliminate that cost. People pay for our call or promise to sell our stock if it goes up. The cost for the put is the loss of appreciation above our strike price.

**Collars =
Protective Puts +
Covered Calls**

Taking Profits

Many investors have highly appreciated stocks that become a large part of their portfolio. Investors know when they are overweighted but may want to wait for a higher price to sell. A good solution for them is to buy a protective put, but puts can be costly. Instead, investors may want to use collars to protect their gains and help pay for the insurance.

Protecting Indexes

Collars can also be used to protect a whole portfolio or indexes. When options on indexes are used, tax rules are different, such as straddle rules noted earlier. Consult with your tax advisor before you use puts, calls, or collars on indexes.

Even the Blue Chips Fall

When we think of big falls, we think they will happen only to Nasdaq stocks, but it happens more and more often to the bluest of the blues. How much do you think a blue chip like Gillette fell? Gillette fell from a high of $64 in March 1999 to $26 in August 2001, or almost 60 percent. Polaroid and Enron went bankrupt in 2001. GE fell over 37 percent.

Long-term investors can usually sustain, 5, 10, even 15 percent falls, but the 60 percent-plus falls in some of the telecommunications stocks in 2000 and 2001 were more than almost any investor can sustain. Volatility is always a risk, whether in the Nasdaq or in the bluest blue chips. Look at the 72 percent Nasdaq fall from March 2000 to March

2001. How long will it take to recover? If you have a 30 percent rally in 2001, 30 percent in 2002, and another 30 percent in 2003, you would still have a 10 percent loss in 2004. A $10,000 invested in the Q (the Nasdaq 100 Index Shares) at its high in 2000 would still be worth only $9,000 in 2004. As bad as that sounds, it is the same situation for hundreds of blue chip stocks.

Many long-term investors are becoming aware that they need to hedge and control risks.

Back to the Basics: A Quick Review

A stock option is a contract that conveys to its holder the right, but not the obligation, to buy or sell shares of the underlying security at a specified price (known as the exercise or strike price) on or before a given date (known as the exercise date).

- *Protective puts:* When prices fall, you can force the put seller to buy your stock because you paid a premium for that right, *no matter how low it falls.*
- *Covered calls:* When prices go up, you are forced to sell your stock to the call buyer, who paid you the premium, *no matter how high it rallies.*
- *Collars:* A combination of protective puts and covered calls.

Covered calls. Covered calls (see Chapter 6) are sold to increase income and generate cash. That income helps offset some of the downside risk and also increases the probability that we would have some decent returns, even in flat markets. The premium from the call can be used to generate income, to buy additional shares of the stock, or *to buy insurance on the stock.*

Letting the call premiums pay for your insurance. If we needed or wanted more protection than calls can provide, the next alternative would be buying a put for maximum protection on the downside. The protective put allows you to sell your stock at a predetermined price, but because the put, the insurance, costs money, it is not perfect either. However, if we expect our stock to trade in a narrow range, be relatively flat, or fall, we may find that collars are a better solution than either puts or calls individually. With collars we combine the calls and puts. We sell the calls to pay for the insurance. To get the best of both worlds, use both put and call strategies simultaneously—known as hedge-wrappers, collars, or combination put and call strategies. These collars control the risk and reduce the cost of protection.

Collars combine covered calls and protective puts simultaneously.

How Do Collars Work?

Assume you own 100 shares of XYZ at $60 per share, which are now trading at $75. You are happy your stock price has gone up so much, but you are nervous, knowing that nothing goes up forever. With your 25 percent return, you have five alternatives:

1. Do you sell, take your profit, and run?
2. Do you try to hold for a better return?
3. Do you sell a call to minimize some of the downside potential?
4. Do you buy a put to protect and lock in your profit?
5. Do you buy a put and also sell a call to pay the premium on the put?

First let's look at alternative 3. We can promise to sell our stock if it goes up to $80 and assume we receive $2 for that call premium. If the stock falls, we have reduced our loss by $2. If it goes up, we have to sell at $82 ($80 + the $2 premium we received).

Second, let's look at alternative 4, buying a put. Assume we buy an XYZ put option expiring in six months with an exercise price of $70 and a premium of $2. You have protected yourself for any downside below $68. ($70 minus the $2 cost of the put.) Your profit would be $68 minus the $60 that you paid for your stock. Although you didn't lock in all your profit, you did protect $8 of the $13.

Third, let's now look at alternative 5. Assume we buy the $70 put and sell the $80 call. The put costs you $2, and the call nets $2, so the collar in this case has a zero cost. You are protected on the downside to $70 and will have capped your upside to $80.

The specifics. To create a collar, the holder of the stock takes these steps.

- Step 1: Sell a call.
- Step 2: Once the call has been sold, use the proceeds to pay for the insurance, or put.
- Step 3: Relax.

Now the investor can sit back, relax, and congratulate herself. If the market falls, she'll be in good shape. If the market goes up, she may have to sell but at a better price than if she sold today. She should be happy no matter what happens; she looks good no matter which way the market goes and can congratulate herself for being bright enough to hold off for a higher price and not sell at the lower price if the stock goes up.

Example. Assume you own 100 shares of a stock that you purchased for $40 a share, and it has risen to $50 per share (assuming no commissions). Let's review your choices.

- Purchase a put option at an exercise price and date that fits into your overall plan. Assume you purchase a $45 put expiring in nine months and you pay a premium for it of $2, a total cost of $200, to cover the 100 shares. (Remember one put contract protects 100 shares.)
- At the same time, sell a call with the same expiration date (it is not necessary to have the same dates but for now assume the same expiration date for both the put and call). Assume you sell a $60 call and get $2, $200 total, for the 100 shares. This is called a zero-cost collar. You received enough from the call to pay for the full cost of the insurance, or put.
- If the stock goes up, you will have to sell at $60 and will have a profit of $20 a share. This is $10 more than if you had sold at the current price of $50.

- If the stock falls, you can either sell the stock or sell the put, but either way you have a profit of $500. (The $45 strike price minus the $40 you paid.)
- If you did not sell the call, your profit would have been only $300 because you would also need to subtract the cost of the insurance from your profit. This is what makes a collar, a better idea for those who do not mind capping the upside because they get the insurance at no cost.

The nice part about puts is that you do not have to sell the stock. You can sell the put and net the same $500 profit, yet keep your stock and collar again.

Zero-Cost Collars

As mentioned above, a zero-cost collar is one in which you receive a call premium that is large enough to pay for the put premium. The collar trades upside appreciation for downside protection. You can structure your collars to net out to zero, but often you may have to sell a call closer in, or "tighter," to get the income you want. Or you may have to buy a put at a lower price with less protection than you might want. Or you could sell calls out a little further in time and take a little time risk and buy shorter-term puts. In the real world, we usually can't get everything—the ideal put and ideal call at no cost. However, surprisingly, it happens more often than you might expect, so the ideal is worth looking for.

Insurance Cost

Remember when I discussed puts and explained that the more insurance you wanted, the higher the insurance premiums. In our example above, if you wanted insurance at $45, or 90 percent of the value of the stock, it would cost you more than if you purchased insurance for 80 percent of the value of the stock. If the insurance costs more, you will have to sell calls that generate more income in order to pay for the more expensive insurance. What does that mean? It means you have to sell calls that are tighter in, that are closer to the current price of the stock, and that will eventually cut off more of your appreciation.

Partial Collar

Assume you have 1,000 shares of XYZ at $50, and you purchase ten of the $45 puts, costing $6 per share. Instead of selling the $65 calls to get the $6, we can sell fewer of the $60 calls. This will cut off the upside on some of the stocks but then allow the rest unlimited upside. Assume we get $7.50 for the $60 calls; then we would have to sell only eight calls to pay for the premium (eight $60 calls @ $7.50 = $6,000; used to pay for the ten $65 puts @ $6 = $6,000).

Credit or Debit Collars

Sometimes everything goes right: The market is going up and people are positive, optimistic, and willing to pay you large premiums for calls. They also are not that nervous about the market falling, so the insurance becomes cheaper. You may be able to sell calls further out or at higher strike prices so that you reduce your costs by giving up less appreciation. You may be able to sell your calls for more than it costs you to pay the insurance. This is called a *credit collar*—you paid for the insurance and have something left over. This is the ideal.

A *debit collar* occurs when you pay for part of the insurance. For example, the put cost you $650 and the call only nets $600, leaving you with a debit of $50.

E-FLEX

If you have accumulated a large amount of stocks (maybe for a company you work for) and you want to protect them, then you may want *flex options*. For many stocks, investors can customize the terms of an options contract to meet a specific objective subject to a 25,000-share minimum. Equity Flexible Exchange Options (E-FLEX) are especially attractive for business owners and executives who own restricted stocks.

You can build in your own features with E-Flexs. For example, you can set the price at a numerical value or as a percentage move, or as a percentage value of the market price of the underlying stock. You can also vary the expiration dates. Regular calls and puts are not sold every month and have limited exercise dates. These flexible options can be just for a day or two or for two years. Styles also vary from American (when you can exercise your stock on any day) to European (when you can only exercise on the final day). As you can see, there is a lot of flexibility with these customized options, thus the name E-Flex.

Monetizing Put Options

Collars and hedging create such a secure investment that they allow you to borrow up to 90 percent of the put's protected price for loans that are not related to purchasing other stocks. Usually, because of the risks related to stocks, you can only borrow up to 50 percent of the value of your stocks.

For example, if most of your assets are tied up in your company stock and you need money, you could sell your stock. But what if the stock is priced so low that you don't want to sell now and think it may rally soon? Maybe you're lucky and the price is so high you want to postpone the sale and the taxes until next year. You still need the money, so if you don't want to sell, you can borrow against these stocks. Normally, the most you can borrow is 50 percent of the stock's value if you use the money to invest in other stocks. But if you have a collared position and you use it to buy a new home or for education or for other reasons, then you can borrow more, as much as 90 percent. This is especially attractive for owners of businesses who cannot sell their stock but need to raise cash. You could not normally borrow that much against a stock portfolio, but because you have made the portfolio so safe and the collateral so secure, you can borrow a much larger amount.

Normally, you could not, and you certainly would not want, to borrow 90 percent of the value of a risky stock, but when you take most of the risk away by collaring the position, then the stock becomes attractive collateral for loans.

When you have very volatile stocks, it is foolish to borrow large amounts against them. Large margin loans destroyed much personal wealth in the 1929 crash. Over the years, regulations have gotten stricter so that individuals can't destroy themselves as easily with margin. Think about what happens if you have a large loan against a stock like Cienna, which fell over 75 percent in the 2000–2001 crash. The stock falls, your collateral becomes almost worthless, and you are forced to pay back your loans early. The exchanges, the bank, or the brokerage firm call in your loan and force you to come up with some money to bring your collateral back to prescribed levels (and you are faced with margin and house calls). But if you have a stable investment that is used for collateral or an insured investment such as a collared stock, then you don't have to worry about such margin calls (of course, only while the collar lasts).

The Costs

Collars can get expensive. Instead of doing one trade with one commission, you are doing three: buying a stock, buying a put, and selling a call. Then if the stock is called away or you put it, there is another commission. If the put is not exercised and you redo your collar, you will have two more commissions. Needless to say, unless you have large amounts of stocks, these strategies are best done in wrap accounts. Most of the major brokerage firms and discount brokerage firms offer wrap accounts for less than 1 percent.* These accounts allow unlimited trades for the flat fee.

The Taxes

The taxes can get a little tricky, especially if you are using collars on indexes (you may want to refer back to Chapter 4). In general, you have to use common sense. In a zero-cost collar, you will normally have no tax consequences on the collar itself if the stock goes up or remains even, as the premium you got for the call will be offset by the loss you have on the put. Normally, if your stock falls and you close out the collar, you would

---

*I do not recommend discount brokerage firms for these types of trades because I think advice is critical!

have a profit on the call and a profit on the put, which could have tax consequences. If you put or exercise the stock, these profits will reduce the tax basis of your stock.

Using collars can have tax advantages. They can allow you to defer selling your stocks into other years or convert short-term to long-term capital gains. You should talk to your tax advisor about the tax consequences and tax straddle rules before and after you utilize these strategies. As with most strategies, there are no clear-cut rules, so you have to look at your individual situation.

Remember that in no way are these few chapters expected to make you an expert on options. They are intended to provide a glimpse of their potential and their risks so you can get a handle on the strategies you wish to employ with your financial advisor. Don't go it alone. The safety you are seeking may be lost with inexperience.

The Pros and Cons of Collars

As we go through the pros and cons of collars, it will seem you have heard them before and you will be right. You heard them when I listed the pros and cons of covered calls and protective puts, respectively. The pros for collars are very similar to the pros for protective puts, but with one important point missing: puts do not cap the upside but collars do. However, protective puts alone cost money, but with collars part of that cost is offset. With collars, the calls pay the bills.

With covered calls, one of the pros was that you generated income; but with collars, you don't receive the extra income because the income is used to pay for the insurance premiums. But with covered calls alone, you have only partial downside protection. With collars you have partial guarantees from the puts. So by combining the puts and calls, you get the best of both and a few of the negatives of both.

The Pros

The advantages of collars include:

- Guarantees of full or partial principal
- Increased collateral, increased liquidity, with 90 percent loan potential
- Possible tax benefits
- Ownership, voting rights, and dividends retained
- Participation in appreciation of stock up to call strike price
- Designing zero-cost collars possibly resulting in no cost for the insurance
- Designing credit collars to possibly give you a little extra cash to buy more stocks, pay off margin debt, or just have fun
- Acts like callable equity-linked CDs or some of the principal-protected investments discussed in Chapter 3

The Cons

The disadvantages of collars include:

- Limited upside
- Costly commissions outside of flat-fee wrap accounts
- Tax consequences if not done properly
- Care required to avoid constructive sale rules
- Subject to tax straddle rules
- No downside protection until stock hits the strike price

With collars, the calls pay the bills, but you no longer have unlimited upside.

The Mechanics

Let's look at XYZ. The numbers I am using here are for a real stock that traded at $120 in 1999 and is now trading at $30. I am sure most owners would have loved to have owned collars then. Why didn't they? Because in most cases they were striving for the big home runs.

Assume we purchased 100 shares of XYZ at $120 and sell a six-month out-of-the-money call promising to sell our stock at $130.

Purchase 100 XYZ at $120 and sell a 6-month call @$130 for $11 premium

Purchase Price	Minus call premium	= net price	Potential profit if called @$130
$120	$11	$109	21/109 = 19%

This is an out-of-the-money call strategy. If the stock is called away or you have to sell, you will have a profit of $21, a 19 percent return ($11 call + 10 appreciation = $21 ÷ $109 results in a return of 19%).

But if XYZ falls, we are protected on the downside by $11. But once the stock falls below $109, we start incurring losses. If we are nervous or need to or want to protect more on the downside, we could buy a put at a strike price of $105 for a cost of $6.

We find we can sell a $130 call for $11 and buy a $105 put for $6.

$$\text{Net cost} = \text{Stock price} - (\text{call premium} - \text{put premium})$$

$$\text{Net cost} = \$120 - (\$11 - 6) = \$115$$

This is a credit collar as we had a $5 credit after we paid for the insurance. We call the difference between the call premium and the put premium our *excess premium*. If it is a credit collar, it will be positive; if it is a debit collar, the excess premium will be negative.

EXCESS PREMIUM = Call premium – Put premium   = _____

NET PRICE = Stock Price – Excess Premium   = _____

WHAT HAPPENS IF CALLED AWAY?

STRIKE PRICE   = _____

NET PROFIT = Strike price – Net cost

_____ – _____   = _____

% return if called away = Net profit / Net cost

_____ / _____   = _____

WHAT HAPPENS IF STOCK DOESN'T CHANGE?

Excess Premium (Call premium – Put premium)   = _____

NET PROFIT = Excess premium

WHAT HAPPENS IF STOCK FALLS?

Downside risk = Net price – Put strike price

_____ – _____   = _____

Profit if called	$130 – $115 = $15	= $15/$115 = 13.04% (not as good as call alone return of 19%—but look at the downside protection)
Loss if falls	$115 – $105 = $10	You have limited your loss to $10, whereas without a put your loss could be as much as $109.
Profit if remains unchanged	$500	$500 profit if unchanged as you keep the excess premium

If you would like to look at collars, a good idea is to rip out the collar worksheet above and copy it so that you can try some yourself. Let's use the previous example of XYZ and fill in the following worksheet. We paid $120 and sold a $130 call with a premium of $11 and bought a $105 put for a $6 premium.

EXCESS PREMIUM = Call premium – Put premium

= $11 – $6   =   **$5**

NET PRICE = Stock Price – Excess Premium

= $120 – $5   = **$115**

WHAT HAPPENS IF CALLED AWAY?

STRIKE PRICE of call   =   **$130**

NET PROFIT = Strike price – Net cost

      $130 – $115   =   **$15**

% return if called away = Net profit / Net cost

         $15 / $115   = **13.04%**

WHAT HAPPENS IF STOCK DOESN'T CHANGE?

NET PROFIT = Excess Premium (Call premium – Put premium)   =   **$5**

WHAT HAPPENS IF STOCK FALLS?

DOWNSIDE RISK = Net price – Put strike price

        $115 – $105   = $10

Summary

Because perfect investments don't exist, we make trade-offs every time we seek more safety. However, if you have large profits you want to protect or are just starting out and want to procure a little safety, think about collars. They work wonders. They are for bears, however, not bulls. But remember that bulls usually have a lot more risk to handle.

CHAPTER 9

Selling Puts to Dollar Cost Average

DEFINITION

Dollar cost averaging is a strategy of investing in intervals over time. Selling puts is a strategy of agreeing to purchase a stock at a lower price in return for a premium. By combining these two strategies, investors can be paid while waiting to purchase future investments.

KEY

Safety: ★★★   Simplicity: ★★

Returns: $$$$ Tax efficiency: –$$

SUMMARY

Safety: Anyone who has sold puts is probably surprised that I claim selling puts can actually increase safety. Usually, selling puts is thought of as a risky way to increase returns. However, selling puts to dollar cost average into a position can actually add safety, especially when you consider using puts as an alternative to limit orders. I also show you one strategy when puts are very risky, but in general this chapter is dedicated to the safer uses of puts.

Returns: Puts can improve returns by paying you while you wait for a stock to fall into the range in which you want to buy.

Simplicity: This strategy is simple to understand, but it does have to be monitored very carefully.

Tax efficiency: Puts in general may result in short-term or long-term capital gains. If stocks are "put" to you, the put premium will reduce the cost basis of your stock. If not put, the entire premium could be taxable. You need to consider the tax consequences, but, again, paying taxes on something is better than paying no taxes on nothing.

Selling Puts

What Are Short Puts?

Shorting is synonymous with selling. *Short puts* are option contracts that obligate us to buy a stock if it falls. When you sell a stock or an option you don't own (either a put or call), you are shorting it, or are short that position. When you buy an option or stock, you say you are "long" that position. So using the term *short put* means we have sold a put for which someone pays us a premium. In Chapter 6, I described buying puts as a form of insurance on our portfolio. We paid someone a premium for the puts to insure us against a market or stock fall because we were worried about protecting the stocks we currently own.

We buy puts as an exit strategy; we sell puts as an entrance strategy.

Sometimes we're not worried about getting out of the market but instead are trying to find safer ways to get into the market. Rather than buying a put to exit gracefully, we can sell a put to help us enter the market slowly and gracefully.*

With protective puts we paid a premium in order to sell our stock at a specified price. When we sell puts, we are the person who gets paid for our willingness to buy the stock if it falls.

In most cases, using puts as a way to buy your stock at a lower price is no riskier than buying the stock at the current price. Actually, so long as you have the cash set aside, it is actually safer. Even if you never own the stock, just selling the puts over and over, year after year, may be beneficial and certainly is better than just sitting, watching, and waiting for the stock to fall. In other words:

Short puts let us get paid for waiting.

---

*In reality, no single person on the other side buys our put, but I use the term *someone* to make it easier to understand. The put goes back into the market, and it is assigned by lottery to another investor.

- Selling puts can be better than waiting to buy.
- Selling puts is better than placing limit orders to buy.
- Selling puts is safer than buying all your stock at the current price.

Who Should Sell Puts?

Aggressive options traders use puts as a way to bet on the direction of the market and take advantage of the ups and downs in stock prices. This can be an attractive strategy for some investors, and I'll show you a real-life example later. This book is dedicated more to the investor, the person trying to make reasonable returns using commonsense strategies to get out and into the market. So although many different types of individuals should consider puts, I use them here for investors who want to dollar cost average into the market, those who want to buy a stock at a lower price, and those who want to improve returns on cash while waiting for desired stocks to falls.

Shorting or selling puts is also for those who want to get back into a position that was sold and for those who need to control a taxable sale. It is also for investors who want a way to increase returns while increasing safety by a small amount, not for investors looking to increase safety by large amounts. It is for investors who have cash and want to leverage their cash. It is for investors who are willing to move slowly, with patience, but who want to get paid for their patience. The way I approach this strategy is not for the aggressive trader, though selling puts is a favorite strategy for such traders.

Why Not Just Buy the Stock?

There are many reasons why you may not want to buy a stock today. Maybe the market is too high or you think the stock is trading too close to its resistance level. Maybe you want to increase the safety of your portfolio by moving slowly or you just want to be paid for the time you are waiting to get back into the market. Maybe you sold a stock when the market was falling with a stop loss or by exercising a put, or maybe it was just an outright sale and now you are waiting to reestablish your position at a lower price. Maybe you don't have the cash now, but in a couple of months you will, so you want to hold off buying. Perhaps, as noted, you are a gambler and want to bet on the direction of the market by trading options.

Where Should You Use Short Puts?

You can buy protective puts for a stock you own in any type of account, including a retirement account, as protective puts are a tool to hedge and increase safety. Although the shorting-puts strategy may be used to construct a little safer portfolio, usually short puts are used as an aggressive, risky strategy. Therefore, short puts are typically not allowed in retirement accounts, children's accounts, or fiduciary accounts. Check with your legal or financial advisor to determine where you can use them.

The Mechanics

Let's start with an example that assumes we sell XYZ at 45 with a stop loss because we think it is overpriced. But at $40 we think it is fairly priced and would not mind buying it back at that price. We could put in a limit order and tell our broker to buy it for us if it falls to $40. Limit orders to buy are placed at a price lower than the current price, which on the surface looks smart and fulfills the first rule of the market to sell high and buy low.

$$XYZ \longrightarrow \text{Sell at } \$45$$
$$\downarrow$$
$$XYZ \longrightarrow \text{Buy at } \$40$$

However, there may be a better way to buy the stock. If we know we want to buy it at $40, why not let someone pay us for a contract that says we will buy the XYZ if it falls to $40? Instead of placing an order to buy the stock at $40, we instead place an order to sell a put with a $40 strike price. That put will obligate us to buy XYZ if it falls to $40. In the meantime, we get paid a premium—let's assume $2—for our willingness to buy. If the price falls, we have to buy the stock at $40 a share minus the $2 premium paid us for a net cost of $38.

$$XYZ \longrightarrow \text{Sell at } \$45$$
$$\downarrow$$
$$XYZ \longrightarrow \text{Buy at } \$40 - \$2 = \$38$$

	XYZ goes up	XYZ stays even	XYZ falls below 40
Limit @ 40	Don't own stock $0 return	Don't own stock $0 return	Own stock at $40
Put @ 40, $2 premium	Don't own stock but keep $200 put premium	Don't own stock but keep the $200 put premium	May be forced to buy stock at a net cost of $38

As you can see, if we decided to buy at $40, we were better off with the put. If the stock fell dramatically to a much lower price we would wish we had not bought it in either case. But with the put we still have $2 less of a loss.

What if the stock never falls? If you had a limit order to buy the stock and it never falls, you may have set your money aside in a money market account and will earn interest on the account. But had you sold the put, you would have earned interest on the account as well as the $200 put premium and even interest on the put premium. So if the stock never falls, you are better off with the short put. As a matter of fact, if the stock doesn't fall, you can sell another put and collect money for that, possibly another $200. Theoretically, you could collect hundreds of put premiums and never own the stock. That is how and why traders often use puts to increase returns. In strong up markets, you can keep collecting puts over and over, but *watch out if the market falls!*

Selling Puts versus Limit Orders and Waiting to Buy

In our example, we are comparing selling a put to a limit order. We are looking at a person who has a set price in mind to buy a stock. This person can wait until it falls to place a buy order; place a limit order; or sell a put.

Selling a put frequently works well even if you are comparing it to a person who was willing to buy the stock at today's price. If the stock falls, the person selling the put will do better than the person who bought the stock. If the stock stays even, the put seller will also do better. If the stock goes up, the person who bought the stock immediately would do better but only if the stock went up more than the put premium. The put seller has only his premium and could miss out on a lot of upside with the stock, even though puts could be sold year after year on the stock. Several stocks over the years, especially in the nineties, you could have sold puts on over and over and never been forced to buy the stocks, that is, had them put to you, until 2001. Intel and Texas Instruments were two that you could have sold many puts on over the years, and by the time you were forced to buy them in 2001, the money you could have made on the puts could have exceeded the cost of buying the stocks. You could actually have had a negative cost basis for them.

Not every stock works out that well, but in the ideal world, even if you never own the stock but are willing to buy it, you could still make money by selling puts.

Stock goes up	Stock falls dramatically	Stock stays even
The stock buyer is the winner, but put seller out-performs the limit order.	Put seller is the winner, even though forced to buy stock. Even if stock falls more, she paid less than the limit order and the person who bought at the current price.	If stock remains flat, the put seller earns more than the person buying immediately and the person with the limit order.

Why Wouldn't You Always Short Puts If You Wanted to Buy a Stock?

If you really wanted to buy a stock and believe the price of its shares might go higher after a short-term dip, an immediate purchase may be better. The stock could fall to your price, and you would get the stock if you had the limit in. But with a put you might not ever own the stock, even if it falls to the strike price, because the owner of the insurance (the put) might not force you to buy the stock when it hits the strike price. If the stock is up at the time the put expires, you may never be forced to buy the stock.

Although it is unlikely that selling a put would ever be a worse strategy than buying a stock or a limit order, it could be more dangerous if the put makes you feel as though you are locked in. If you bought the stock at the market price, but it started to fall and you no longer wanted it, you would sell the stock. Yet somehow, when investors sell puts, they don't often realize it is the same situation. If the stock falls and you no longer want it, you can close out the put. Sometimes you may even have less of a loss than you would if you owned the stock and sold that.

Remember our situation: the investor has cash or government bonds set aside to buy the stock. If an investor is on margin or borrowing money to buy stocks, the risk is increased dramatically by selling puts, not decreased as in our example. The best reason for not selling puts is that often investors get too aggressive. They think the puts are a free ride, and they overextend by selling more puts than they really need. It becomes addictive, and you feel as though you are just collecting free money.

Only sell puts on stocks you want to own, and always have the money set aside to buy the stocks.

Sell Puts to Dollar Cost Average into a Stock

Considerable debate occurs whether dollar cost averaging is a better strategy than investing all your money at once. Several studies have shown that if you invested your full amount on the worst day of the year for ten years, you would be better off than people who added one-tenth each year—dollar cost averaged—into the market, even if they went in on the lowest day. Statistics and numbers can be viewed from many different perspectives, and I'm not sure it is worth debating the merits of dollar cost averaging. Buying all at once may result in better returns, but dollar cost averaging is safer. If it makes you feel more comfortable moving in slowly, then dollar cost averaging is for you.

Let's look at an example. You have $10,000. Do you buy all of XYZ today, or do you buy a little at a time over the year, trying to capture some of both the downside and the upside?

- If XYZ goes straight up, the person who bought all the stock immediately would be better off.
- If XYZ falls, the put seller would be better off by waiting for the lower price and was paid while waiting.

Let's assume that XYZ is trading at $50 a share and you decide you want to invest one-half of your money now at $50 and wait to invest the other half at $45. Let's assume you sell a put at a strike price of $45 and get a $3 premium. To make the example simple, let's forget about the interest earned while you're waiting to buy.

Invest $10,000 XYZ @ $50 Put and limit are @ 45	Scenario 1 Invest in two parts: ½ at $50, ½ at $45 limit	Scenario 2 Invest in stock @ $50 and sell $45 put @ $3	Scenario 3 Invest in all the stock now at $50	And the winner is . . .
If stock falls to $45 and then goes to $60	First $5,000 grows to $6,000. The $4,500 purchase grows to → $6,000 + $500 not invested = $12,500	First $5,000 grows to $6,000 + $300 put + $500 not invested. The $4,500 grows to $6,000 = $12,800	$10,000 → = $12,000	**Scenario 2 selling put**
If stock stays even	$10,000	$10,300 = $5,000 stock, $5,000 cash + $300 put premium	$10,000	**Scenario 2 selling put**
Stock↑ $60	$11,000	$11,300	$12,000	*Scenario 3 Buying now*
If stock falls to $40	$8,500	$8,800	$8,000	**Scenario 2 selling put**

Interpreting the three scenarios. *If the stock falls,* selling the put is the winner. *If the stock goes up* immediately to $60, then the individual who invested all the money immediately would be the winner, with a profit of $2,000. *If the stock stays even,* the person who sold the put would be the winner, with $5,000 invested in the stock and $5,000 in cash, plus $300 from the put premium, or $10,300. In addition, $5,300 would be earning interest.

If stock falls to $40, the person who sold the put would still be better off than both the stock buyer and the limit holder. In the case of the limit holder, the first $5,000 position fell to $4,000, and the second $4,500 position fell to $4,000. The investor would still have $500 in cash and is still better off than the person who purchased all the shares today. The put seller, however, fares best, with $500 in cash, $300 from the put premium, and the interest earned on the cash, including the put premium, until the day of purchase.

Increasing Safety

In Chapter 2, I showed you how increasing the number of investments increases your safety because of diversification. Even adding two risky investments will give you more safety than one safe investment and decreases the standard deviation of your portfolio. Let's look at our example above again. If we spend all our money on one stock, you may make more money if the stock goes up, but you will have all your money in one investment with no downside cushion. On the other hand, if you were to buy only 100 shares of the stock, keep the other $5,000 in cash, and sell a put, you would immediately increase your safety because you would now have three investments: cash, stock, and the put. Albeit the put is an artificial investment, it still adds safety. As you can see from the example above, if the stock price stays even or falls, diversification made the portfolio safer. In addition, in a flat market the put can increase your return because it generates additional income. It also increases safety by allowing the purchase of part of the stock at a lower price. Increasing safety is relative. Even if you have a loss, you have increased your safety if your loss is less. I am not saying this is safe, but rather it is *safer* than buying all your stock at once or using limit orders.

Another Approach: Selling Puts against Government Bonds

Let's assume you have $100,000 but think the market is high and would rather wait until it falls 10 percent. In our scenario, let's assume you will be paid 10 percent in put premiums for your willingness to buy your stocks at a 10 percent discount to today's prices.
Let's look at the numbers.

- $100,000 to invest
- Buy $100,000 worth of government bonds at 5 percent interest for one year
- Sell puts to purchase stocks priced today at $100,000 but with strike prices totaling $90,000
- Put premiums are $10,000

Buying stocks at the beginning of the year. If you had purchased all the stocks at the beginning of the year and they fell 10 percent, they would be worth $90,000—a $10,000 loss compared with to the gain of $15,000 from purchasing bonds and selling puts to purchase stocks at a 10 percent lower price. Even if the stocks fell 10 percent and are put to you, you still get to keep the $15,000 put premiums and the interest from the bonds. In addition, you only need to spend $90,000 as that is what you contracted to buy.

If the stocks fell 10 percent to $90,000, the stock buyer would have a $10,000 loss. The put seller, even after a 10% fall, would still have a $15,000 profit. (In reality the return would be even higher for the put seller as interest would have been earned on the $10,000 in put premiums as well.)

IF STOCKS STAY EVEN OR FALL LESS THAN 10%.

	Beginning of year	End of year
Bond :	$100,000 $\longrightarrow$	$100,000 + $5,000 interest = $105,000
Put Premium:	$10,000 $\longrightarrow$	$10,000

If stocks are not put, you earn $5,000 interest on government bonds and $10,000 in put premiums or $15,000 = 15%.

IF STOCKS FALL 10% and you have to spend $90,000 to purchase stocks.

	Beginning of year	End of Year
BOND:	$100,000 $\longrightarrow$	$10,000 left over + $5,000 interest = $15,000 ($90,000 used to buy stocks)
PREMIUM:	$10,000 $\longrightarrow$	$10,000
Stocks	0 $\longrightarrow$	$90,000

Total value at end of year = $115,000 or gain of $15,000 versus loss of $10,000 for the person who purchased all at beginning of year.

What's Wrong with this Picture?

- If the stocks fall or stay even, you were better off with the puts. However, if the stocks were to rally more than 15 percent, you would have been better off purchasing the stocks immediately.
- There is tremendous downside risk, but less so than purchasing all the stocks.
- This can be an extremely risky strategy if used in a fast-falling market, if done on margin, or if you're overextended in sales of puts.
- Be careful; again I caution you to use this strategy wisely. It not only can increase your returns dramatically but can add safety. However, it can destroy your portfolio if you use it incorrectly.

Pat K.

In Chapter 1, I told you about Pat K., a brilliant retired lawyer and friend who taught me that a little risk is a good thing. When I first started to work with him, we purchased mostly government bonds, but he wanted to get into the stock market. The market was high and overpriced, so I suggested moving into the market slowly, in steps—buying a little stock, selling puts for part, and collaring a third part. He liked the strategy and learned quickly. Sometimes I think too quickly, because soon he saw that the real money to be made in an up market was selling puts. Soon Pat discarded the calls and collars and started using only puts. He grew an account from $200,000 in 1998 to over $1,995,000 by March 2000. He became more aggressive than I could handle, but I admired him.

Pat understood his risk tolerance; he didn't want to lose his original $200,000, but anything above that was paper money. He loved the challenge and picking the stocks, and he was good at it. However, he went on margin, eliminated his bonds, and soon stocks were being put to him in late 2000 and 2001. One stock after another would fall, and he got house call after house call, margin call after margin call, and he was forced to keep selling off his good stocks. His account fell from a high in March 2000 of $1,995,432 to a little over $66,000 by March 2001.

Because Pat owned mostly aggressive technology stocks, his account would have fallen even without the puts to $450,000. The puts were very dangerous, but without them he would never have been able to build the account up to nearly $2,000,000. Had he closed out the puts and just kept the stocks, he would have had more than $370,000 more money. By July 2001, he had brought his account back to more than $200,000. He's smart and will probably have his account back up to $2 million again.

There are a lot of Pat's out there—people who can handle large amounts of risk. But if you're not one of them, can't handle extreme volatility and risks, and need safety and peace of mind, then don't fool around with margin or sell puts on stocks you don't want to own nor have the money set aside to buy. Stick to selling puts as a means of diversifying and dollar cost averaging.

> **If you start selling puts other than for averaging into a stock, remember Pat. No matter how bright you are, the market has destroyed many portfolios of geniuses, including a famous Nobel Prize winner.***

Selling Puts to Postpone Taxes

Selling puts can also be used to time tax sales. Investors who have large losses in a stock and want to establish a tax loss this year may sell an unprofitable long position, realize the loss, and simultaneously write a put option on that stock. The put cannot be deep in-the-money or the put will be treated as a contract to purchase the stock, and the sale will be considered a wash sale—

---

*Robert Merton, a partner in Long Term Capital Partners.

that is, you sell and purchase back a stock within 30 days. If you purchase the stock too quickly, the IRS won't allow you to write off the loss.

- *If the stock price rises after you sell the stock:* The short put will give you some income to minimize the impact of the lost opportunity in the stock's increase in price; for example, the stock goes up $5 after you sell it. If you received $2 for the put, your lost opportunity is only $3. If you sold the stock and did nothing, you would have lost the entire $5 opportunity.
- *If the stock stays at the same price:* You have collected the income from the put and will be able to purchase the stock after 30 days.
- *If the stock falls:* You will have to buy it, but it will be at a lower price, because it will include the income from the put.

After the 30-day wash sale period expires, you can repurchase your put and buy your stock. Be careful that you only use out-of-the money puts. The IRS has indicated that any in-the-money put will result in a wash rule, so consult your tax advisor about the tax implications.

Summary

We sell puts when we want:

- To increase the safety of our portfolio versus being fully invested
- To dollar cost average into a stock
- To buy a stock at a lower price
- To reestablish a position we sold
- To be paid while we wait for the stock to fall to our price
- To assure that we are paid something if the stocks goes up and we don't own it
- To sell stocks we have for tax reasons and need to reestablish a position

CHAPTER 10

Seeking Value and Teaching Old Dogs New Tricks

DEFINITION

Value investing has a variety of definitions, but for our purpose it means investing in companies with solid valuations and earnings. Value investing is finding companies at a bargain, the "dogs," namely, out-of-favor stocks that are inexpensive relative to their earnings and assets.

KEY

Safety: ★★★★   Simplicity: ★★★

High returns: $$$ Tax Consequences: +$–S

SUMMARY

Safety: As I constantly remind you, safety is relative. Compared with growth stocks, value stocks have historically been much safer. In addition, value stocks that have fallen out of favor and strategies that focus on the value have been even less volatile than strategies that focus on growth stocks.

High returns: Over the long run the investment strategies in this chapter should outperform bonds and the Dow index, but there is an ongoing debate whether they can outperform the more growth-oriented indexes over the long term.

Simplicity: All of the following strategies are easy to understand and relatively easy to employ.

Tax implications: These strategies can have unfavorable tax consequences and should generally be used in pensions, IRAs, and low-tax-bracket accounts. However, the tax consequences can be reduced by holding for longer periods. We will note the tax consequences of each of them.

This chapter looks at the popular debate about value versus growth. I show you some old value strategies that fell out of favor over the last few years as well as how to improve those strategies to make them more viable—in other words, how to super-charge them and make the old dogs howl again. By using these strategies, you can increase returns and minimize some of the recent volatility in the market.

What Is Value?

The debate between the "value" camps and "growth" camps is ongoing. Value investments have outperformed growth 78 percent of the time, and value has a much lower risk (a standard deviation of 14.3 percent compared with growth's 17.5 percent). But when growth does well, it does so well that it has compounded wealth to a much higher level. Some investors are so stubborn that they insist on having only one style, but sometimes value does better and sometimes growth does better. The older value companies have consistency, wisdom, maturity, and financial strength. The new young growth companies offer strength, agility, and the ability to get into new markets and to grow quickly.

What Do Value and Growth Offer?

Growth offers excitement. Think of a baby boy as he grows through the years. When he is young, he has the most growth and physical ability and is the most exciting, yet at the same time he is the most fragile. The lack of experience and huge unknowns lead to the greatest potential to fail. In his teens and 20s, this young, healthy male has a much better chance to win great races, score more goals, and achieve more daring feats than he will later in life. As he matures, he becomes stronger and more reliable; he has more relationships, more experience, and more places to turn for financial support.

Value offers substance, maturity, and stability. As he approaches middle age, our boy becomes (or should become) more and more predictable, more set in his ways with fewer surprises and disappointments. He is solid, a man of substance. But the reality is that at some time he may run out of energy and may not age gracefully. He may become too tired to compete. The excitement he had to offer in his youth, the strength and consistency he had to offer in his 20s and 30s, and the value and experience he had to offer later in life may fade as he approaches his 90s. A young child will be able to outrun and maybe even outthink him. At some point, companies, like people, may no longer be able to compete.

Even though a company is older or has been around for a long time, we cannot always assume they will have the best returns. In the stock market, as in life, the younger, growth-oriented companies tend to offer the most potential for growth and appreciation, whereas the older value companies tend to offer more reliability and consistency.

Combine a Little Value and a Little Growth in Your Portfolio

For a rich life, surround yourself with diversity. When investing, also diversify among a variety of different stocks in varying sizes, styles and sectors.

Don't hang around with children only because you'll miss out on the wisdom of maturity. Don't hang around with elderly people only, because you'll miss out on the excitement and growth of the young. *And* don't get caught up in the debate over which is better, growth or value. Both have a place and you want both of them in your portfolio.

Different Strategies and Different Approaches

You have to approach value and growth companies differently. Just as you don't treat a 5-year-old child the same way you treat a 50-year-old adult, you shouldn't treat your mature value stocks and your young growth stocks the same either. You use different measurements and look for different benefits from them. You also use different strategies. This chapter looks at value investing and some of the ways to approach and benefit from it. The value, or more mature, company needs less protection because it has proven itself over time. The next chapter looks at growth companies, which often need more protection and more control but can have more home runs.

Who Should Consider Value?

My answer is obvious: all investors. If you believe that over time the economy and market change, then several outstanding value strategies are for you. They include:

- The Top Ten
- The Dogs of the Dow, one of the most popular strategies that is also called the Low Five, Basic Dow 5, Focus 5, or Dow 5
- The Penultimate Dow
- The Combo: The marriage of the Dow and the S&P
- The S&P Dividend Strategy
- The Triple Play
- The Supercharged Dogs

Value versus Growth

The debate between value investors and growth investors leads to this question: Do you buy stocks because they are undervalued or because they have superior growth potential?

James O'Shaughnessy, president of the investment advisory firm O'Shaughnessy Capital Management, has written about the battle between value and growth in his book *What Works on Wall Street: A Guide to the Best-Performing Investment Strategies of All Times.* O'Shaughnessy's conclusions are similar to those of other studies: both growth and value work, but they work better or worse at different times and for different stocks. Value strategies tend to work best with large company stocks, whereas a more growth-focused approach is better for smaller stocks. He suggests picking value stocks from the top large cap companies and picking growth stocks from smaller stocks as well as larger cap stocks.

Previous chapters mentioned some of the risk analysis done by many other analysts that showed value has much less volatility whereas growth has a higher potential for capital appreciation. For controlling risk, I showed that it was important to have investments with different characteristics and low or negative correlations. Having some growth *and* some value is probably the best solution because there has never been clear-cut proof that one strategy is better than the other, leaving us to believe there is room for both.

Avoid growth stocks when PEs are high. Many studies that focus on value stocks base their valuations on price-earnings ratios, or PEs. The lower the PE, the better the value. When the spread between PEs for growth and value widens, then shifting more to value is attractive.

PEs are not so relevant for growth stocks, but the spread between PEs for growth versus PEs for value is important. When that spread is high compared with historic averages, the growth sector will have a long hard struggle to rally. When the PEs for growth fall closer to those of value, then value becomes less attractive and growth more attractive.

Evaluating value. The criteria we use to evaluate stocks depends on, to a large degree, whether they are growth stocks or value stocks. When we look at growth, we focus more on PEGs. When we focus on value stocks, we look at PEs, yields, and dividends. For growth stocks, looking at yields and dividends has little value in helping us with our selections, but for value stocks they can be very important. For example, when looking at large value stocks, dividends should be high; but when looking at small value stocks, dividends should be lower. For growth stocks, they are irrelevant.*

When looking for value stocks, in addition to looking for low PEs and high yields, you may also want to look for low ratios in price to book and price to cash flow, for example.

In the next chapter's focus on growth stocks, the criteria to help us select good growth stocks are PEGs and momentum, or relative strength. In addition, with growth stocks you are not concerned that price-to-book ratios may be a little high, but for both value and growth, price-to-sales ratios should be low.

Some of the factors that help determine when value is attractive are:

Earnings	Want them high for value
PEs	Want low
Yields	Want high
Price-to-book	Want low
Price-to-cash flow	Want low
Price-to-sales	Want low

When looking at growth stocks, we look at different criteria:

Earnings	Not as important as *growth* in earnings
PEGs	Want them low, preferably under 2
Yields	Irrelevant
Price to book	Can be higher than for value
Price to sales	Low

PEs

Price-earnings ratios are probably the most often used statistic when evaluating value stocks. They are simply a company's price divided by its earnings. For example, if company stock is $100 and earnings are $2, the PE is 50.

$$PE = P/E = Price\ /\ Earnings = 100/2 = 50$$

The problem with PEs is that they are only part of the story. If you are looking for a consistently mature company whose earnings are expected to be stable in the future, then PEs are a good guide. However, if we look at two companies that have the same PEs, does it mean they are both equally attractive? Unfortunately, it's not that easy, especially if one

---

*James O'Shaughnessy, *AAII Journal,* November 1997.

is a young growth company that has promise of increasing earnings dramatically over the years, and the other is a mature stable company with steady, but not increasing, earnings. PEs do not mean a lot unless you are comparing similar companies in similar sectors with similar styles.

What should a PE be? 1, 10, 100? A PE of 15 means the stock is selling at 15 times earnings. Is that good? Again, it's relative. Before you can determine the worth of the PE, you need to look at the average PE for that stock, for the industry, and for the market. You have to compare it relative to some benchmark. Everything is relative in the stock market. To say a PE is 2 means little unless we have a benchmark against which to compare it. Try to find the PE of the Dow and sectors, as well as the average P/E of the stock, before you make a decision on your stock.

How to Use PEs to Evaluate Stocks

- Step 1: A good starting point is to look at the current PE of your stock.
- Step 2: Find the PE for the sector that your stock belongs in. For example, if you are considering Merck, look at the health care sector's PE.
- Step 3: Look at the PE for the Dow. You want to get a sense if your stock is over-valued against the market.
- Step 4: Look at historical PEs or the five-year average PE. Because PEs of stocks as well as other valuation criteria tend to revert back to the mean, or average, we can expect that when PEs are higher than normal or than average PEs, they will eventually revert to the average. This is why it is so important that you don't look at PEs without also looking at how they relate to their average PE.

When PEs are 30 percent higher than the average, start placing stop losses 10 percent under the current price. If PEs are over 60 percent higher than historical averages, place stops 5 percent under the current price. If they are higher than that, start selling off parts, buying puts, selling calls, or creating collars.

Where Do You Find PEs?

You can find PEs and average PEs in most research reports and financial publications. Below are some of the PEs from summer 2001 compared with their average PEs for the previous five years. This information came from Morningstar.com, a great source of such information for PEs, PEGS, and so on.

Sector PEs

Sector	Utilities	Financials	Technology	Health
Current PE	14.9	24.3	43.0	30.0
5-yr avg PE	11.5	15.0	38.8	29.0

At first glance, technology seems the most overpriced. But if we look at the variance between the average PEs, we see that financials may indeed be the most overpriced relative to their averages.

Stocks, the market, the economy, sectors, and interest rates tend to revert to their mean (average). That means that when the market or a stock trades higher than its average value, it is more likely to falter than to continue forward.

The Problem: There Are Lies, There Are Very Bad Lies, and then There Are Statistics

The problem with PEs is that we are often trying to predict earnings into the future.

No matter how much we would love to believe in quantitative data, *don't*. Always use common sense, and always assume that the data are flawed. Be especially careful if the data are based on estimates of future earnings, or growth. Use it, but use it with care and an awareness that even though this is the best that is available, for now it is still not perfect.

High Yields

I noted earlier some of the theories of why markets fall and rise. Analysts such as Robert Shiller,[*] who looked at dividend yields over the world, found that over the years, as yields of the market fall, the likelihood of the market's falling increases. When yields are high, there is a greater likelihood that the market will rise. High yields imply that stocks are undervalued and the price of stocks are low compared with their earnings or yields.

The higher the yields, the more likely the stock will rise.

Yields are considered an attractive forecasting tool for predicting market as well as individual stock moves. When yields are high, they attract investors; and when yields are low, investors look elsewhere for better returns. This is in theory, but it also holds true in reality for much of the world in most instances. Applying this theory to the real world is relatively simple and frequently employed. The Dogs of the Dow, for example, is one of the most popular strategies based on the theory that high yields attract money.

The strategies in the following sections were made famous during the 1980s by Michael O'Higgins in his book *Beating the Dow,* and I adapt these strategies to encompass the new volatility in the market.

---

[*]John Y. Campbell and Robert J. Shiller. "Valuation Ratios and the Long-Run Market Outlook." *The Journal of Portfolio Management.* Winter 1998.

The Top Ten

The strategy of the Top Ten finds the ten highest-yielding stocks in the Dow. Investors purchase those top-ten-yielding stocks at the beginning of each year and sell them at the end of the year. In the next year, they buy the top ten highest-yielding again. This strategy was a little disappointing during the late 1990s though highly profitable for the 1980s and early 1990s. Although the top ten did not perform as well during the 1990s as did the low five or the Dow, it was an attractive strategy in that it had only 1 down year in the last 21 years. Because it is also more diversified, it tends to have less specific risk. If you believe that stocks go through dramatic swings, and if you believe that high dividends indeed do attract investors, then this is a strategy that you should seriously consider including in part of your portfolio.

How to Determine the Top Ten?

The Top Ten strategy is made up of the ten highest-yielding stocks in the Dow—the biggest and best-known companies in the world. The formula for determining which companies make up the top ten is very simple. Just find the ten stocks in the 30 Dow stocks with the highest dividend yield. (The dividend yield is the dividend per share divided by the share price.) The dividend information is available on nearly all research and quotation systems, such as Zacks, Value Line, SPAR, and so forth. This information is critical in analyzing stocks, and all worthwhile research reports and newspaper financial sections also include it.

Step 1: First look at the Dow stocks. When this book was written in 2001, the 30 stocks that made up the Dow Jones Industrial Average were the following:

Alcoa (AA)	Honeywell (HON)
American Express (AXP)	Intel (INTC)
AT&T (T)	IBM (IBM)
Boeing (BA)	International Paper (IP)
Caterpillar (CAT)	Johnson & Johnson (JNJ)
Citigroup (C)	McDonald's (MCD)
Coke (KO)	Merck (MRK)
Disney (DIS)	Microsoft (MSFT)
Dupont (DD)	Minnesota Mining & Mfg (MMM)
Eastman Kodak (EK)	Morgan, J.P. (JPM)
Exxon Mobile (XOM)	Philip Morris (MO)
General Electric (GE)	Proctor & Gamble (PG)
General Motors (GM)	SBC Communications (SBC)
Hewlett – Packard (HWP)	United Technologies (UTX)
Home Depot (HD)	Walmart (WMT)

Step 2: Find the ten highest yielding stocks from the list above.

Step 3: Invest one-tenth of your money in each of these stocks.

Step 4: Sit back and relax for a year, and then do the same thing again.
The two basic reasons why the Dog strategy tends to work:

1. Stocks that are high tend to fall when they become overvalued, and stocks at the bottom tend to eventually rally when they are perceived as undervalued.
2. High yields indicate that a stock may be undervalued and thus will attract investors.

The Dogs of the Dow

The Dogs of the Dow strategy takes the Top Ten strategy one step further. It is an annual investment plan that concentrates on the five cheapest of the ten highest-yielding stocks of the 30 companies that make up the Dow Jones Industrial Average (DJIA). These companies have long histories and widespread investor recognition with such long-term track records that often, even when they fall from glory, it is easy for them to get financing and to restructure, turning their companies around. Unlike young new growth companies that fall on hard times, these companies usually find it easy to raise the capital they need to make a comeback. But be careful; even some of the best-known companies can never get their act together. For example, look at Xerox and Polaroid. Like aging gentlemen, some companies get tired, so use your common sense; if old companies have legitimate fundamental problems, you may want to avoid their weak stocks, no matter how low their price. Be especially careful if there is news that yields are going to be cut.

Dogs of the Dow Strategy = Appreciation + High Dividends for income

In the past we could expect dividend income to account for almost 40 percent of return, but the yields have been much lower in recent years and do not add as much to the return.

Step 1: We start with the ten highest-yielding stocks, looking for those that offer the attractive yields that make them appear undervalued.

Step 2: Find the five cheapest stocks within the top ten group and invest one-fifth of your money in each of them.

Step 3: Sit back and relax. Wait a year, sell your stocks, and then go through Steps 1 and 2. Frequently, you may find that some of the same stocks will still be on your lists, so create the list before you sell. However, sell any shares that would create a starting position of more than 20 percent.

The Dow as a Measure of Value

As more and more growth stocks find their way into the Dow, Dow-focused strategies will become more and more difficult. Nothing is wrong with the Dogs of the Dow strategy or the premise behind it, but the problem lies with the universe of stocks that we use for selection. Instead of using the Dow as the basis for selecting our stocks in future years, we may have to use other value indexes or value recommendations from research departments.

Past Performance

Many investors gave up on the Dogs of the Dow strategy when it didn't do well in 1999, but it has been extremely successful over the long run. Value in general had problems as money was rushing into hot technology and growth stocks. It is unlikely that it or any other strategy will outperform all the time. The past success of this strategy, however, has made it a strategy that anyone who believes in value should consider.

The Low Five strategy is basically an alternative to more difficult timing and trading strategies. At the end of 1998, trusts that employed this strategy held more than $20 billion in assets, according to the Investments Company Institute.

Look at Figure 10.1. As you can see, the Top Ten and the Dogs of the Dow strategies have both outperformed 20 years' compounded returns of the DJIA.

When you look at this table, it seems as though the dogs performed better in 9 of the 21 years, the DJIA outperformed 6 times, and the top ten outperformed 6 times. Statistically, there seems little argument to be made for the Top Ten strategy over the Dow; even luck could account for the outperformance of the dogs. The differences are not so significant that we could easily determine the best strategy. However, when you look at the differences in dollar amounts, the Dogs strategy appears much more attractive. Let's look at the 1990s when growth actually outperformed value for most of that period. The dogs outperformed only four times. In spite of that, the total dollar amounts argue strongly for the Dogs of the Dow strategy.

Over the ten years, the DJIA grew to $314,104 @ 14.78%, the top ten grew to $290,068 @ 14.45%, and the low five grew to $453,123 @ 16.48%.

Although the top ten did not outperform, you still might want to consider the Top Ten strategy as it appears to have the fewest down years. You need to consider not just the returns but the risk/reward ratio. You have to determine where you are getting the greatest return per unit of risk that you take. When you look at it from a risk/reward standpoint, the top ten and the dogs still look very attractive.

FIGURE 10.1 Twenty Years of Compounded Returns of the DJIA Compared with the Top Ten and Low Five

Year	DJIA Total Return	Top Ten Total	Low Five Total
1979	10.52	**12.99**	9.91
1980	21.41	27.23	**40.52**
1981	−3.40	**7.52**	3.63
1982	25.79	26.04	**41.88**
1983	25.68	**38.91**	36.11
1984	1.06	6.43	**10.88**
1985	32.78	29.44	**37.84**
1986	26.91	**34.79**	30.32
1987	6.02	6.07	**11.06**
1988	15.95	**24.54**	21.64
1989	**31.71**	26.45	10.49
1990	**−0.57**	−7.57	−15.27
1991	23.93	35.09	**61.80**
1992	7.35	7.85	**23.01**
1993	16.71	26.92	**33.85**
1994	4.93	4.15	**8.56**
1995	36.20	**36.48**	30.25
1996	**28.57**	28.08	25.96
1997	**24.78**	21.62	19.95
1998	**18.14**	10.63	12.34
1999	**27.01**	1.01	−7.15
2000	−4.74	3.11	**8.05**

The Penultimate Dow

One of the premises of most of these value strategies is to find ways to beat the returns of the indexes. The returns of the indexes are not that bad, but there is always competition to beat them, so new strategies and refinements to old ones constantly arise. The Penultimate Dow strategy is a refinement of the Dogs of the Dow.

Over the years, many of the Dow stocks have fallen by the wayside. To decrease the risk that you might have found a real dog and a stock that could never recover, many investors drop the lowest-priced stock and double up on the second lowest, the *penultimate stock.* The logic here is that the lowest may have a lot of fundamental problems that could hold back any upside or maybe even cut its dividend. The Penultimate strategy, which was once hailed as one of the best, focuses on the second lowest-priced stock. Statistically, it is believed to offer a 1 to 1.7 percent better annual return than the Dow 5 strategy. It is worth considering because even small incremental improvements in returns over time from compounding can dramatically increase wealth. Although this strategy has not been as successful during the last few years, it is likely to do better when value starts outpacing growth in the future. Many investors select the penultimate stock only. I feel uncomfortable with that because dealing with one stock increases specific risk.

When growth stocks do better than value stocks, these strategies often don't do so well when compared with the Dow. Because so many growth stocks are in the Dow now, the Dow 30 stocks have a better chance of outperforming these pure value plays.

Can You Really Use Just the Dow Stocks Anymore?

We used to think of the Dow as our indicator of value and the S&P as a good indicator of growth. Today, however, the Dow looks much different than it did years ago. Many stocks now have little or no yields. Many strategies, including the Top Ten, the Dogs of the Dow, and the Penultimate, have to be carefully evaluated each year to see if there are sufficient dividend-paying stocks in the Dow to make these strategies viable. As the Dow changes, these strategies will fall out of favor.

If the Dow moves more into growth stocks, you are going to need to find a new universe of value stocks to select from. You may find a new approach by going to Value Line or another research source, find its top 50 picks for value, and then sift through those stocks for the best yields. You can use Value Line's top 50 value stock picks, selecting the 10 with the highest yields. The premise is the same as that of all the above strategies. You are looking for value that offers high yields. The high yields imply that the stocks are undervalued. You can go one step further and select the five cheapest. You can use as many different strategies as there are for the Dow stocks. You are still looking for high yields and value, but the universe of stocks will differ a little.

The S&P Dividend Strategy

The S&P Dividend strategy is made up of 15 high-yielding stocks found in the S&P 500. Value is not necessarily found only in Dow stocks. The Dow has many growth stocks now, and the S&P 500 has at any given time hundreds of value stocks. Because there are so many stocks in the S&P 500, the S&P Dividend is a much more difficult strategy to employ, but many firms offer it prepackaged in trust, so it is worth reviewing. Trusts work well for value strategies. Although hidden fees are always a problem, especially when dealing with trusts that hold just four or five stocks, as do those using the Penultimate and Dog strategies. However, the S&P Dividend strategy, because of the complexity in selecting 15 stocks, could be less expensive than paying commissions each year on this many stocks. If you were to use this strategy, a trust may be the best way to go. I also like using trusts because you can combine many different strategies.

The Dow and S&P Combo

When deciding whether to go with value to have a little more safety and consistency or to go with growth to have a better shot at higher returns, you could well ask if there's any reason why you can't have the best of both worlds. In past chapters, you've seen the advantages of combining equities with bonds to give you a little more safety. You can also combine different styles of stocks not only to improve safety but also improve returns. Combining growth and value helps an investor create a well-balanced and diversified portfolio in one simple investment.

The Easy Way

Again, there are trusts that provide packages of Dow stocks and some that give you packages of S&P stocks, making it easy to combine both growth and value. Some brokerage firms even offer convenient packages that combine the Top Ten and the Dogs of the Dow strategies with the top stocks in the S&P.

The Supercharged Dogs: Covering the Dogs

Selling covered calls not only increases safety, but the additional income makes the strategy attractive for pensions. If the dogs fall, you have the dividends to offset the downside and in addition have the covered call premiums.

One of the main concerns of covered call strategies is that you may cut off more upside potential than you want. However, with this strategy we want stocks to be called, because the theory is to sell the best-performing stocks at the end of the year and repurchase lower-costing stocks. If the stocks were called away, it would mean you made a 15 to 20 percent return in a year. Remember that you want to sell stocks after they rally, as you are trying to sell at the top, and the following year buy at the bottom. If ever there was a time and place to use covered calls, it is with this strategy, which works well because we incorporate so many known factors. For example:

- We take profits on stocks that rally.
- Value investors tend to look for stocks at the bottom, driving those stocks back up.
- High yields have historically attracted investors and add to total return.
- Growth tends to do better at the end of the year, and value does better during the summer months, so the calls tend to minimize the year-end pullbacks in value.
- Call premiums not only add safety but increase the probability of a good return.

SUPERCHARGED DOGS = APPRECIATION + DIVIDENDS + CALL PREMIUMS
= TOTAL RETURN.

Triple Play Strategy

This strategy combines three of the previous strategies and includes:

- The Top Ten, the ten highest-yielding stocks in the Dow Jones Industrial Average
- Dogs of the Dow, the five lowest of the Top Ten's highest-yielding stocks
- Penultimate Pick, the second lowest-priced stock of the five stocks in the Dogs of the Dow

Divide the money you want to invest according to this strategy as follows:

- 10 percent in the Top Ten
- 56 percent in the Dow's Dogs
- 34 percent in the Penultimate Pick

The concept behind this combination is simple: It is to create a portfolio that combines several winning strategies. Not all strategies work all the time, but by combining these strategies, the probability of one performing well is enhanced. Even though there are now several growth stocks in the Dow, this strategy weeds them out and typically will be very value oriented.

The best way to participate in this strategy is through trusts. If you invested $10,000 in the Dow in 1975, it was worth $200,000 in 1995. If, however, you invested according to the Triple Play, you would have had over $840,000. Over the long run, a combination of several good strategies, these or others, should work better than any single strategy.

Trusts. Again it is worth considering prepackaged trusts that take all the work out of these strategies. If you are considering more complicated strategies that will involve a lot of transactions, a trust is extremely attractive. For the Triple Play, trusts are particularly attractive. You may also want to consider using trusts for the Top Ten or the Low Five with calls, because of the number of trades. A trust purchases the stocks, sells the calls, and in 6, 12, 13, or 18 months will roll your stocks into newer buy recommendations.

The Last Few Years Were Unique

If you believe that the last few years were unique, then you may want to step back in time and look at the past. Let's see what the numbers looked like before the new paradigms or before the tech euphoria so overwhelmed the markets.

From 1976 to 1996:

S&P	$153,489	14.21%
DJIA	$137,138	13.25%
Top Ten of Dow	$270,695	17.62%
Top 15 S&P	$326,968	19.05%
Low Five—Dow	$441,689	20.18%
Triple Play	$840,000	21.96%

The best strategy was the Triple Play, which was a combination of the Penultimate Pick, the Dogs of the Dow, and the Top Ten.

Summary

The debate between value and growth will continue for many more years, although the conclusion will most likely be the same as it is today. Value tends to be safer, and growth tends to offer a little better return. After the poor market performances in 2000 and 2001, Dr. A. Craig MacKinley at the Wharton School shows that between 1979 and 2000 value has actually had an average return of 16.5 percent and growth an average return of 15.9 percent. Better still, the standard deviation, or volatility, was only 14.3 percent for value compared with 17.5 percent for growth. In addition, if you used the Sharpe ratio, which measures reward versus risk, value has a .66 ratio and growth a .51 ratio. On a reward/risk ratio, value looks better, but each of us should probably consider both strategies and styles in our portfolios. As discussed earlier, high yields provide reasons to believe that stocks will rally until their yields fall enough to make them less competitive with other investments. The Dow Dogs have outperformed both the Top Ten and the DJIA for the last 10, 15, and 21 years, but covering the Dogs could theoretically add even another 2 to 8 percent in call premiums alone. If the Dow stocks were to rally strongly, you could cut off some upside, but over a long period these should add extra value and get those dogs howling.

FIGURE 10.2 Growth vs Value

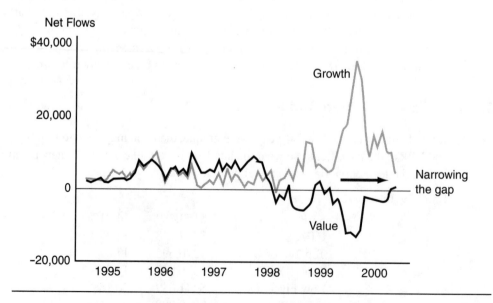

CHAPTER 11

PE/Growth

DEFINITION

PEGs—price-earnings to growth—are ratios of the price of a stock to its earnings and to the growth rate. These ratios warn us when stocks are priced too high. PEGs also help us buy stocks at reasonable prices.

KEY

Safety: ★★★   Simplicity: ★★★

Returns: $$$$$ Tax efficiency: $$$$

SUMMARY

Safety: Monitoring PEGs, PE/growth ratios, can increase safety dramatically.

Returns: Monitoring PEGs ratios not only increases safety but also dramatically increases returns.

Simplicity: This strategy is simple to understand, but it does have to be monitored very carefully.

Tax efficiency: Using PEGs as a means of selecting growth stocks can help to build a tax-efficient portfolio because long-term growth stocks can usually be taxed at capital gains rates. Growth stocks historically have fewer tax consequences than value stocks, the latter often paying dividends, that are taxed at ordinary income rates.

Those who should consider this strategy include:

- Anyone and everyone who has ever considered growth stocks for their portfolio.
- Anyone who is looking for additional tools to help build a more tax-efficient portfolio.
- Investors seeking higher returns with less risk.

Balancing Growth and Value

In this case, as in many others, knowledge is the factor that controls risk. Think back to our story of the two sailboats. When someone yelled "Man overboard," all seven brothers rushed to save him and thus tipped the boat over, but everyone moved in different directions on the tourists' boat and kept the boat in balance.

When we have negative correlation, with different investments going in different directions, it's easy to keep our accounts in balance. However, if all the investments move in the same direction, volatility can be extreme. It is difficult to find investments with negative correlation, but even investments with low correlation can help stabilize an account. With low correlation, stocks may move in the same direction but not at the same speed. In the market, the boat may be shaky, but it is unlikely to tip over if all investments move at different speeds in the same direction.

Therefore, even though growth and value may move in the same direction, it is the speed at which they move that makes it attractive to have a balance between them. We use PEs and PEGs to help us determine what that balance should be.

GROWTH VERSUS VALUE: TOTAL ANNUALIZED RETURNS FROM 12/31/79 to 12/31/00

Russell 1000 Growth = 17.3%, Russell Value = 17.1%*

---

*Source: Frank Russell Co. Russell 1000 Growth Index is commonly used to measure growth-oriented stock performance and the Russell 1000 Value for value. Using different indexes changes the numbers slightly.

Although value and growth indexes perform similarly, when looking for the best return you need to look at growth. Growth has the highest risk so the many losers pull down the averages, but good growth stocks are more likely to outperform the stable, mature value stock.

What Is PEGs Strategy?

PEGs are simply the PE of a stock divided by its projected five-year earnings and are to growth stocks what PEs are to value stocks.

As discussed in the previous chapter, after many years of debates concerning the merits of growth versus value stocks, most analysts have discovered that, at some point, all of us have to accept that they both have merits. Growth tends to offer the potential for higher capital gains, and value tends to offer more safety.* We need ways to help us select the best stocks in both categories. Though the benefit of a growth portfolio is that it should outperform value, growth will certainly underperform a value portfolio if you pick lousy growth stocks. A value portfolio with poorly performing value stocks will always underperform a growth portfolio with terrific growth stocks. However, after decades of debate, there is probably some consensus that if you are searching for stocks with the potential for the highest returns, then you need to look in the growth sector. That does not mean that all growth stocks will do well but just that if you are looking for gold, you look for it in a gold mine, not in a coal mine.

PEGs are tools that help us discover the best growth stocks. When evaluating value stocks, we look at PEs, yields, and other quantitative factors, but these tools and criteria are not applicable to growth stocks. If we looked only at PEs, we would have to discard almost all the new young growth stocks. Because growth stocks typically have no yields and possibly even no earnings, it is unlikely that their PEs will have much validity. In addition, when we buy growth stocks, we are paying for future earnings, not current earnings. We need to find some way to discount those future values into today's dollars. It is unlikely we would buy a value stock that had no earnings. But, if a growth company has losses and the losses are decreasing or the company has the potential for future earnings, we may still buy after we look for patterns in the *growth* in those earnings or decreases in the losses. This is where PEGs come into play.

Using PEGs is the easy part; the hard part is collecting accurate data. In general, we look for lower PEGs and want to find stocks that are trading at a discount to the S&P or other growth indexes. Perhaps we want to compare the PEGs of various stocks and find

---

*With the dividends from value, pretax, value and growth look neck and neck. After tax, however, growth returns tend to look a little better. Also, growth with covered calls tends to offer higher returns than value with calls, as the premiums for growth stocks are much higher than those for value stocks.

those that have a relatively lower PEG. It is more beneficial to view PEGs compared with a benchmark, but it also can be useful just viewing the PEG itself. Look for PEGs lower than 1. Historically, PEGS on midcap and small cap growth companies that are lower than three-quarters of a percent result in the best returns.

The search. In your search for great growth stocks, you can calculate the PEGs easily. These numbers are especially important in the midcap and small cap areas. If you are looking for a little more safety, stick with midcaps over small caps as the returns on mid-caps and small caps are close (approximately 12 percent) and the volatility is 20 percent less for midcaps, according to University of Chicago Professor Claudia Mott.

Assume for the time being that you agree with me that low PEGs are attractive. Also assume that it is difficult to find midcap stocks with a good earnings track record because most young companies have low or no earnings. How do you find opportunities?

In the past, searching for low PEGs was a great strategy for finding stocks to buy and will probably be great again when the economy stabilizes. But in 2000 and 2001 the estimated earnings that are used to calculate PEs and PEGs became very unreliable because of the difficult economic picture. However, PEGs are still useful compared with a benchmark, and they are also useful in helping us discard overvalued growth stocks. Higher PEGs stocks should be avoided; however, just because a PEG is low no longer means that the stock is necessarily a good buy. You have to dig a little deeper and investigate the estimates that underlie the PEGs. In sum:

- PEGs are a great tool for warning us when growth stocks are overpriced.
- PEGs are a great tool for helping us know when to exit a stock.
- PEGs are still attractive to help us determine which stocks to buy, but a low PEG no longer means we can buy without further research.

Claudia Mott, small-cap quantitative research director at Prudential Securities, in an attempt to determine whether investors were paying too much or too little for future growth on a relative basis, designed guidelines that were published in the June 1997 issue of *Money.* Her basic premise is that stocks with low PEGs should outperform the market. Mott targeted midcap stocks. Her data went back to 1982, covering PEGs on more than 2,000 small cap and midcap stocks and showed that on average, from 1982 to 1997, if the PEG is

$$<.75 \text{ the returns} = 19.2\%$$

$$\text{Between 1 and 1.25 the returns} = 16.55\%$$

$$>2 \text{ the returns} = 10.8\%$$

Therefore, although past performance is never a guarantee of future performance, this study provides guidance in our search for value in growth stocks.

Calculating PEGs

Do it yourself. To find a PEG, we simply divide the current PE by the forecasted five-year earnings growth rate. The lower it is, the cheaper the company's growth is being priced in the market. Theoretically, the lower the PEG, the higher the potential. In reality, as Mott's study showed, low PEGs indeed go hand in hand with high returns. It is basically a strategy of buying growth at reasonable prices.

You can break down the calculation into the following steps:

- Step 1: Find the PE of your stock.
- Step 2: Find the five-year estimated growth in earnings.
- Step 3: Divide the PE by the five-year estimated growth rate to get the PEG.

And voila . . . it's that simple! Well, maybe not that simple.

- Step 4: Unfortunately, turbulent times make it more difficult to gather accurate data, so you need to evaluate the data, the earnings, and the growth rates carefully. See if they have been updated recently or if there are new surprises. Also check to see if the estimated earnings have a history of surprises. If a company keeps surprising us with either better-than-expected earnings or disappointing earnings, the surprises decrease the likelihood that the data will be accurate. If there are few surprises in the past and no fundamental changes in the stock or the market, the numbers become more viable.

Low-PEG stocks appreciate nearly twice as much as higher-PEG stocks.

It sounds simple. If you found stocks with low PEGs, then you probably have found the stocks that you can hold for long-term growth, the ones with the highest probability to have the best long-term returns.

How to Use PEGs

PEGs almost always are attractive tools for warning us when to sell but can also be used to help in the buy decision.

Although PEGs are no longer a guarantee that you are purchasing a stock at a good price, they are nonetheless useful in helping us exit gracefully.

As with betas, PEs, and other valuation measures, we want to look at the movements in PEGs. If the PEG of your stock is increasing faster than the market or is at a much higher level than past averages or higher than comparable stocks, you should consider the exit strategies explored in previous chapters. There are no hard-and-fast rules, but some rules I have found useful are as follows:

- If PEGs are higher than 3, start getting defensive; use stop losses and covered calls.
- If PEGs are higher than 4, consider purchasing puts.

- If PEGs are 50 percent above their historic averages, consider protective puts, calls, or stop losses.

The good points. This is a great strategy, and if you go back and test it, you'll find it holds true. Low PEG stocks have the best returns. High PEGs are a good warning to start protecting and exiting high-priced stocks and eliminating them from buy lists.

The problem. The problem is the same as that with most statistics we use in evaluating companies. It results from the fact that we are often working with estimates on future earnings and PEs; and when estimates are involved, the data become less and less valuable.

How do we get those estimates? Companies, analysts, research teams all have input, but unfortunately no one can really predict them. A lot of past data are used to predict future performance, but what happened in the past can be drastically different from what could happen in the future.

We compound the problem even more with PEGs because we are dividing an estimate of a PE by another estimate (the estimated five-year growth rate of the stock), and the more estimates involved, the less and less valuable the data are. The further out into the future the projections extend, the less reliable they are. With all these estimates, our equation for PEG = P/?/? That is not the kind of ratio to give you confidence that you have a valid piece of information for assessing value or growth.

Just as with computers, we have to remember the GIGO rule: Garbage in, garbage out. The numbers we rely on are only as valid as the variables we use. When the market is very volatile, as it was in 2000 and 2001, many analysts were not even updating their estimates on growth, so you could not begin to calculate the PEGs. However, with that said, do we want to discard PEGs? No. They may not be perfect, but they are the best we have to evaluate growth stocks. As absolute numbers, they may not be attractive, but for use in comparison with other estimated data, they can be very valuable. PEGs are an excellent starting place, and when the volatility of the market and event risk is low, the information is usually much more reliable. In spite of the problems related to PEGs, they probably are our best way to view some of the younger growth companies. We know that PEGs definitely determine success, and we know that the math of PEGs is simple, but we have to be careful of the data we use in the calculations.

The Advantages and Disadvantages of PEGs

The pros:

- PEGs are simple to calculate.
- PEGs give us a starting point to evaluate growth.
- PEGs are better than looking at PEs alone.
- PEGs give us a tool to evaluate young new companies.

The cons:

- Finding accurate estimated earnings rates is nearly impossible.
- You still need to look at fundamental, quantitative, and technical issues when selecting stocks.

Another Approach to Growth

In the previous chapter on value, I discussed O'Shaughnessy's criteria for evaluating value stocks. He also has criteria that he uses to look at growth stocks. Over the long run, he believes that the higher returns on growth do not justify the high risk. The exceptions, however, are stocks that have relative strength and persistent earnings growth.

O'Shaughnessy suggests looking for stocks not with the highest earnings growth but with the most consistent or "persistent" earnings growth—yearly increases over a five-year period. He also looks at relative strength (one-year price changes). Stocks with high relative strength (the highest price changes over the prior year) produced the highest returns the following year. O'Shaughnessy's momentum indicators did not do so well in 2000 and 2001, but then almost no indicators did. O'Shaughnessy's indicators are still extremely popular and can be found for every stock in *Investor's Business Daily* and other publications. Many believe these indicators work over the long run because investors flock to stocks that go higher and avoid past losers.

Add some of O'Shaughnessy recommendations to Mott's and those of other growth managers, and you have a basis for finding good growth stocks, including those of companies with these characteristics:

- PEGs lower than 2
- Capitalization of $150 million or more
- Earnings gains five years in a row with the potential for future growth
- Price-sales ratios of 1.5 or below
- Ranking among the highest in relative strength
- Potential to increase market share
- Weak earnings in economies coming out of recession

With this approach, it is important to combine low price-to-sales ratios with high relative strength.

Price-sales is to assure that growth stocks are bought when they are cheap. *Relative strength* is used to assure that they are also purchased at a time when the market is starting to realize they have been overlooked. The problem with great stocks, especially those of small companies, is that they go unnoticed. Most major brokerage firms follow larger companies, and small companies are often not worth researching when there is little or no interest in them. If no one notices them, they can be the best company with the best earnings, but you need to know their relative strength to prove that people are watching and buying. Comparing the price changes of stocks with their peers is one way to determine which stocks are moving up the fastest.

Relative strength, the one-year price changes of a stock relative to other stocks, can be found in financial publications such as *Investor's Business Daily.* Stocks with the highest relative strength (i.e., the highest price changes over the previous year) often have the highest returns the following year if, and that is a big *if,* the market is strong. You should always look at a stock's relative strength and momentum, but they should never be the only criteria used to select a stock. However, combining relative strength, with PEGs lower than 2, price-sales ratios of 1.5 or below, fundamental analysis, and technical analysis, makes an attractive addition to the arsenal of tools used in finding value in growth stocks.

There is a big difference between great companies and great stocks. Usually the difference is in being noticed.

Recessions and Declining Earnings

Many studies have shown that value stocks usually do better when earnings are increasing because value purchases are based on *current earnings.* Growth stocks do best when earnings are declining. There is a reason this sounds counterintuitive. When the economy is coming out of recession, people and companies start buying again. The greatest benefactors of optimistic consumers and buyers are growth companies. When earnings are stable or increasing, value stocks do better; but when earnings are decreasing and the Fed is lowering rates, then ultimately the market feels the economy will turn. When investors see the light at the end of the tunnel, they want to move before they get out of the tunnel, so they move into growth stocks that will benefit from a strengthening economy. Expectations of future potential and bargains found in growth usually cause the market to move 6 to 12 months ahead of the economy. Remember with growth that you are not buying current earnings as you are with value. Growth is purchase on anticipation and expectations of *future earnings.* Growth and the market in general do better after the market has experienced declining earnings with the potential for future growth in earnings.

The Leuthold Group, an investment research group, studied the entire postwar period—more than 53 years—and found when earnings were falling the most, that, ironically, is when the S&P 500 did the very best. As a matter of fact, during the nine years when earnings fell more than 5 percent, the S&P was up every year over 20 percent. When earnings were up over 22 percent, the S&P was up only 10 percent. There are many variables that contribute to these numbers, but it is interesting and important to not shy away from growth when earnings are declining.

Summary

In order to select quality stocks at reasonable prices, we need criteria to judge those prices. With value stocks we want low PEs, high yields, and low price-to-book, price-to-cash flow, and price-to-sales. With growth stocks, however, these tools are not valid. Many growth stocks don't have earnings, and their PEs have to be based on estimates; but, in addition, earnings aren't as important as growth in earnings, growth in sales, and low PEGs. Yields are irrelevant. Price-to-sales should be low, but price-to-book can be higher than for value stocks. Momentum and relative strength are also critical for growth stocks but have little relevance for value stocks. Additionally, declining earnings offer potential for future returns with growth stocks.

Overall, portfolios with growth and value positions create a good balance. However, the safety of portfolios balanced between growth and value is not as great as the safety of portfolios balanced between stocks and bonds, or stocks and real estate, or domestic and international stocks. Many years ago it was believed that growth and value moved in opposite directions. In fact, they have a relatively low correlation, but it certainly is not negative and certainly not as low as was once believed. Value doesn't tend to fall when growth rallies; instead, value may just rally less. Growth does not necessarily fall when value rallies; it just tends to underperform. There are, however, many seasonal trends, such as growth performing well at the end of the year and value performing better in the summer months. If you are seeking a truly balanced account, you can't think of it just in terms of growth and value, but you have to also include income or deflation investments and inflation hedges, the premise of the next chapter on asset allocation.

Use PEGs as a way to measure a stock's risk. The higher the PEG, the higher the risk. You may also want to look at other risk measurements, such as the Sharpe ratio, which measures a stock's risk premium over its standard deviation, and the Treynor ratio, which measures the risk premium over the beta.

CHAPTER 12

Asset Allocation

DEFINITION

Asset allocation is the process of proportionately balancing different classes of assets, such as stocks and bonds, in an attempt to achieve the best returns for any given level of risk.

KEY

Safety: ★★★★   Simplicity: ★★

Returns: $$$ Tax efficiency: $$$$

SUMMARY

Safety: Historical data show that investors can control risk by adding diversification and balance. Proper allocation can reduce specific, sector, credit, inflation, market, and opportunity risk. It can also reduce event risk but to a lesser degree.

Returns: Historical data also show that asset allocation accounts for over 90 percent of a portfolio's performance and, if done properly, can substantially increase returns for any given amount of risk.*

---

*Gary P. Brinsom, Randolph Hood, and Gilbert L. Beebower, "Determinants of Portfolio Performance," *Financial Analysts Journal* (July/August 1986).

Simplicity: Although this strategy takes a lot of planning, it is becoming easier to set up well-balanced asset allocation programs with the advances in financial planning and computer analysis.

Tax efficiency: This strategy assumes that you will build a well-balanced portfolio that requires minimum transactions, and thus it is tax efficient.

In general, we have two choices in our approach to investing; we can buy and hold or we can trade. When we buy and hold, we need assurance that our assets are properly balanced and diversified to avoid constantly fine-tuning and trading. For the buy-and-hold approach, concentrate on asset allocation and tax-balancing strategies. This chapter explores asset allocation, and Chapter 15 looks at tax-balancing strategy. For the trading approach, I explore timing and sector rotation strategies in Chapters 13 and 14.

Who, What, Where, and Why

Who Needs Asset Allocation?

Asset allocation is always important, but more so for individuals who are seeking tax efficiency and limited trading activity. It is for both the risk-averse and the risk-tolerant investor because it helps define the best combination of assets for any given risk level.

What Is an Asset Allocation Program?

Asset allocation is a concept that has been around for centuries. Miguel de Cervantes is credited with advising investors "not to put all their eggs in one basket," and that was in 1605!

Asset allocation strategies help relieve stress for the buy-and-hold investor. Over the last few years, the extreme market volatility has made it particularly difficult to sit by and watch your investments fall and rise without being tempted to sell in a panic. This grin-and-bear-it approach has led to depression and extreme stress for many investors, especially those who were not well balanced and diversified.

Asset allocation is a combination of diversification and balance. Many times investors think they are well balanced when they are well diversified or have many different investments. But being well balanced is more than just being well diversified. *Diversification* means having many different investments. *Balance* means having many different investments that have different types of risks and move in different directions (negative or low correlation). Having many investments adds diversification and some safety. Having many *different investments* that move in different directions creates balance and even more safety. If all your investments are similar, such as all technology stocks or all utility stocks, you may be diversified but you are not balanced.

Asset allocation is a strategy that trades one risk for another. To avoid the temptation to sell in a panic, it is critical to have a portfolio that can ride through most market fluctuations and has low or negative correlation. I introduced the concept of negative correlation with the two sailboats. It is better to find investments that are not closely related to each other if you are seeking safety. Your primary task, then, is to find investments that have little in common and move in different directions.

An asset allocation program seeks to find the best combination of investments for *any given risk level.* Your allocation may not always have the best returns, but it is meant to have the best returns for your personality and your unique tax and risk situation. It requires you to look carefully at how you allocate your investments among large companies, mid-size companies, small companies, domestic stocks, and international stocks, as well as between value and growth, between equities and bonds, between inflation and deflation hedges, and among various sectors.

With an asset allocation program, you must first determine your risk level and then find the best combination of investments for that risk level.

Look at the return/risk graph in Figure 12.1. The returns are shown on the vertical line, the risks along the horizontal line. At what point would you like to be: A, B, C, or D?

Asset allocation is not striving for the best return. It is striving for the best return for any given level of risk.

FIGURE 12.1 Risk Measured against Returns

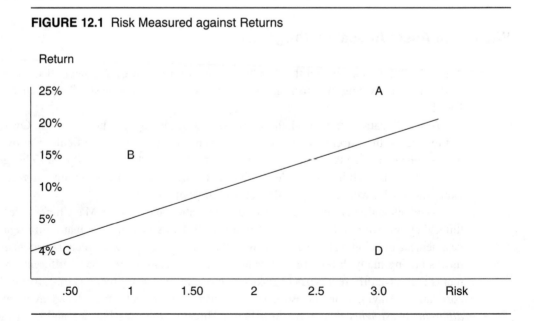

As you can see:

- A has a 25 percent return and 3 units of risk.
- B has a 15 percent return and 1 unit of risk.
- C has a 4 percent return and 0 units of risk.
- D has a 4 percent return and 3 units of risk.

A has the highest return at 25 percent. Is that what you want?

Now let's look at the risk. Both A and D have three units of risk. It is obvious that because both A and D have the same three units of risk, you would prefer A over D as A offers a 25 percent return and D offers less than a 4 percent return.

However, now compare A with B. A has three times as much risk as B. Is it worth taking three times as much risk to earn 25 percent versus 15 percent? There is no correct answer as your risk tolerance determines how much risk you are willing to take. If you really want 25 percent and are not risk averse, A may be fine. But if you look at it from a different perspective and try to assess how much additional return you would get for each unit of risk you take, then B would be a more attractive choice.

For one unit of risk in B, you get a 15 percent return. For each unit of risk you add, you get only 5 percent more return. Moving along the line from B to A does give you more return but at a proportionately much higher risk.*

Would you ever select C? Our graph shows that you can get 4 percent with no risk. Although no investment is completely risk free, we'll assume that money market accounts and Treasury bills are. They do have inflation and opportunity risk, but for our example we are only concerned with market risk. Because C has no volatility and is so stable, a risk–averse investor may select C, willing to settle for lower returns in exchange for the benefit of little or no market risk.

Would you ever select D? No rational investor would willingly select D, which has higher risk and the same return as the risk-free investments. Unfortunately, we often end up at D, though not by choice.

The best possible return may have too much risk for you. It is your job to understand the amount of risk you can take. It is the asset allocation's job to find the best package of investments to achieve the best return for your risk level.

Where Should You Use Asset Allocation?

Asset allocation is especially important in taxable buy-and-hold accounts as this strategy minimizes transactions and thus minimizes taxes.

---

*For those who want to know more, look at the Sharpe ratios or the ratios that compare various rewards per unit of risk. Sharpe ratio = return of portfolio − risk-free rate of return/risk of portfolio. A's Sharpe ratio would be 25% − 4%/3 or 7 units of return for one unit of risk. B's Sharpe ratio would be 15% − 4%/1 or 11, or 11 units of return for one unit of risk. Thus, B would be more attractive for the purely rational investor.

Why Should You Use Asset Allocation?

Because different investments perform differently over time, you need to know how each fits into your life's plans and goals. Asset allocation plans are designed to take into consideration your age, risk level, and liquidity needs. Most financial magazines and financial institutions offer asset allocation guidelines for you, but unless you understand the basics of how the plans fit into your unique situation, you won't be able to provide the correct input, such as your risk tolerance.

Balance and Diversification

Diversification, as noted earlier, is one of the key elements in improving safety and controlling risk. Adding just one or two additional positions to a portfolio can increase safety dramatically. If they have negative correlation, it adds even more safety. Asset allocation strategy combines both diversification and correlation or balance.

Ideal Diversification

Studies demonstrate that you can start to reduce most of the specific risk in a portfolio with just six or seven stocks. The more stocks you add, the less risk you should have. If you have 25 to 35 stocks, you can ideally achieve the best amount of diversification to eliminate the specific risk in a portfolio. However, once you start adding more stocks, you start to weaken manageability. Having more stocks may reduce your risk slightly, but too many stocks or investments can become too difficult and too costly to manage.

Balance

Although increasing the number of stocks decreases specific risk, you can decrease risk even further by considering the correlation of your stocks. Balance can be even more important than diversification.

I would tease my dad all the time that he needed more than just AT&T in his portfolio and that he shouldn't put all his money in one stock. When AT&T was divested, he showed me that he was indeed diversified because he now had several stocks. His safety did increase a little because now there were companies with different management and different earning potential. However, I couldn't convince him that just because he now had several telephone stocks and was technically diversified, he was not actually balanced. All his stocks were likely to respond similarly to market conditions.

At that time, I appeared every morning on a television show in Norfolk. One snowy morning, I had to take my two young children to the studio with me. We put them on the stage and when the host of the show asked a question about Government National Association securities (GNMAs or Ginnie Maes), my six-year-old son, to our amazement, explained to her all the pros and cons of Ginnie Maes, adding that even though they were safe, you need many different colored eggs in your basket. We were in shock that he knew so much and had absorbed so many of my comments over the years. My eight-year-old daughter, could not be outdone by her six-year-old brother and added her comments: "But of course you know you still need to be balanced and you need more than 12 eggs; they also have to be in different baskets and move differently." Obviously, she had heard my repeated warnings to my dad.

Having different colored eggs in different baskets is probably a pretty good definition of diversification, but having different colored eggs doesn't necessarily give you balance. Owning 12 stocks may give you a diversified portfolio, but it is not balance if they are 12 phone companies. Owning 12 government bonds may be diversification, but they are not adequately balanced if they have the same maturity date. The same holds true for mutual funds; diversification or balance is not adequate if they are all large cap growth. To be balanced or adequately diversified, investments not only have to be different from each other but they have to move differently in different baskets. They have to have different betas and correlation and different responses to economic factors. In fact:

- *Diversification* is having 12 eggs.
- *Adequate diversification* is having 12 different-colored eggs.
- *Balance* is having 12 items in 12 different baskets that move in different directions at different times. The less related the items, the better the balance.

Even without a perfect number or combination of investments for all of us, if you have some investments that respond well in inflationary times, some that respond well in deflationary scenarios, some that do well when the market is strong, and some that do well when the market is weak, historically you should be fine.

The Pie Charts

I am sure most of you have seen the colorful little pie charts in financial magazines and financial brochures like those in Figure 12.2. They claim to offer the magic solution to all of the market's problems. In theory, they could, but in reality they are just a beginning. Each color theoretically represents an investment or asset class that offsets some of the risk of the other classes, such as cash, bonds, and stocks. Without different categories, we expose ourselves to large risks, but even with them there is risk, especially event risk.

How Do They Create Those Little Pie Charts? Asset allocation pie charts are probably the most popular financial planning tool today. But how do people come up with them, and why are certain investments selected? As mentioned earlier, it is now an accepted financial practice to assume that asset allocation determines most of the varia-

FIGURE 12.2 Pie Charts

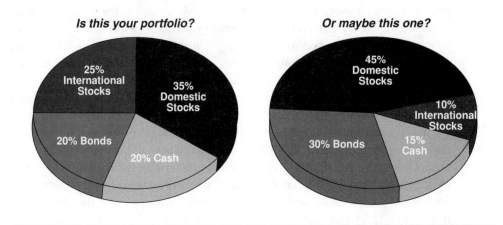

tion of different portfolios' performance. One of the most popular studies showed that 92 percent of performance is the result of asset allocation, 6 percent from stock selection, and 2 percent from timing.* Many authors, professional managers, and other theorists feel that these numbers exaggerate the benefits of asset allocation and discount the benefits of stock selection and timing. However, few doubt that asset allocation is the major contributor to a portfolio's return.

Asset allocation charts start by looking at age, risk tolerance, and liquidity needs. For any given amount of risk, there is one and only one combination of stocks, bonds, and cash that will give the best return. That best combination is what the pie chart theoretically represents.

Most asset allocation goes even further and provides a breakdown of the stock asset classes by international and domestic, by style (value and growth), and by the size of stocks. Bonds are broken down by international and domestic and then by the durations or maturities of bonds. Some asset allocation programs go even further and look at sectors within the categories. Because your portfolio's performance is so closely tied to allocation, it is only logical that this is where most investors begin their portfolio construction.

Look at the pie charts in Figure 12.2. These charts indicating allocations are based on different risk tolerances, which are often assumed by the creators of charts to be related to your age. The more aggressive allocations have the best long-term returns based on the past history of different sectors in the economy. However, the higher expected returns come at the cost of higher risk.

---

*Gary P. Brinson, Randolph Hood, and Gilbert L Beebower, "Determinants of Portfolio Performance," *Financial Analysts Journal* (July/August 1986).

Because age is not the only consideration when evaluating risk, you need to consult with a financial advisor to develop a more accurate picture for yourself. Your risk might be still high when you are older if you have a large portfolio and are more interested in saving for your heirs and estate planning. Even if you are young, your risk tolerance may be very low as you may need the money soon for a home or a child's education. Many financial programs and Internet sites can help you get a better handle on your portfolio's allocation, but in the final analysis you have to determine your risk level.

Making the pie The numbers that make up these pie charts are based on the risk/reward ratios that stemmed from the well-known and credible work done by Dr. Harry Markowitz in the 1950s. His early work laid the foundation for diversification and asset allocation programs, and he was rewarded with a Nobel prize for his work on the efficient frontier curve, which shows us the best allocation for any given amount of risk.

As you can see from the efficient frontier curve in Figure 12.3,* the more risk you are willing to take, the higher your returns will be. Each point or dot on the curve represents one of those colorful little pie charts. The pie charts in turn depict the best combinations of various investments for any given amount of risk. There are, of course, many

FIGURE 12.3 Efficient Frontier Curve

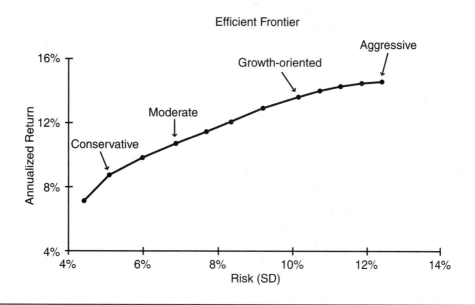

---

*Developed from the work done by Dr. Harry Markowitz. See Harry Markowitz and Andre F. Perold, "Portfolio Analysis with Factors and Scenarios," *Journal of Finance* (September 1981).

other combinations that don't fall on the efficient frontier curve, but they would have lower returns for the amount of risk you selected. The curve is called "efficient" because it represents only the best return for any given level of risk.

Your risk tolerance determines the proportion of asset classes and where you are on the efficient frontier curve.

Asset allocators calculate the various combinations of the returns and risk of various asset classes and create the mathematical data that appear on the asset allocation charts or on the efficient frontier curve. If you were more risk tolerant, your portfolio would be in a very different place on the chart than would the portfolio of a conservative investor. The more risk tolerant you are, the more you would move to the right on the efficient frontier curve. For the higher degree of risk you would be willing to take, you would theoretically have a higher return in the long run, although the probability of greater falls and dips in the short run is likely to increase. You would probably see a recommendation that was much more heavily weighted to stocks, with little or no bonds. It would be to the far right of the curve.

There is probably no more widely accepted belief in investing than that proposed by Dr. Markowitz: the higher the returns, the higher the risks. If you are willing to take more risk, then you can expect to achieve higher returns:

EXPECTED RETURNS = Risk-free returns + Beta (risk premium)*

More aggressive portfolios have none of the theoretically safer bonds and fixed income assets and also have much more invested in small cap stocks because, historically, small caps have outperformed larger caps and bonds. Therefore, if you are striving for higher growth, you need to be in sectors that have provided higher returns in the past.

The efficient frontier curve takes into consideration trade-offs for risks, balancing risks based on the correlation of the underlying investments. Once we determine where we belong on the efficient frontier curve, we then find the pie chart (i.e., the asset allocation) that makes us comfortable and finally select the investments that fit into each of the categories.

The Probability of Achieving Your Expected Return

What is the probability that after you do all your research you'll end up with the return depicted on the efficient frontier curve? With decades of data behind us, analysts are able to predict with a high degree of success the probability of achieving a targeted return over a long period. One of the greatest problems with most retirement planning and financial

---

*This is the formula in Chapter 3. The returns you can expect for your portfolio will equal the returns on the current risk-free investments (Treasury bills) plus the amount of risk you are willing to take (beta) times the risk premium (the difference between historic returns on the stock market minus the risk-free returns of Treasury bills).

planning packages is that they assume an average return over the years yet don't look at the probability of achieving those returns over a specified period. The longer the time frame, theoretically the more likely you are to achieve the predicted return.

But the market goes up and down, and *when* you invest in the market makes a big difference; the timing of those ups and downs can have a huge impact on the probability of your achieving your targeted return in a certain time frame. Many programs now include probability analysis (such as Monte Carlo) into their planning. These programs can depict the probability of portfolios composed of hundreds of investments. Figure 12.4 shows the probability of your achieving your targeted return on the basis of only two investments: stocks and bonds.

The Probability of Achieving Your Target

The probabilities in Figure 12.4 are the same no matter where the data come from. I took these figures from Rittenhouse Financial Services, Inc., of Radnor, Pennsylvania (800-847-6369). Although the figure is limited to stocks and bonds, it is interesting to see the likely returns for some of the combinations.

The numbers represent the probability of various combinations of bonds and stocks achieving the likely average return. Past performance over the last 50 years shows a 95 percent chance that a portfolio's return in any one year will fall between the highs and lows shown in Figure 12.4.

Only two asset classes are used, but realistically you should have more than stocks and bonds in your portfolio. However, what is important here is to understand how changing the proportions or combinations changes the likely return. Notice that as you

FIGURE 12.4 Probabilities

% in stocks	% in bonds	Likely low	Likely average	Likely high
100%	0%	−21.3%	14.7%	50.6%
90	10	−18.8	13.8	46.4
80	20	−16.4	13.0	42.3
70	30	−14.0	12.1	38.2
60	40	−11.8	11.3	34.3
50	50	−9.7	10.4	30.6
40	60	−8.0	9.6	27.1
30	70	−6.6	8.7	24.1
20	80	−5.9	7.9	21.7
10	90	**−6.1**	7.0	20.2
5	95	**−6.6**	6.6	19.8
0	100	**−7.3**	6.2	19.7

increase the bond portion to 80 percent, the likely low decreases. Thus, adding bonds decreases the risk of the portfolio but only to a certain point. When you reduce stocks to less than 20 percent of the portfolio, your risk actually starts to increase!

Investors often think that having only bonds is the safest portfolio, but you can see the safest portfolio for a given amount of risk and reward is a combination of 80 percent bonds and 20 percent stocks. As you increase bonds to 90 percent, your risk (the likely low) actually increases (from −5.9 percent as a likely low to −6.1 percent). When you reach 100 percent bonds, the likely low increases to −7.3 percent, making a zero percent stock/100 percent bond portfolio much riskier.

Size Matters

According to Ibbotson Associates, from 1925 to 2000, small cap companies returned more than 12.4 percent; large cap companies returned more than 11 percent; long-term bonds returned more than 5.3 percent; and inflation was 3.1 percent.

The 12.4 percent for small caps doesn't sound like much more than the 11 percent for large companies, especially if you don't like the idea of risk. However, if you look at it from the point of view of a dollar, you would see how much difference 1.4 percent can make: $1 invested over 75 years grew to $2,587 in large cap stocks, but grew to $6,402 in small cap stocks.

Thus, you see that 1.4 percent can make a tremendous difference and may make you think differently about risk and help you understand the trade-off between risk and reward.

Sectors Matter Too!

According to Lipper Analytical Services, the sector you select can also make a dramatic difference in your return. For example, returns on an investment of $10,000 in the following over a ten-year period from 12/31/88 to 12/31/98 would look like this:

The Lipper Science and Technology Funds average grew to	$86,972
The Lipper Health/Biotech Funds average grew to	$79,087
The Lipper Financial Service Funds average grew to	$73,019
The S&P 500 grew to	$57,928

Another Way to View Asset Allocation

Many years ago, I needed an easy way to explain asset allocation to my clients. I wanted to show investments that offset the risk of one investment with another and respond differently to market conditions. To create asset allocation pie charts you need sophisticated computer models that can handle inputs of thousands of variables and that rely on the correlation of many different investment classes. Not only are those correlation numbers not available to most of us, but the number of variables are overwhelming. I created my own chart as a way to easily view the many different levels of risk and the concept of asset allocation.

My chart helps me visualize many of the components needed for asset allocation. I like to divide my chart into four categories: *inflation hedges, deflation hedges, value investments,* and *growth* investments. Make sure all portfolios include some of each category or class, and then decide which investments are most suitable for you. For example, if you decide on bonds, you should then decide the maturities and quality of the bonds. If you decide on growth stocks, you should determine the amount in various growth categories,

FIGURE 12.4 Asset Allocation: A Different View

such as technology or telecommunications. I use my chart as a way to determine how well balanced my clients' portfolios are. You can do the same by marking off the main classes and then the individual investments you have. You will then be able to see how balanced your accounts are. You need to use different charts for taxable accounts and tax-deferred accounts (to be discussed in Chapter 15).

I have included only a few examples of each investment in different classes to make the chart easier to use here. I like this approach because it encourages me to look at strategies such as sector rotation, buy and hold, emergency funds, laddering, and various individual investments. It helps ensure I have investments that protect me no matter what happens in the market. It also ensures that I have inflation as well as deflation hedges, along with value and growth, in addition to different sectors and strategies. Look at the chart yourself, and check off or highlight the investments and categories that you have. You can easily tell that you aren't well balanced if all your investments are in one section of the chart. Make your own chart, writing down all the investments you have that fit under growth and value, and under inflation and deflation hedges.

Again, this is only a starting point for building a portfolio and guiding me in making sure all my bases are covered.

Risk Review

As I noted above, my chart is meant to complement traditional pie charts, not serve as a substitute for them. It can also be used to help control risks. Some of the risks I look at and investments I use to offset them are:

- Opportunity risk, for which I include growth investments
- Inflation risk, for which I include stocks, oils, real estate, commodities, and the like
- Deflation or recession risk, for which I include bonds
- Interest rate risk, for which I include laddering strategies and cash
- Reinvestment risk, for which I include laddering and long-term securities
- Market risk, for which I include hedges and guaranteed vehicles

Make sure that you have investments in the areas that give you inflation protection, deflation protection, growth, and value. If you are more risk oriented and younger, you might have nearly all your investments on the growth and inflation side. If you are older and nervous, you may want more in the hedge, income, and value areas.

Diversification also adds additional safety. Four basic approaches to investing in stocks and bonds are buying individual stocks and bonds, trusts, mutual funds, and relying on money managers. Individual stocks have more specific risk than funds, managed accounts, and trusts because poor earnings, lawsuits, credit risk, and hundreds of other variables can affect a stock's price. We can reduce specific risk, whether good or bad risk, by buying groups of stocks rather than individual stocks. Trusts and mutual funds have allowed individual investors to get the diversification they need with smaller amounts of money. Money management accounts, on the other hand, usually require a minimum of $100,000 or more.

Passive Management versus Active Management

You need two different types of asset allocation portfolios: one for taxable accounts and one for tax-deferred or nontaxable accounts. You may find that for your given risk you need in both your individual and IRA accounts the same proportions in inflation hedges, value stocks, growth stocks, and so on. The type of investment you use for each of those categories, however, will have a big impact on your taxes. For taxable accounts, *passive* investments are probably the best, but for nontaxable accounts *actively managed* investments are often the best. Active management implies frequent monitoring, fine-tuning, and trading. In a passive investment securities are bought and held for certain periods. In the determination of the asset allocation for a taxable account, relatively passive investments are preferable to assure that the investments in your portfolio are not creating negative tax consequences. Examples of passive investments are index mutual funds, bonds, or trusts that buy and hold securities.

After you have done your work to select an appropriate asset allocation for a taxable account, it may all be for naught if you have investments that are constantly creating tax consequences through active trading. You should usually try to avoid actively managed investments, such as mutual funds and covered-call writing programs.

Passive investments, such as trusts or index funds, are usually more attractive in taxable accounts because they don't require constant trading and transactions that have tax consequences. However, passive investments such as indexes, funds, and trusts are just that: passive because no one is reviewing, trading, or monitoring the investments. Passive trusts are usually attractive for conservative bonds and stocks, but when dealing with aggressive sectors, such as small cap stocks or international securities, you might want managed mutual funds instead of passive indexes. For risky investments, you want someone with experience and in-depth information and research looking out for your interests.

General rules for active versus passive investments include these.

- Use passive investments for asset allocation programs in taxable accounts.
- In both taxable and tax-deferred accounts, use mutual funds when the underlying investments are risky. Consider active management for international, small, and mid-cap investments. Even though taxes are a concern, don't trade the advantages of active management for tax savings.
- In retirement plans, such as IRAs and 401(k)s, you can use mutual funds and investments that have much higher tax consequences. In retirement accounts, look for the best investments and strategies and don't worry about the tax consequences.

Mutual funds are actively managed; trusts are passively managed.

There is much debate about whether funds or trusts perform better, but there is little debate that both tend to do better than does holding a few individual stocks.

Mutual Fund Drift

As attractive as mutual funds are for asset allocation programs, funds have a problem. When you see that a fund is a large cap growth fund, you assume it is large cap growth, but in fact it may have small cap, large cap, value, international stocks, cash, and the like in it. In 2001, funds were required to name their funds to describe more accurately the underlying investments. For example, bond funds had to actually hold bonds and not equities. However, there was no requirement for the description of styles. For example, Legg Mason's Value Fund is often accused of being a growth fund even though its name implies value. Funds often drift from one style to another, which may or may not benefit investors. The problem arises when investors are trying to build balanced portfolios. If they don't know exactly what a fund holds, it is difficult to use it in asset allocation programs as there may be overlapping among the funds.

Dr. A. Craig MacKinley, a professor of finance at the Wharton School, studied the dangers of a style-based approach when evaluating mutual funds. He investigated how funds calling themselves one type may actually be another type. For example, when value was out of favor in the 1990s, many value managers added growth stocks to their portfolios and small caps were added to large cap funds. These managers felt they couldn't strictly adhere to the style that their titles implied. Dr. MacKinley found that value funds during the 1990s had as little as 61 percent in value stocks and the rest in growth stocks. Growth funds stuck closer to their style classifications with over 70 percent in growth stocks. As growth becomes more unpredictable, growth managers may feel a need to sneak in more value stocks. What does this mean to you? It means that when you set your asset allocation percentages, be aware that you may actually not hit your targets by just viewing titles or Morningstar's characteristics of funds.

Let's assume your asset allocation plan calls for 40 percent growth, 40 percent value, and 20 percent cash. If you select a growth mutual fund that is actually only 70 percent growth, 10 percent value, and 20 percent cash and you select a value fund that is 60 percent value and 40 percent growth, then your actual percentages would be 44 percent growth, 28 percent value, and 28 percent cash.

Although Dr. Craig uses return analysis to determine the true style of funds, it is often too difficult for individual investors to employ this kind of analysis. Therefore, a simple solution is to assume that when growth is good, value funds will try and add some growth stocks to their portfolios to capture the strength in growth. Although it sounds counter-intuitive, once you determine your percentages, add a little more to value funds when growth is strong and add a little extra to growth mutual funds when value is strong.

Trusts

Because of the difficulty in managing taxes and the style drift in mutual funds, an explosive growth in the use of trusts and passive index funds has occurred. I prefer using funds in retirement accounts where taxes are not a concern and where sector rotation, timing, and rebalancing are attractive strategies. Mutual funds are also attractive for dollar cost averaging, which typically occurs in retirement accounts. But trusts and passive index funds tend to be more attractive in taxable accounts as they are passively managed and have little or no transactions and therefore little or no tax consequences.

Trusts and passive index funds come in a variety of packages. Some are packages of bonds and stocks that can be sold and purchased at the end of the day. Others can be traded on the stock exchanges, the American usually, just like stocks.

S&P 500 trusts. S&P 500 depositary receipts are modeled after Standard & Poor's 500-stock index and trade under the symbol SPY.

iShares. iShares trade on the American Exchange just like stocks. They can be traded in round lots of 100 or in even smaller amounts. You can use market orders, limit orders, and stop losses just as you can with stocks. iShares cover over 50 different domestic indexes.

- The Dow Jones, basic materials, chemicals, consumer cyclical sector, noncyclical, energy, financial, health care, industrial, Internet, real estate, technology, telecommunications, total market, utilities, and more
- iShares also has an S&P 500 index and segments of the S&P.
- S&P 500/BARRA Growth Index Fund, iShares 500/BARRA Value Index Fund, iShares
- S&P MidCap 400 Index Fund and so on

Over 50 different countries are covered by iShares, and they usually invest in the same stocks as the major indexes in those countries. You can build your own international portfolio by dividing your assets among several different countries.

Advantages and Disadvantages

Pros:

- Diversification
- Minimal fees
- Minimal taxes
- Ability to trade like stocks
- Some have options
- Ability to borrow against them in most cases
- Attractive for asset allocation programs
- Cover almost every equity class
- Can get information easily <www.ishares.com>
- Can clearly see accurate diversification

Cons:

- Passive management could be a negative, especially in bad markets.

Asset allocation is not perfect. It is a starting point, not the final answer.

Simplistic allocations often don't offer the best protection or the potential for higher returns but usually are the best we have. There are so many variables and event risks that asset allocation cannot account for all of them. But for all their drawbacks, simplistic allocations are still a good way to start thinking about how to allocate your assets among various investment classes. The days of buy and hold are becoming more and more difficult to tolerate, whereas asset allocation strategies can add safety and balance. In addition, once set up, these strategies are relatively easy to monitor and execute. For long-term core accounts, asset allocation is crucial, because the last few years have made even the calmest of investors shudder. No matter how tough it is to hold, many investors need core buy-and-hold strategies for tax reasons, and for buy and hold you need asset allocation. Even though simple little charts are not the final answer, they are a good starting point.

Asset allocation not for those seeking the highest returns. Theoretically, if your asset allocation is done correctly, you will never achieve the highest returns, but you will receive the highest returns for the amount of risk you are willing to take. Because asset allocation strategies should include investments that move in the opposite direction from each other—investments that go up while others are falling—it is difficult for these portfolios to outperform the market. If done correctly, asset allocation can lead to peace of mind and performances that match the S&P 500.

Even asset allocation may not work in broad market declines. Asset allocation programs are not perfect. There are times when they don't work well. If there is a broad market decline in which all asset classes fall, then asset allocation programs may not work well in the short run. However, over the long run they offer the best solution for investors who want or need to build a portfolio based on sound risk versus reward principles. In markets such as the one in early 2000, even well-balanced portfolios suffered, as nearly all asset classes suffered from the broad economic decline. Although balance did not appear to offer much relief in mid-2000, when both stocks and bonds suffered, once interest rates started to fall, bonds balanced off some of the losses in stocks.

The Difficulty of Assessing Risk Levels

It is important that investors remind themselves frequently that asset allocation programs give you the best combination of assets for the given amount of risk you select. However, too often investors select allocation packages without a lot of thought. Over the years, I have found that most investors do not fully understand risk. Too often investors think they can handle large amounts of risk, and so they select more aggressive portfolios. Usually, they think they can handle risk when the market is going up. However, when the market falls and they experience high degrees of volatility, these investors suddenly realize that they wanted high returns but were not prepared or willing to take the risk necessary to achieve those returns.

Summary

You cannot have both high returns and low risk. There is always a trade-off, which is why you need to understand who you are and understand the chapters on risks. Low and negative correlation adds safety but usually can limit the upside. Asset allocation is meant to be a buy-and-hold strategy in which you select investments from many different industries and asset classes so that you balance the risk of one asset with another. However, your investments are not designed to sit without adjustments that bring the risk and allocations back into balance.

CHAPTER 13

Timing

A Strategy to Increase Returns and Avoid the Big Downside

DEFINITION

Timing is a strategy that attempts to buy low and sell high. It is the opposite of the buy-and-hold or grin-and-bear-it strategy.

KEY

Safety: ★★★★   Simplicity: ★★

Returns: $$$$ Tax efficiency: –$$

SUMMARY

Safety: Historically, there is no doubt that if investors could avoid the large downside falls in the market, they could dramatically improve their safety and returns, but if avoiding falls is not timed correctly, risk could be increased dramatically.

Returns: A Value Line study shows that over a 20-year period covering the 1980s and 1990s, a buy-and-hold strategy with the S&P 500 averaged 17 percent, whereas a timing strategy returned over 27 percent.

Simplicity: It is very difficult to time because of the large amount of variables, guesses, data, and analysis that is needed. However, automated timing strategies will help you buy near the bottom and sell near the top without emotion. These automated strategies are the topic of this chapter.

Tax efficiency: As with all trading strategies, the tax consequences of timing can be severe.

I love that quotation because it tells the whole story of the market and why timing is often futile and yet extremely important. This chapter focuses on entering and exit strategies for stocks and the market. Chapter 14 concentrates on sectors. I won't depend on forecasting strategies for timing the market but instead on automatic strategies that take the emotion and decision making out of timing.

> "October. This is one of the peculiarly dangerous months to speculate in stocks. The others are July, January, September, April, November, May, March, June, December, August, and February."
> —Mark Twain

Timing provides strategies for avoiding panic selling or the roller-coaster strategy of buying low, watching stocks rally, and then watching them fall lower and lower and lower before they rally again. We know the roller coaster will eventually come back up, but we might not like the ride. Or even worse, you may need your money before the roller coaster heads back up. The following strategies are for those who think it is more fun to take some profits at the top, not necessarily the best profits but good profits.

We often think of timing as using technical forecasting programs. Of course, using those programs is a fine strategy when it works, but few of us have the time and talent to develop sophisticated computer programs. Although timing can dramatically reduce risk, it can actually expose us to more risk if not done with automatic programs and without emotion.

Many noted authorities rightly claim that timing accounts for only 2 percent of a portfolio's performance. The poor track record of timers also makes arguments for timing less credible. However, it is not the strategy that is lacking. It is the implementation that is flawed. A new school of credible analysts is showing that timing in fact does add safety to a portfolio and may increase returns dramatically.

In this chapter I use timing as a way to increase the safety of portfolios without claiming it will get you out at the top or provide the best returns. What timing does do is show you how not to lose the money you've made and give you some commonsense criteria and tools to help you determine when your stocks or the market are overvalued. I use these same criteria for sector rotation but add additional exit and entrance strategies more suitable for sectors and funds. The concepts presented in the previous chapters are building blocks for you to use in timing and sector rotation strategies.

Who Should Consider This Strategy?

Timing is for investors who believe taking profits is more rewarding than buy-and-hold strategies. It is for those who want to protect the profits they have, avoid some downside, and make good returns, but it is not for those trying to hit home runs. It is for those who want to control their life and money, believe that success in investing depends to a large degree in buying low and selling high, and are tired of the grin-and-bear-it strategy. Most important, it is for those who believe that the markets and stocks revert to their average or mean.

What Is Timing?

Simply, timing is trying to buy low and sell high. I view it as buying at reasonable prices and learning to take reasonable profits.

Where Should You Consider Using Timing?

Because taxes can be high when you are moving in and out of the market, timing strategy is best for tax-deferred accounts where taxes are not an issue and avoiding losses is critical. However, even in taxable accounts it is often better to take a profit and pay taxes than to sit and wait until you have a profit. In an earlier chapter I told you about Martha and her Qualcomm. She would never sell it because her profits were so high . . . well, she doesn't have that problem anymore—she now has a 60 percent loss! Don't wait, even in a taxable account, to take some profits; it is more fun and more rewarding to have small profits than big losses.

Time-In versus Time-Out

Arguments against Timing

Because I agree with many of the numerous arguments against timing. I suggest using timing strategies for only part of a portfolio as an approach to taking profits and stopping losses before they destroy the portfolio. Although I concentrate more on exit strategies, many of the criteria I use will help you to enter the market at low prices also.

Even though reasonable arguments can be made for and against timing, I think you'll find the arguments in favor of timing strong enough to consider timing strategies for part of your portfolio.

Argument 1: Missing the best days. Probably the most popular argument against timing is the difficulty in recovering losses if you miss the few best days a year. During the 1980s, almost every investment seminar or publication started with the famous Datastream, Ibbotson Associates, and Sanford C. Bernstein charts showing that if you were invested in the S&P 500 during the entire decade, your return was 17.5 percent.

> If you missed the 10 best days, your return dropped from 17.5% to 12.6%.
> If you missed the 20 best days, it dropped to 9.3%.
> If you missed the 30 best days, it dropped to 6.5%.
> If you missed the 40 best days, it dropped to 3.9%.

Had you missed just four of the best days each year, your return would have been worse than that from a money market account. Later, we'll see why these data are a little skewed toward the buy-and-hold argument, but for now they show that timing may be dangerous. If you miss out on the best days, you won't share in the higher returns of the market.

In the 1990s, the numbers, according to Putnam Investors, are even more impressive. If you were fully invested, your average return was 18.21 percent.

If you missed just the 40 best days in the 1980s, your return would have fallen from 17.5 percent to 3.9 percent.

> If you missed the 10 best days, your return dropped to 13.84%.
> If you missed the 20 best days, your return dropped to 10.80%.
> If you missed the 30 best days, your return dropped to 8.26%.
> If you missed the 40 best days, your return dropped to 5.95%.

One of the worst one-day falls in the Dow Jones was on October 27, 1997, when the Dow fell 554 points. It was even worse than the 508 point fall on October 19, 1987. But it was followed one day later by the third best gain of 337 points. Had you sold out and not gotten back in the next day, you would have missed a golden opportunity, one of the strongest rallies that year. Or, as the argument goes, what if you had missed the best one-day gain ever in the Dow's history, on March 16, 2000, when it rose 499 points? Obviously, missing these days would have influenced your performance.

Argument 2: Even the best have failed at predicting the economy and the markets. Have you ever noticed that even though we get statistics each month describing the economy, earnings, unemployment, and so on, months later these numbers are revised. No matter how sophisticated computers are, it is still impossible to gather all the data and review the many variables needed to give an accurate picture of the past, never mind the future. It seems that once investors, the government, the Federal Reserve Board, and businesses have based their plans and strategies on these numbers . . . they change! They are revised over and over again. It takes the National Bureau of Economic Research six months to tell us what happened in the past, so it is unlikely that it or anyone will be able to tell us what will happen in the future.

The Federal Reserve Board, even with the best research, couldn't predict how fast the economy would expand with its easy money in 1999. Worse yet, it was not able to see how interest rate increases would bring the world into a tailspin in 2000 and 2001.

So my second argument against timing is that it is naïve for any of us to believe that we can predict the future. With so much event risk and the inability of companies to understand even their own outlook, how can we assume we have some special talent that will let us forecast better?

Argument 3: Brinson, Singer and Beebower study.* One of the more popular studies of investing shows that 92 percent of a portfolio's performance is related to its asset allocation—that is, how assets are divided among various styles, sectors, and sizes of investments. Picking individual stocks or investments accounts for only 6 percent of performance and timing the stocks accounts for only 2 percent. Therefore, with such a small part of success attributed to timing, it's not worth expending time or effort on it.

Argument 4: MIT. Few, if any, forecasting programs can take into consideration all event risks. The programs can work well with known variables, but there are so many unknowns that not even computers can provide accurate insight. In 1972 and 1973, my husband and I were working on our master's degrees. As a navy carrier pilot sent to the Middle East, he started to realize that the probable reason he was sent there was to protect our oil interests. His letters were filled with discussions about oil, even though the media were not picking up on the stories. At that time, I was assigned in one of my master's degree courses to forecast the price of coal and wood-burning stoves in ten years. We were to use one of the most sophisticated computer programs in the world that was created by the brightest of the bright MIT mathematicians. As I wrote my paper, I remembered the oil crisis, and in spite of the results of the computer program, I argued that event risk could throw the whole forecasting program off. Two weeks later there was an oil embargo! Although the purpose of the course was to show how successful sophisticated forecasting programs had become, my professor agreed that even with the most advanced computer programs, no method can accurately forecast the future, so timing can be fraught with difficulties.

Argument 5: Odean study. Individual investors often get so excited about trading that they forget it is not the trading, but the result that matters. When Terrance Odean, a behavioral economist at the University of California, examined 10,000 accounts at a discount brokerage firm from 1987 to 1993, he found that the average annual turnover rate was

---

*"Determinants of Portfolio Performance: An Update." Based on ten-year returns of 82 pension funds, *Financial Analyst Journal* (May/June 1991).

78 percent. The turnover itself would not have been so bad, even though fees were probably excessive, but the problem resulted from the fact that the stocks that were sold outperformed the ones subsequently purchased by 3 percent that year (before commissions).

Argument 6: Information is disseminated so fast. Because we have such easy access to information at the same time, it is difficult for any of us to discover the hidden value in most stocks. In 2001, securities laws were enacted that required companies to distribute information to everyone at the same time. Thus, shareholders and the public get information now at the same time investment bankers, analysts, and money managers get it. Even the brokerage firms that have relationships with companies no longer have an edge. With everyone getting information so quickly, can investors act fast enough to get in and out? The answer is probably no, which is why I argue not to wait for the top but rather set realistic goals and take reasonable profits.

Are You Still Interested in Timing?

Many often argue that it is time-in the market that is so important, not timing it. Before you give up on timing as a strategy, I would like to remind you there are just as many arguments in favor of timing; and if you lived through the 2000 and 2001 crash, you can appreciate how great it would have been to have gotten out and not lived through the nightmare.

Arguments for Timing

Argument 1: The market crash of 2000 and 2001. I think this needs no more comment. How many of you enjoyed that crash? Avoiding it would have made a big difference in the life of most investors.

Argument 2: Time does not solve all problems. We hear many statistics showing how well the market has done over the long run and predictions that in the long run the market will come back. Yet Nobel Prize–winning economists, such as Paul Samuelson and Robert Merton, also show that because average returns have been positive over the long run doesn't mean we'll end up with positive returns and increased wealth over the long run. Not everyone makes money in the market, and if you are one of those who doesn't, then you can't sit and hope for time to erase all problems. If you have suffered from negative returns year after year, your terminal wealth (how much money you had at the end), would be greatly diminished. When things are going fine, buy and hold works; but when things go sour, buying and holding can be disastrous, so you have to know when to pull out.

Argument 3: Missing the bad days is more important than missing the good days. If you could be in the market only in the months it was going up and out in the months it was going down, I'm sure you would agree your portfolio would show larger returns. If you had invested $1 in 1926 in Treasury bills and let it sit until December 2000, it would have grown to $16.61. If you had invested $1 in the S&P 500, it would have grown to $2,586.31. Not bad! The risk premium of the market was great.

Risk premium means how much more you earned by taking a risk and investing in the stock market instead of investing in a risk-free investment such as Treasuries. You received $2,586.31 instead of $16.61 for taking the risk and going into the market. But what if you had a crystal ball and were able to miss all the bad months and be invested in only the good months? Earlier, I told you about Professor A. Craig MacKinlay's study that showed with perfect hindsight how your $1 would have grown to $9,668,522,667. If you were out of the market on all the down months, your $1 would have grown to over $9 billion . . . that is billion with a *B!**

Most of us realize that we would be better off missing the bad days, but when you put it in perspective, missing them is a lot more important than we often realize.

$1 in Treasuries	$16.61
$1 in stock you buy and hold	$2,586.31
$1 invested with perfect timing	$9,668,522,667.00

Why even mention a number like that? No one has perfect timing and no one ever will. However, a little timing can go a long way, and that is what I hope to show you in this chapter.

Argument 4: Timing is everything in life. For dancers, comedians, and actors, timing is critical . . . it is everything. It's the same in the financial world. I would like to remind you of my dad's AT&T stock, which my sisters and brother let me sell shortly after his death. I sold most of it around $60 a share. My sister Joan later found some reinvested shares that we didn't know about so we fought with AT&T to liquidate them. By the time they were finally sold, we got $51 a share, or over 20 percent less. At the same time, I was advising a family with a similar portfolio: AT&T, its spin-offs, and a little GE; but the family couldn't agree. When their dad passed away, they had more than $432,000 worth of shares. When they finally agreed to sell, the shares were worth less than $20 a share, less than $164,000. Ask them if timing is important and I think they will tell you it is everything.

Argument 5: Value Line study. Because it is assumed that timing adds only 2 percent to a total portfolio's success, it seems hardly worth the time worrying about it.[†] But that argument is made because timing is difficult to do and is often done poorly. Those

---

*Data from Ibbotson and Professor A. Craig MacKinlay, the Wharton School. CIMA program presented on June 28th, London, Ontario.

†Although the Brinson, Singer and Beebower study on performance attribution is popular and credible, it is questionable if it is applicable today for individual investors. This is the study quoted here often that showed 92 percent of a portfolio's performance is related to asset allocation. However, Stuart R. Veale points out the study was based on only 91 pensions. The pension managers used a limited number of

who take timing seriously, however, can improve their returns, not by trying to forecast the future in a crystal ball, but by using strict guidelines to help them exit gracefully. Value Line's study showing that over the last 20 years a buy-and-hold strategy in the S&P would have resulted in a 17 percent return also showed that a timing strategy would have resulted in a 27 percent return, and a sector rotation strategy would have returned 34 percent. Of course, this is assuming you have a successful program that gets you out of the market before dramatic falls and gets you back in on time. It does not assume that you miss every bad day and capture every good day, only that you just miss most of the downside and capture most of the upside.

Argument 6: Statistics can be deceiving. The first argument above against timing relied on the fall of the Dow Jones on October 27, 1997, of 554 points and rallying one day later with the third best gain ever of 337 points. So the argument goes: had you missed that second-day rally, it would have taken you years to recover. Therefore, you should buy and hold to avoid missing such golden opportunities as the rally of 337 points.

Does this argument strike you as odd? What if you had missed the 554-point fall? Even if you had missed the 337 point rally, wouldn't you still have been 217 points better off had you missed the fall?

Argument 7: Revisiting 1987. In earlier chapters, I told you how I used stop losses while commuting from Puerto Rico each week. On the Friday before the 1987 crash, I was stopped out of nearly everything when the market fell 109 points. On the next Monday, the market fell another 508 points. Wouldn't it be nice to miss some of those terrible falls? Octobers and Septembers are notoriously dangerous. Wouldn't it be nice to have some protection during those months?

Argument 8: Marty Zweig. Marty Zweig, one of the more famous market timers, has often not been able to time the market as well as he would like, but he is correct when he notes that the media often concentrate so much on missing the good days that they forget how important it is to also miss the bad days. The press always seems willing to defend buy-and-hold strategies, but what about "taking-some-profit strategies"?

> **If you missed the 40 worst days over ten years, you would have done 9 percent better than the market!**

For example, if you missed the ten best days, your return would have dropped to 4 percent. But if you missed the 10 worst days in the 1980s, your return would have increased by 9 percent to 27 percent.

---

stocks because of fiduciary responsibility, so stock selection probably did not get the attention it deserved. In addition, the timing of stocks then was limited because of constraints on pension funds and was probably not applicable to other situations. When you consider the increased volatility in the market the last few years, you may feel there is more than just buy and hold that works. Some strategies work some of the time, but none works all of the time.

Argument 9: Philip Morris. Perhaps the best argument for timing is that when you get to the top, there is always someone else who wants to get there too. In 1990 Philip Morris was at the top, but by 1993 it was the worst of the Dow Jones Industrial Average stocks. It is not only difficult to be the winner every year, but companies at the top often quickly become overvalued. When they are knocked off their pedestal, they have a long way to fall. Stocks that have spectacular growth, way above their averages, have a tendency to fall back to those averages. In addition to the natural ebb and flow from top to bottom, fundamental problems can occur, such as Philip Morris's litigation woes. These fundamental issues should again make you consider timing or exit strategies.

Argument 10: Active management versus passive management. If you feel that an actively managed portfolio is better than a passively managed one, then you believe in timing. There is an element of timing, stock selection, and asset allocation in all actively managed accounts.

Argument 11: The most important argument—we all do it now. Every time we buy or sell a stock or any other investment, an element of timing is involved. We can either time haphazardly or we can have a strategy. You can either go blindfolded without a strategy or with your eyes wide open.

> After all the arguments, the pros and cons, if you still want to try to time, I can offer some simple strategies.

How to Enter and Exit the Market and Buy and Sell Stocks

Later in this chapter I advise you *when* to get in and out of the markets and stocks. But first you need to know *how* to get in and out. I've discussed most of the "hows" and exit strategies already. When you feel economic information or criteria tell you it's time to get out, you may not want to make any rash moves but instead use some of the exit and entrance strategies explained previously.

For example, assume you use the interest rate timing strategy, and you see signals that make you want to decrease your market position. You can just sell immediately, which would be timing in its purest form. However, I suggest that you monitor the warning signals and instead of immediately selling, employ one of the exit or entrance strategies explained in previous chapters.

Exiting to Take Profits

Covered calls. If you still feel comfortable with your profit and you don't detect any sell signals, consider covered calls. This could be an ideal exit strategy if you want to hold on for a while longer but at the same time get a little downside protection. However, if your stocks fall quickly, you may have a loss larger than your call premium, so don't forget to watch the downside closely.

Exiting to Protect Yourself from Large Losses

Protective puts. This is probably the best way to exit if you detect sell signals but still aren't sure that the excitement in the market might not carry it higher, as in the 1990s. You still get to participate in all of the upside minus the cost of your insurance, but now if the indicators are correct, you can exit gracefully on your own terms; you're in control.

Collars. Collars are also an excellent strategy because the calls pay for the insurance. However, collars can cut off some of the upside, so be comfortable with your sell signals and the exit price just in case the market goes higher.

Stop losses. Moving stop losses up closer and closer to the stock price can also be a great exit strategy, but they may not get you out fast enough in a dramatic fall.

Entering Strategies

Selling puts. After you have been sold out of your stocks and want to buy back at a lower price, selling puts can help you get back in.

Exit and Entrance Strategies for the Market and for Funds

In the next chapter I discuss the following strategies for sectors such as automatic rebalancing, dollar cost averaging, and value cost investing in depth.

All of these are good exit strategies, although you might notice many *howevers* or *buts* with each of them. That is because they are attractive but not perfect, and it is important that you understand the good and the bad of all strategies. You should never have only one or two strategies in place because time changes all things.

Traditional versus Automated Timing

Traditional Timing

Some timing strategies look at the economy and fundamental data to determine which way the market is going. Other timing strategies look at technical factors to predict the future. Both of these strategies are fine, but for the average investor the amount of data, the number of variables, and the extensive amount of research involved make them impractical.

Automatic Timing

Because of the difficulty with some of the traditional timing techniques, I look at a few relatively simple techniques that will help you remove emotion from your decision-making process and make the most of your automatic moves.

Why Not the Traditional Way

Most timers look at economic data or technical data and make decisions whether to get in and out of the market based on chart patterns, valuations, growth rate, volume, momentum, break-out points, trend lines, pivot points, and support and resistance levels. Although I touch a little on these, they constitute a world for the sophisticated, dedicated, technical trader, not for the average investor. Instead I use simple economic and valuation tools that help signal when to get out without emotion or decision making.

Increased Volatility

Over the long run, market volatility seems to be fairly consistent, although it has increased dramatically the last few years. Many different opinions have tried to explain this increase in volatility. It could be the automated trading systems or the fact that the laws have changed so that companies must disburse news to all institutions, individuals, and traders at the same time. It could be that as soon as CNBC mentions a stock, everyone rushes to trade, which increases the swings on both the upside and downside. It could be that everyone is more knowledgeable about the market and feels they can time the market. Phoenix Investors performed a study in June 2000, according to The Leuthold Group, showing that the moves of over 1 percent a day in the past occurred about 16 percent of the time. However, 1 percent moves occurred 44 percent of the time in 2000 and extreme moves of over 3 percent a day have increased from 0.2 percent to 4 percent of the time.

	2000	1999	Historically
Moves of 1% or more occurred	44%	37%	16.0%
Ultravolatility—moves of 2% or more	15	9	1.6
Extreme moves—3% or more	4	0	.2

But if you think the volatility on the S&P was remarkable, look at the volatility on the Nasdaq. In 2000 the Nasdaq market had moves of 3 percent or more on 76 of 252 trading days. That was over 30 percent of the time, so almost 1 of every 3 days you could face a 3 percent rally or a 3 percent fall.

	2000	1999	Historically
Moves of 1% or more	75%	58%	16.7%
Moves of 2% or more	49	25	2.0
Extreme moves—3% or more	30	8	0.4

You can use these volatility numbers to justify that trying to time markets with such extreme volatility will give even the weathered veteran whiplash. Even the autopilot strategies outlined in the following section don't work well in these extreme markets. You can use these numbers as evidence that despite the difficulty of timing, it is more imperative than ever to have set floors and ceilings and strategies to take profits off the table.

I think it is ludicrous to buy and hold and watch assets fall. Times change, companies change, laws change, the economy changes, and life is not static, so we need to consider those changes. On the other hand, I also think it is impossible to time the market. The best have tried and failed. For that reason, I use a middle-of-the road approach, whereby we look at the criteria but don't immediately buy or sell when we get the signals. Instead, we assume that we could be wrong at times and right at times, so we employ exit strategies and entrance strategies when we get trading signals. Some timing signals we use are determined by individual requirements instead of market-related criteria. For example, you may be willing to sell once you achieve a specified return.

Going on Autopilot: Warning Signals to Look For

Many factors need to be considered when determining whether to buy or sell a stock. Every buy and sell decision is a timing decision also. I break down timing and sector rotation decisions to five elements.

1. Economic inputs: Interest increase
2. Valuations: Dividend yields, PEs, and PEGs
3. Technical inputs: Support and resistance, relative strength, and seasonality
4. Fundamentals: A company's market, goal, and competitiveness along with confidence levels, media attention, and the like
5. Weightings: Acceptable targets, profit and losses, and acceptable weighting

Many more factors could be put in each category, but I concentrate on these to make the strategies workable.

Economic Inputs

Hundreds of items of economic data influence the economy and the stock market. Probably the most important are interest rates, economic health, and consumer confidence.

Interest rate increases. If you decide to take advantage of economic changes, then watch interest rates, which are probably the best tools for market timing. The market tends to perform the very best when interest rates are falling and the worst when interest rates are increasing.

When interest rates are increasing, decrease your investment in equities and bonds. When interest rates are decreasing, increase your investment in equities and bonds.

The Federal Reserve Board raises rates for a reason, usually to slow down businesses and the economy. Businesses know that and so react to create a self-fulfilling prophecy as they did in 2000. As soon as the Fed raised rates in February 2000, businesses were surveyed and 85 percent responded that they saw a recession or slowdown coming. What do you think happened? They started cutting back on inventories and stopped buying and hiring. Even if the rates hadn't slowed the economy, just the fear of rate increases causes businesses to slow, if not halt.

The Fed usually drops rates to avoid a recession. It wants to stimulate the economy, pull it back from the brink of disaster, and help prevent a hard landing.

How do you use this information? First, how do you know what the Fed will do? And if you do, then wouldn't everyone else? Therefore, I don't suggest that you sell immediately or buy, but for every anticipated quarter-point increase in interest rates, bring your stop losses up tighter and buy puts. If you have mutual funds, you may want to dollar cost average out of your position by 3 to 5 percent. If interest rates increase 5 percent, then you would be 80 percent in cash and only 20 percent in the market. If rates start to fall, move back in.

Valuation Inputs

Some of the easiest tools for individual investors to use when trying to determine whether to buy, sell, or hold are PEs, PEGs, and yields. They are easy to find and in most markets have been very reliable. Had you paid attention to these valuations in 1999 and 2000, you would have probably saved yourself a lot of downside. Some problems do occur with these valuations in the short run, however. The ability to predict earnings and growth has been hurt dramatically by the extreme nature of the economic fall the last two years. Nonetheless, valuations are still valuable tools to tell you when to get out, but we have to use them with caution when trying to decide when to get back in because of their potential inaccuracy.

Watching dividend yields. Low market yields mean the market is overpriced, and investors will seek other alternatives. Campbell and Shiller* found that if dividend yields are higher than historic yields, the return on stocks are likely to be high in the future because stocks are priced below average prices. Thus, the prices of stocks will rise so that dividend yields will fall in relation to stocks. Historically, the market has been "mean reverting," which means it tends to revert back to the average or mean. When prices in relation to yields are low, it would imply that prices are due to rise. On the other hand, a low dividend yield is a sign that prices are overvalued and stock prices are inclined to fall. Campbell looked at countries all over the world and found that in 9 out of 12 countries these trends held true. Dividend yields that are low in contrast to their average are a warning signal, as they were in 1999. Higher yields provide a good clue that it is time to move back into the market.

> **If dividends are low, decrease your investment in equities. If dividends are high, increase your investment in equities.**

How do you use this information? Dividend yield is another tool, or signal, to help you determine when to get in or out of your stock or the market. When the dividend yield is high, increase your position in the market or stock. When the dividend yield is low, start using exit strategies, such as stop losses. Dividend yields are better for longer-term trends than for short-term trends. They are useful for investors but not for day traders. When yields are higher than average, think about collars. Collars will sell you out if the market rallies, but also, over the long run, they will help you exit near the top and still avoid the big downside. The Dow Dog Strategies are an easy way to implement the yield strategy.

Watching PEs and PEGs. High value measures are a warning to sell. The most popular measures of a stock's value or market value are PEs and PEGs. PEs are used to measure whether stocks are overvalued or if their price is too high. They are a better measure for value stocks, and PEGs are a better measure for growth stocks.

Eugene I. Fama and Kenneth R. French, in the June 2001 *Journal of Finance,* explain why we have to be weary of high PEs. When price-earnings ratios are high, we can expect the market to fall. The large buildup in PEs may be justified by some productivity increases, but over the long run you cannot justify large increases. Fama and French point out that PEs have risen from 10 in 1926 to over 25 today. What makes stocks worth that much more? Probably not much. Expecting PEs to fall within reasonable levels means either the price would have to fall in our ratio or the earnings would have to increase dramatically. Although there may be some growth in earnings, it is unlikely there will be enough to bring the ratios in line with historic returns.

> **When PEs increase, decrease your equities.**

---

*John Y. Campbell and Robert J. Shiller. "Valuation Ratios and the Long-Run Stock Market Outlook." *The Journal of Portfolio Management.* Winter 1998.

Many other studies show that the market historically will regress to its mean or average. Brown (no relation), Goetzman, and Ross show that the U.S. market has been so high historically that the likelihood for underperformance over this decade increases. Because the market has always had a tendency to come back to normal levels to revert to its averages, it is likely that we will be in for further declines if PEs stay high.

With the PE of the S&P in 2000 hovering around 24 and the PEG at 1.71, the market has looked a little overvalued even after its terrible fall from 1999. If PEGs and PEs are viewed over their historic averages, then you may want to protect or hedge your stocks on the basis of the likelihood of their underperforming. Also, when the S&P PE is trading higher than the ten-year average of the S&P 500, you should think about reducing your exposure to the market.

How do you use this information? When PEs and PEGs are high compared with their historical averages, use stop losses, covered calls, and protective puts, and keep automatic rebalancing programs in place, shifting from high PE stocks to lower PE and beta stocks. I would not suggest selling out or shifting dramatically because the market may not recognize or react to these numbers in the short run. But do become more aware and keep your protective strategies in place.

- If your PEs or PEGs are 30% higher than average, use stop losses.
- If your PEs or PEGs are 50% higher than average, use puts or collars.
- If the PEGs are lower than .50 or the stocks look undervalued, then buy.
- If the PEGs are between .50 to 1 or fairly valued, then hold.
- If the PEGs are between 1 and 2 or look overvalued, start using stop losses.
- If the PEGs are over 2, then start moving stops up very tight, 2 to 3% away, and start buying puts or collars.

Technical Inputs

Stocks tend to move in patterns, hundreds of which technical analysts use. I decided against putting them in this book as they are difficult to use and require massive amounts of data. However, stocks and the markets have historically followed certain trends. Trading ranges with support and resistance levels can often be easily distinguished, so I review these again in the following chapter as well as certain seasonal trading patterns that I use in the timing and sector rotation chapters.

Holiday investing. Are you getting bored with these dull strategies? Some fun ones look at more interesting events such as when the NFC wins the Super Bowl, if it snows in Boston before Christmas, or if women's hemlines get shorter. There is supposedly a rationale behind all of these. If women's hemlines are shorter, it means that women have to buy new clothes, men are happier, and so the economy looks brighter.

Another popular strategy that may have a little more validity is the holiday strategy. When the markets are closed for three days on holidays, traders, according to the theory, will not want to go home with long positions on their books. They are afraid that some event risk or unforeseen news could surface when the markets are closed. It is probably true that traders, a tougher breed than most, don't want any surprises when they get back from a long weekend. I know when I'm out of the office or there's a holiday, I like having a little more cash, and tighter stop losses and puts. Traders usually sell before holidays, causing stock prices to fall. The holiday theory assumes that when prices are low is a good time for investors to buy at depressed prices.

You can either sell right after the postholiday bounce, wait for the next holiday and buy again, continue getting in and out on holidays, or wait until the end of the year and sell. Usually, you'll find that buying one day before as opposed to two days before a holiday is the best. StockCharts.com supplies information on this strategy, basing its research on the S&P 500 for 50 years from 1928 to 1975 and concluding, much like Ibbotson and other statisticians, that had you put $10,000 in the S&P index in January 1928 and sold it in December 1975, you would have had $51,441. However, here is where timing comes in. If instead you had invested one-ninth of your money just before each preholiday period and then sold at the end of the year, you would have had $1,440,716.

With that kind of return you might want to look at the holiday strategy. If you have money to invest during the year, think about investing it before the holidays, when traders are typically selling. If you want to take profits off the table, sell your positions at the end of the year and redo and invest one-ninth of your money before each holiday.

Holiday	Buy two days before and sell at end of year	Buy one day before and sell at year-end
Presidents' Day	−0.1%	12.2%
Good Friday	7.3	17.8
Memorial Day	−4.7	22.8
Independence Day	13.3	37.3
Labor Day	16.8	33.7
Election Day	17.9	4.6
Thanksgiving	4.3	1.1
Christmas	−7.1	15.2
New Year's Day	31.1	19.6

StockCharts.com goes further and shows that this strategy not only works for the broad market but also for stocks.

How to use this information. My recommendation is to use only a little of a timing strategy like this. It's clever but limited. Nor am I recommending this strategy all the time and for everyone. However, if you are planning on investing new money, it could be beneficial to hold off for a couple of days before a holiday and buy when the traders are selling before the long weekends.

Problems. The reason you are getting holiday bargains is that traders are afraid that breaking news, as noted earlier, could be announced when the markets are closed. Do traders know something that you should think about? If holiday investing were such a great strategy, why are the pros getting out when you are getting in? You may want to consider this timing only on stocks and indexes that you planned on buying anyhow and using the strategy as an entry point.

Seasonal hedging. One of the strategies that has worked well for me over the last 20 years is market seasonality. Historically, more than 80 percent of market returns occur between November and April. Knowing that and knowing that the summer is usually a tough time for technology stocks and that September and October are notoriously weak, I try to avoid those months. You may want to be fully invested during the November to April cycles and then take profits with stop losses starting in April. Because September is historically the worst month and the greatest falls occur in October, I tend to be a lot more cautious then and usually buy puts in May or August as protection for those months. There are reasons why these patterns occur, but none that can be relied on all the time. Almost half of mutual funds end their fiscal year in October and so need to take their tax losses by the end of October. If September or the summer is bad, funds may take a lot of losses and sell in October.

After the stocks are sold, investors buy back into the stocks that were sold, usually causing November to be an attractive month. January tends to be a good month, but because many investors know that, they try to get into the market before January, so the January effect often comes in November or December. Pension monies come into the market in January, tending to make January look even better.

Over the last 50 years, if you had invested $10,000 in the market in early May and sold out at the end of September each year, you would have netted just $3,000 in profit during the whole 50 years. However, had you invested the same $10,000 from November to May each of the 50 years, you would have made a profit of over $595,000.*

Although this strategy has worked very well for many years and I rely on it a lot, it did not work in 2000 and may not work in the new paradigm.

What do you do with this information? This is what you should do.

- Be defensive in weak months, using puts, calls, or collars from April through October.
- Start with stop loss orders in March at 10 percent away; move up to 5 percent away in April; by June start buying some October puts on one-fourth of your portfolio; by August buy puts on another fourth. It doesn't work all the time, but it helps a lot to be able to make money on the puts during the weak summer months. Remember that you can take profits on puts instead of selling the underlying stocks.
- Be more heavily invested from November to April and don't cap your inside or use calls. (But you may want to use stop losses or a small amount of put insurance.)

---

*Ned Davis, Ned Davis Research, Venice, Florida; *Business Week,* 2 July 2001.

Fundamental Inputs

We need to look at how the market and stocks are viewed by the public, watching for changes in market share and the competition. We also need to continually look at the product. A big part of what will influence buy and sell decisions is based on a company's ability to stay competitive. We need to watch for crises, such as the Ford Explorer accidents, tobacco litigation, and new competing products—a new drug discovery for one biotech company, for example, may hurt another biotech company.

Viewing the media. This is a contrarian strategy, whose logic is that when people get too excited they are relying on emotion rather than reason, and the market is doomed to fall as investors get more and more enthusiastic. The easiest way to see this enthusiasm is in the media. For years the most famous theory was probably the *Time* magazine covers theory: if *Time* had a bear on the cover, within one month the market would stop falling and the last of the sellers would have pulled out; within six months, the market would have reversed course and started upward.

Does it really work? Ironically, the answer is usually yes. It seems that the press always picks up on the misery of investors when the market is at its worst. That's when the stories sell. The media get everyone so nervous that when the last diehards are finally ready to throw up their hands and just give in, that is your buy signal—when the capitulation is finally here. After the last weak owner has been driven out of the market, the bottom fishers come in. The bulls start trampling over the bears, and the market turns. Thus, one of the best contrarian indicators has been the cover of business magazines or the *Time* magazine cover story. The time to come back into the market is when the covers are the scariest.

When I first wrote this chapter, I knew of no scientific data to support what has been recognized as one of the best contrarian market indicators until I found an article written on March 19, 2001, by Gibbons Burke, who reviewed a study done by Paul Montgomery, an analyst at Legg Mason. Montgomery went back to the late 1920s to find that this contrarian indicator was 85 percent accurate. If the cover of *Time* implies the market is terrible and things look bleak and if there is a bear somewhere on the cover, then shortly after that the market has rallied 85 percent of the time.

When one business magazine has a cover like that, it is likely that the others will soon follow. It is the terrible news and the fear it creates that finally cause the last investors to give in, no matter how brave they are; the market falls a little more until finally everybody is out except those last few diehards who will never move out no matter what happens. After almost everyone has been scared out, the market can start its move back up.

Problem. I think there is a lot of validity to this theory, but the problem is that someday that fear may be justified, and it should only be used in conjunction with PEs and other measurements of value.

Stock splits. Although stock splits are often not considered a timing strategy, they can be used as a way to time getting in and out of some stocks and certainly as a way to break a tie when you are trying to decide which stock to purchase. Many stocks start to have dramatic moves when they trade in the $80 to $100 range, because investors often anticipate splits at that level. If a stock has a history of splitting, this could be a range to consider.

With this strategy you watch for stock splits. Rice University and Tulane University conducted two separate studies to determine the impact of stock splits. Both studies noted that stocks rose 3.5 percent the day a split was announced, outperformed the market by 8 percent in the following year, and outperformed it 12 percent over the next three years. A split is often interpreted as management's confidence in a company's fundamentals, and it releases pent-up demand for a desirable, but high-priced, stock that investors have been coveting for some time but couldn't afford to buy. If all things are equal between two stocks, you can use stock splits as your tiebreaker.

When the fundamentals or markets change. When you hear stories that the cellular phone industry may be suffering from oversupply, you may want to start placing stop orders or buy put insurance. You may not want to sell, but you should always look at the fundamentals of companies and the market. If you are nervous, consider exit strategies.

Weightings and Profit

I believe one of the most important tools in timing is your personal input. How much profit will make you happy, how much loss can you handle, and how over- or underweighted is your portfolio in the sectors or stocks you want or need? Using these inputs can help you determine better than anyone else when you should time your exits and entrances.

Watching your profits. Traditionally, we don't think of taking profits as a timing strategy, but that is in fact the whole purpose of timing—to take profits. So set guidelines and determine returns that would make you happy. Because in the past 20 years the S&P has only earned 17 percent a year, maybe you should be grateful if you earn more than 20 percent in any one year. You are not looking at the economy or valuations to give you hints on when to get out; you are looking instead at your own targets.

To exit when you are willing to take profits, stop loss orders could be a good solution. As the market or your stock goes up in value, move your stop loss orders up. As soon as you have a 20 percent profit, move your stops to 5 percent away. When the market or your stock starts to turn south, your order will become a market order and you'll be sold out it's hoped before the losses are too high.

How to use this strategy. This is a strategy in which you have to develop your own criteria. However, some that I have used in the past and have worked well were:

- 20% profit—start using stop losses 5% away.

- 40% profit—start using puts on half 5% away.
- 50% profit—start using collars on half your position.
- 100% profit—sell three-fourths of your position if it's not already called away.

Getting back in. Watch your stock or the market. When either starts trading below or at its historic PE or PEG, move back in. Consider selling puts to repurchase your position.

Summary

Even if timing is not perfect, for many of us it is something we should consider. You can look at economic and value measurements to determine when to exit and enter. When you use these tools, remove the emotion. When you get the signals, listen and act; *do not second-guess.* When using timing strategies, you don't have to sell and buy immediately, but instead start using exit strategies, such as stop losses, calls, collars, puts, and the like.

CHAPTER 14

Sector Rotation

DEFINITION

Sector rotation is simply timing when to exit one sector and enter another.

KEY

Safety: ★★★   Simplicity: ★

Returns: $$$$$ Tax efficiency: –$

SUMMARY

Safety: If done properly, sector rotation can add a high degree of safety to a portfolio. The trick is to do it properly.

Returns: Successful sector rotation strategies in their most sophisticated forms are likely to lead to the highest returns of all the strategies discussed. The strategies I use are simple and have the ability to increase returns, albeit by smaller amounts.

Simplicity: This strategy is simple to understand but does require constant monitoring. The simple strategies I've opted to use put you on autopilot, which nonetheless are more time consuming than some other strategies.

Tax efficiency: There is no tax efficiency. The taxes are terrible! But I'll show you ways to minimize and work around them.

Who and What

Who Should Consider Sector Rotation?

This strategy should be considered by anyone who believes the economy changes over time and that businesses go through cycles. It is for someone seeking higher returns than possible using a buy-and-hold strategy and is willing to do a little more work.

What Is Sector Rotation?

The term *sector rotation* is self-explanatory; it is rotating among sectors, which means frequent transactions and thus taxes. Therefore, this is a strategy best suited for tax-sheltered and tax-deferred accounts.

> Sector rotation → moving sectors → many transactions → tax consequences → need to utilize in tax-deferred accounts.

The terms *timing* and *sector rotation* are used to describe a broad variety of strategies. This book limits discussion to just a small portion of many strategies, usually those that the average investor can use without sophisticated computer forecasting programs. Sector rotation is essentially the same as timing, but instead of determining when to exit or enter stocks, we are determining when to *exit one sector and enter another.* Moreover, sector rotation uses many of the same tools as timing. In discussing timing, I focused on the merits of individual stocks and whether to be in or out of a stock or the market. With sector rotation the focus is on which sector or segment of the market is best.

Rotation occurs everywhere: businesses shift employees to gain experience in different fields; hospitals rotate shifts; farmers rotate crops. Rotation revitalizes weary troops, allowing them time to regroup. The same happens in the market. The sectors run, get tired, meet resistance, and then fall back to regroup.

Companies and industries too have to refuel and rebuild their bases. They can lead the way for a while, but other companies see how well they are doing and increase the competition. Therefore, it is natural for companies and sectors to rally strongly, become overvalued, run out of steam, and fall behind new leaders. We then want to move into undervalued sectors or companies that are on the move again but have had time to reinvent or reinvigorate themselves.

As with timing, many sophisticated strategies for sector rotation are available. Typically, the more sophisticated strategies involve technical analysis and depend on your ability to find, interpret and make decisions on the basis of economic data, technical moves, charts, and especially *relative strength.* These strategies are time-consuming, difficult, and fraught with mistakes and judgment calls. Therefore, in this chapter, I explore simpler strategies that require less interpretation of technical data but provide rigid rules governing when to move. For those using sector rotation to keep their portfolios in line with their original goals and asset allocation, I'll review rebalancing and dollar cost averaging strategies. For those interested in exploiting the potential of trading one sector for another, I'll explore:

- The best of the best strategy
- Dollar cost averaging
- Value cost averaging
- The best of the worst strategy
- Exiting on economic, valuation, weighting, and profit measurements
- Seasonal trading using stop losses, protective puts, and covered calls

These strategies should increase a portfolio's safety and increase returns by avoiding much of the downside. These simpler strategies take the emotion and impulse decision making out of sector rotation.

Being in the Right Place

The premise of sector rotation is to be in the right place at the right time. When it works well, the results could be the best of any of the strategies discussed. In extreme cases, sector rotation can result in unbelievable returns. If you had perfect foresight and could be in the right sectors every month, you could be compounding at 34 percent-plus and have billions of dollars more than the person who bought and held. None of us, however, have perfect foresight. Even worse, if we have poor foresight and capture most of the down months, we could be at the other extreme and go bankrupt quickly. If sector rotation and timing were easy, we would all time sectors and stocks all the time.

The problem with sector rotation is not the concept. It is the difficulty in doing it correctly, which is why I opted to use the more basic automatic strategies to help you take profits and avoid losses.

Timing versus Sector Rotation

Although timing and sector rotation are based on the same premise and often use the same tools, there are important differences in how we use them. For example:

- I confine timing in this book to stocks, trusts, funds, and market indexes. I confine sector rotation to mutual funds and trusts.
- Timing usually implies selling your stocks at the top and buying at the bottom or being invested when the market is rallying and moving to cash when the mar-

ket is falling. With sector rotation you are selling one sector at the top while simultaneously buying another at the bottom.*

> **Sector rotation strategy is similar to timing strategy and uses many of the same tools.**

- I recommend using sector mutual funds with sector rotation to eliminate specific risks of investing in stocks. Because this strategy eliminates the need to look at all the valuations, fundamentals, and technical factors of stocks, sector rotation should theoretically be less tedious and safer. Much of the transaction cost can be eliminated by using funds and exchange-traded funds (ETFs) and trusts in lieu of stocks.
- Sector rotation strategies traditionally take a top-down approach, looking at the total picture. Unlike bottom-up approaches, they don't focus on individual stocks.

Striving for the Best Returns

Percentages Often Do Not Give the Whole Picture

When I tell seminar participants that small caps averaged 12.4 percent versus 11 percent for large company stocks, they are impressed but not often aware how much that difference makes in dollar terms.[†] At one seminar, a woman didn't seem impressed and asked me if I thought it was really worth all that work for 1.5 percent. If you compound at 12.4 percent versus 11 percent over 75 years, the difference is tremendous; $1,000 grew to $6,402,000 versus $2,587,000. Compounding even with smaller amounts can have a dramatic impact on total ending values. Even for five or ten years, small incremental improvements in returns can have a tremendous impact on the actual dollar amount.

If there is that much difference between an 11 percent and 12.4 percent return, think of the difference if you could add 3 or 4 percent to your overall return. Value Line Mutual Fund Advisor conducted a study in June 1994 showing that sector rotation returned 34 percent; timing returned 27 percent; and buy and hold in the S&P returned 11 percent. Those numbers sound impressive but often investors don't fully realize the benefits until we discuss them in dollar terms.

Assume you invested $10,000 for 21 years from 1973 to 1994.

Buy and hold @11% =	$96,000
Market timing @ 27%	$1,500,000
Sector rotation @ 34%	$4,700,000

---

*This may be a moot point because if you think of cash or money markets as asset classes, then timing is selling one sector and buying another.

[†]Data from Ibbotson Associates, *Yearbook 2000: Stocks, Bonds, Bills, and Inflation.*

If you could compound at 34 percent, you would have nearly $4.6 million dollars more than if you compounded at 11 percent. Compounding at 11 percent results in less than $100,000 over those 20 years. These numbers are extreme, but perhaps using these extreme cases gets more attention and starts you thinking about the benefits. I wouldn't suggest that you could ever achieve those extreme returns with these strategies.

But what if you could capture even a small amount of the benefits of changing sectors? The strategies I use are not going to result in large home runs, but they can offer you insight into improving your returns by 0.50 percent to 4 percent or more in ideal situations. Even a 0.25 percent improvement is worth taking the time to achieve, especially if it increases safety at the same time. If you improved your return by 1 percent a year, you would have $112,394 versus $96,000. If you could improve the returns by 2 percent, you would have $138,916 versus $96,000, or over 40 percent more. Even improving by 0.50 percent adds up to almost $6,000. Because of compounding, even small improvements in returns have big impacts on the bottom line. When you consider the large differences in total dollar amounts despite its requiring a lot of work and time and a good chance you may never get it right, the rewards versus the risks make sector rotation worth a try.

Defining Sectors

Sectors are groups of companies that do business in similar ways, tending to move together with a high correlation. Sectors are often broken down into smaller groups called industries. Value Line uses 98, Standard & Poor's 11 sectors and 115 industries, and Ibbotson 10 sectors. I'm going to use Ibbotson's 10 sectors:

- Health care
- Finance
- Technology
- Consumer staples
- Consumer cyclicals
- Capital goods
- Basic materials
- Utilities
- Energy
- Transportation

When It Is Good, It Is Very Good, but When It Is Bad, It Is Very Bad

The premise of sector rotation is that you hold only a few sectors at a time and are not as well diversified as an asset allocation program would suggest. To get adequate diversification, it is generally assumed you need at least eight sectors. This should be adequate diversification if you have low or negative correlation. However, although eight sectors are appropriate for an asset allocation program, eight is often a little difficult to handle in sector rotation strategies, so I usually limit it to four or five at the maximum. Balanced or asset allocation accounts need more diversification because you are buying and holding for long periods of time. The diversification balances off poorly performing assets with better-performing assets. However, in sector rotation accounts and trading accounts, we are not seeking to offset bad-performing sectors as we are attempting to eliminate bad sectors.

Sector rotation works because sectors rotate. It's that simple. For example:

- Health care was the best sector in 1991 and 1995 but the worst in 1992 and 1993.
- Finance was the best in 1992 and 1997 but the third worst in 1993.
- Technology was the best in 1993, 1994, 1996, 1998 and 1999, but the worst in 2000.
- Utilities were the best in 2000 but halfway through 2001 were one of the worst and were down more than 20 percent.

The Phoenix Investment Partners' chart in Figure 14.1 is one of my favorites for making it clear how dramatic rotations can be.

FIGURE 14.1 Sector Diversification

BEST	'91	'92	'93	'94	'95	'96	'97	'98	'99	'00
	Health Care	Finance	Tech	Tech	Health Care	Tech	Finance	Tech	Tech	Utilities
	Transport	Consumer Cyclicals	Capital Goods	Health Care	Finance	Finance	Health Care	Health Care	Basic Materials	Health Care
	Finance	Utilities	Transport	Consumer Staples	Capital Goods	Capital Goods	Consumer Cyclicals	Consumer Cyclicals	Consumer Cyclicals	Finance
	Consumer Staples	Basic Materials	Energy	Basic Materials	Transport	Energy	Utilities	Utilities	Capital Goods	Transport
	Consumer Cyclicals	Capital Goods	Utilities	Energy	Utilities	Consumer Staples	Consumer Staples	Consumer Staples	Energy	Energy
	Basic Materials	Transport	Consumer Cyclicals	Capital Goods	Tech	Health Care	Transport	Finance	Utilities	Consumer Staples
	Capital Goods	Consumer Staples	Basic Materials	Finance	Consumer Staples	Basic Materials	Tech	Capital Goods	Finance	Capital Goods
	Utilities	Tech	Finance	Utilities	Energy	Transport	Capital Goods	Energy	Transport	Basic Materials
	Tech	Energy	Consumer Staples	Consumer Cyclicals	Basic Materials	Consumer Cyclicals	Energy	Transport	Health Care	Consumer Cyclicals
WORST	Energy	Health Care	Health Care	Transport	Consumer Cyclicals	Utilities	Basic Materials	Basic Materials	Consumer Staples	Tech

Source: Zweig Advisors

Stock rotation. Not only do sectors rotate but stocks, styles, and indexes also rotate. Remember the Dogs of the Dow strategy? That was basically a stock rotation strategy. The main reason that it worked so well for so long was that stocks rally till they get overvalued and then fall back, often to the bottom. With the Dogs of the Dow strategy, it was those bottom stocks, the losers, that we were seeking because they had a high probability of rallying.

When good companies fall, investors perceive them as having value and buy the stocks at the bottom, causing them to rally. This rotation goes on and on. The top stocks are sold and the bottom ones purchased. It doesn't happen to every stock, and it doesn't happen all the time, but it happens enough that it is a trend worth exploiting. Again, stocks gravitate or revert to the mean, or average, and this concept is the foundation of the Dogs strategy: timing and sector rotation.

Style rotation. *Style* is a relative and vague term usually referring to growth, value, balance, hedging, and international investment. As noted in previous chapters, over the long run growth investments tend to result in higher total wealth than do value investments. But value has outperformed growth 78 percent of the time. If we compare both growth and value to the S&P, we find that during the 1980s, value tended to outperform, whereas in the 1990s growth outperformed.

Value outperformed in 1978 through part of 1979, again in 1981, in most of 1982, 1983, 1984, 1986, and most of 1987 and 1988.* The '80s were a good time for value, but then the '90s saw a dramatic reversal with value outperforming in 1992 and 1993 and growth outperforming the rest of the time. Value did shine again in 2000, and thus the rotation goes on. For instance, Russell 1000 growth was down −22.4 percent in 2000, and the Russell 2000 growth was also down over −22.4 percent, while the Russell 1000 value was up 7 percent, and the Russell 2000 value was up 22.8 percent! Whose turn is next?

Growth fell back to its average, and value rose to its average.

Money usually follows too late. Ironically, investors have a knack for after-the-fact investing. They tend to wait until a sector has already run before they invest in it. When growth was outperforming in the 1990s, many investors were putting money in value funds on the basis of past performance. When growth peaked in 1999, the bulk of money started to flow into growth funds, again because investors saw that growth had been doing well for a while, and they based their purchases on the past few years' performance. This is just when they should have been moving to value. By the time the market fell in 2000, value already had its rally, but the money still flowed into value in 2001. Investors have a tendency to go into the sectors that have done the best in the past, but often that is the least attractive strategy.†

Size rotation. As you can see in Figure 14.2, not only did sectors change dramatically during the last 20 years, but styles, such as growth and value, also rotated. The size of the

---

*Brandywine Asset Management updates on Ibbotson data.
†Morningstar, January 1995 through Nov 2000—Phoenix Investment Partners.

FIGURE 14.2 Diversification Is Key

BEST → WORST	1986	1987	1988	1989	1990	1991	1992	1993	1994	1995	1996	1997	1998	1999	2000
BEST	Int'l 69.4	Int'l 24.5	Int'l 28.3	Large-Cap Growth 35.9	Large-Cap Growth -0.3	Small-Cap 46.1	Small-Cap 18.4	Int'l 32.6	Int'l 7.8	Large-Cap Value 38.4	Large-Cap Growth 23.3	Large-Cap Value 35.2	Large-Cap Growth 38.7	Large-Cap Growth 33.2	Mid-Cap 8.2
	Large-Cap Value 20.0	Large-Cap Growth 5.3	Small-Cap 24.9	S&P 500 31.7	S&P 500 -3.1	Mid-Cap 41.5	Mid-Cap 16.3	Small-Cap 18.9	Large-Cap Growth 2.7	S&P 500 37.5	S&P 500 23.0	S&P 500 33.4	S&P 500 28.6	Int'l ??	Large-Cap Value 7.0
	S&P 500 18.7	S&P 500 5.3	Large-Cap Value 23.2	Mid-Cap 26.3	Large-Cap Value -8.1	Large-Cap Growth 41.2	Large-Cap Value 13.8	Large-Cap Value 18.1	S&P 500 1.3	Large-Cap Growth 37.2	Large-Cap Value 21.6	Large-Cap Growth 30.5	Int'l ??	Small-Cap 21.3	Small-Cap -3.0
	Mid-Cap 18.2	Large-Cap Value 0.5	Mid-Cap 19.8	Large-Cap Value 25.2	Mid-Cap -11.5	S&P 500 30.5	S&P 500 7.6	Mid-Cap 14.3	Small-Cap -1.8	Mid-Cap 34.5	Mid-Cap 19.0	Mid-Cap 29.0	Large-Cap Value 15.6	S&P 500 21.1	S&P 500 -9.2
	Large-Cap Growth 15.4	Mid-Cap 0.2	S&P 500 16.6	Small-Cap 16.2	Small-Cap -19.5	Large-Cap Value 24.6	Large-Cap Growth 5.0	S&P 500 10.1	Large-Cap Value -2.0	Small-Cap 28.4	Small-Cap 16.5	Small-Cap 22.4	Mid-Cap 10.1	Mid-Cap 18.2	Int'l ??
WORST	Small-Cap 5.7	Small-Cap -8.8	Large-Cap Growth 11.3	Int'l 10.5	Int'l -23.5	Int'l 12.1	Int'l -10.2	Large-Cap Growth 2.9	Mid-Cap -2.1	Int'l 11.2	Int'l ??	Int'l ??	Small-Cap -2.6	Large-Cap Value 7.4	Large-Cap Growth -22.4

Source: Phoenix Equity Planning Corporation

companies that led the way also changed dramatically. Sometimes mid-cap value shines, other times large cap value. In 1990, for example, the best style was large cap growth even though it was down three-tenths of a percent. Everything was down that year, with international faring the worst at more than −23.5 percent on the downside. But in 1991 everything recovered, and, as usual, growth led the way with small cap growth taking first place at more than 46.1 percent on the upside.

Index rotation. Another way to look at rotation is by looking at moves among the indexes, such as the S&P 500, S&P 100, Nasdaq, Dow, midcap, Russell 2000 value, Morgan Stanley Capital International Europe, Australia, and Far East Index (MSCI-EAFE), and more, as shown in Figure 14.3. We can categorize stocks in as many ways as there are stocks.

Why Rotate Sectors?

Whether we look at the markets, sectors, stocks, indexes, or styles, historically all of them revert to their averages at some point. It may take a month, a year, even ten years, but eventually they fall back or move up to their historic returns.

So if I told you that the average return on the S&P from 1926 to 2000 was 11.1 percent and from 1995 to 2000 it was 21.3 percent, in which direction would you guess the market is likely to lean? Some believe we are in a new pattern and stocks will now trade at much higher averages. But even many proponents of the new paradigm who once believed that the increased productivity could sustain higher PEs and PEGs no longer believe they can be sustained at these high levels. Many noted academics as well as many analysts believe we will see only 9 percent growth in the early 2000s.*

What do you believe? If you think we are in for volatility, then many of the previous strategies should work for you. If you believe there will be a lot of rotation in and out of sectors, then sector rotation should also be considered. Funds and sectors have seen extreme volatility, and most of the returns we witnessed in 1999 in Internet stocks were wiped out in 2000 and 2001. Wouldn't it have been nice to have taken some profits at the top? So many times I have found investors who think they can handle 20 percent declines . . . until it happens! They love the stock market until they lose money. They have had such positive returns for so long that they don't believe the market can rotate. Unless investors were in the market during the fall of 1974, they were shocked in 2000 and 2001, having never really experienced markets with that much downside. Most investors think the market falls quickly and recovers. When they think of bad markets, they remember 1987 with its big fall in October and its ending up 5.2 percent at the end of the year.† They come to expect V-shaped markets that tend to fall quickly and come back quickly.

---

*Dr. Jeff Jaffe of the Wharton School.
†Dow Jones; Ibbotson Associates.

FIGURE 14.3 The Callan Periodic Table of Investment Returns

Annual Returns for Key Indices (1981–2000)

Ranked in order of performance (Best to Worst)

1981	1982	1983	1984	1985	1986	1987	1988	1989	1990	1991	1992	1993	1994	1995	1996	1997	1998	1999	2000
Russell 2000 Value 14.85%	LB Agg 32.65%	Russell 2000 Value 38.63%	LB Agg 15.15%	MSCI EAFE 56.14%	MSCI EAFE 69.46%	MSCI EAFE 24.64%	Russell 2000 Value 29.47%	S&P/BARRA 500 Growth 36.40%	LB Agg 8.96%	Russell 2000 Growth 51.18%	Russell 2000 Value 29.15%	MSCI EAFE 32.57%	MSCI EAFE 7.78%	S&P/BARRA 500 Growth 38.13%	S&P/BARRA 500 Growth 23.97%	S&P/BARRA 500 Growth 36.52%	S&P/BARRA 500 Growth 42.16%	Russell 2000 Growth 43.09%	Russell 2000 Value 22.83%
LB Agg 6.26%	Russell 2000 Value 28.52%	Russell 2000 29.13%	S&P/BARRA 500 Value 10.52%	S&P/BARRA 500 Growth 33.31%	S&P/BARRA 500 Value 21.67%	S&P/BARRA 500 Growth 6.50%	MSCI EAFE 28.26%	S&P 500 Index 31.69%	S&P/BARRA 500 Growth 0.20%	Russell 2000 46.05%	Russell 2000 18.42%	Russell 2000 Value 23.86%	S&P/BARRA 500 Growth 3.14%	S&P 500 Index 37.58%	S&P 500 Index 22.96%	S&P 500 Index 33.36%	S&P 500 Index 28.58%	S&P/BARRA 500 Growth 28.25%	LB Agg 11.63%
Russell 2000 2.03%	Russell 2000 24.95%	S&P/BARRA 500 Value 28.89%	MSCI EAFE 7.41%	S&P 500 Index 31.73%	S&P 500 Index 18.67%	S&P 500 Index 5.25%	Russell 2000 24.89%	S&P/BARRA 500 Value 26.13%	S&P 500 Index -3.11%	Russell 2000 Value 41.70%	S&P/BARRA 500 Value 10.52%	Russell 2000 18.89%	S&P 500 Index 1.32%	S&P/BARRA 500 Value 36.99%	S&P/BARRA 500 Value 22.00%	Russell 2000 Value 31.78%	MSCI EAFE 20.00%	MSCI EAFE 26.96%	S&P/BARRA 500 Value 6.08%
S&P/BARRA 500 Value 0.02%	S&P/BARRA 500 Value 22.03%	MSCI EAFE 23.69%	S&P 500 Index 6.27%	Russell 2000 Value 31.04%	LB Agg 15.30%	S&P/BARRA 500 Value 3.68%	S&P/BARRA 500 Value 21.67%	Russell 2000 Growth 20.16%	S&P/BARRA 500 Value -6.85%	S&P/BARRA 500 Growth 38.37%	Russell 2000 Growth 7.77%	S&P/BARRA 500 Value 18.61%	S&P/BARRA 500 Value -0.64%	Russell 2000 Growth 31.04%	Russell 2000 Value 21.37%	S&P/BARRA 500 Value 29.98%	S&P/BARRA 500 Value 14.69%	Russell 2000 21.26%	Russell 2000 -3.02%
MSCI EAFE -2.27%	S&P 500 Index 21.55%	S&P 500 Index 22.56%	S&P/BARRA 500 Growth 2.33%	Russell 2000 31.01%	S&P/BARRA 500 Growth 14.50%	LB Agg 2.75%	Russell 2000 Growth 20.38%	Russell 2000 16.25%	Russell 2000 Growth -17.42%	S&P 500 Index 30.47%	S&P 500 Index 7.62%	Russell 2000 Growth 13.37%	Russell 2000 -1.55%	Russell 2000 28.44%	Russell 2000 16.53%	Russell 2000 22.36%	LB Agg 8.70%	S&P 500 Index 21.04%	S&P 500 Index -9.10%
S&P 500 Index -4.92%	S&P/BARRA 500 Growth 21.04%	Russell 2000 Growth 20.14%	Russell 2000 Value 2.27%	Russell 2000 Growth 30.97%	Russell 2000 Value 7.41%	Russell 2000 Growth -7.12%	S&P 500 Index 16.61%	LB Agg 14.53%	Russell 2000 -19.50%	S&P/BARRA 500 Value 22.56%	LB Agg 7.40%	S&P 500 Index 10.08%	Russell 2000 Growth -1.81%	Russell 2000 Value 25.75%	Russell 2000 Growth 11.32%	Russell 2000 Growth 12.93%	Russell 2000 Growth 1.23%	S&P/BARRA 500 Value 12.72%	MSCI EAFE -14.17%
Russell 2000 Growth -9.23%	Russell 2000 Growth 29.99%	S&P/BARRA 500 Growth 16.24%	Russell 2000 -7.13%	S&P/BARRA 500 Value 29.68%	Russell 2000 5.69%	Russell 2000 -8.76%	S&P/BARRA 500 Growth 11.95%	Russell 2000 Value 12.43%	Russell 2000 Value -21.77%	LB Agg 16.00%	S&P/BARRA 500 Growth 5.06%	LB Agg 9.75%	Russell 2000 Value -2.44%	LB Agg 18.46%	MSCI EAFE 6.05%	LB Agg 9.64%	Russell 2000 -2.55%	LB Agg -0.82%	S&P/BARRA 500 Growth -22.07%
S&P/BARRA 500 Growth -9.81%	MSCI EAFE -1.86%	LB Agg 8.19%	Russell 2000 Growth -15.84%	LB Agg 22.13%	Russell 2000 Growth 3.59%	Russell 2000 Value -10.48%	LB Agg 7.89%	MSCI EAFE 10.53%	MSCI EAFE -23.45%	MSCI EAFE 12.14%	MSCI EAFE -12.18%	S&P/BARRA 500 Growth 1.68%	LB Agg -2.92%	MSCI EAFE 11.21%	LB Agg 3.64%	MSCI EAFE 1.78%	Russell 2000 Value -6.46%	Russell 2000 Value -1.48%	Russell 2000 Growth -22.43%

Source: Callan Associates Inc.

Times have changed! In the 1990s, most investors were petrified to sell and take profits for fear that the market would rally and they'd miss it. Now, most investors are petrified to buy, afraid the market may fall even more. If you know that you should not get out of the market but are still afraid the market may fall more and pull you down with it, you then might want to consider sector rotation.

You can argue both ways: diversify or rotate. You can use the violent 2000 market rotation and the other dramatic changes in sectors to argue that you should be diversified and well balanced. You can use them to argue that you should have rotated out of growth and moved into value when you saw that the PEGs and PEs were so far above their averages. Both arguments are valid. If done correctly, it is obvious that sector rotation would have resulted in higher returns.

One of the most important things to remember about markets is that markets tend to revert to their averages (mean), just as sectors and stock do.

The Higher They Climb, The Greater They Fall

The ideal situation would be to avoid those big drops. Sector rotation is an attempt to control those swings and exploit them, trying to be in the best sectors when they are hot and out of them before they become the worst sectors. A daunting feat not easily accomplished. I'm not proposing that I have easy solutions, but I am proposing that if you can exit bad sectors before they become miserable sectors, you can reduce the pain. If you can get into good sectors before they get to the top, you can achieve higher returns.

The tools you need to get started. We have looked at all the tools you need to start automated sector rotations, which are basically the same as those for timing: valuation; risk measurements; technical, economic, and fundamental analysis; and weightings.

Exiting gracefully. As with timing, we also use many of the same exit strategies: stop losses, calls, collars, protective puts, dollar cost averaging, rebalancing, and value cost averaging.

In this chapter we look at strategies that help us time the exit from sectors. All the caveats I gave for timing stocks and the market apply to sectors as well.

Getting Started

Sector rotation strategies are going to be confined here to relatively simple strategies. When using mutual funds, I use such exit strategies as value cost averaging, rebalancing, exiting on valuations and weightings, best of the best, best of the worst, and seasonal trading. For exchange-traded funds, indexes, trusts, and stocks, I also use exit strategies—puts, collars, calls, limit orders, and stop losses—and warning signals such as support and resistance levels, relative strength, valuations, and weightings. Exchange traded funds have more flexibility than open-ended mutual funds.

The best returns can probably be achieved the hard way, that is, through technical analysis, but this requires a lot of research and perhaps a crystal ball. I'm going to skip the hard way and go straight to the easy way! Instead of technical analysis, you can use some of the valuation, economic, fundamental, and weighting tools described earlier.

Tools for Determining When to Move

Economic tools to aid in deciding when to rotate include the following:

- Interest rate hikes: If interest rates increase, reduce stocks and rotate to cash and bonds.
- Seasons: Invest in growth from November to April and in value during the spring and summer. Overweight in small-cap value from November to January.

Valuation tools to help in deciding when to rotate:

- PEs: If they get too high relative to their averages, move out of those sectors into sectors with low valuations compared with their averages.
- PEGs in the case of growth sectors: If the PEGs you're monitoring are relatively high compared with the average PEGs for the market or other sectors, switch to value sectors or lower PEG sectors.
- The spread between PEs for growth and PEs for value: As the spreads widen, switch to the lower PEs and value.

Fundamental criteria to help in deciding when to rotate:

- Inventory: If a sector such as telecommunications is finding that it has an over-supply of inventory, then move into a sector that is in favor.

Weighting and profits as aids in the decision to rotate:

- My favorite reasons to move out of a sector are having a large profit and much-higher-than-average returns for that sector.
- In addition, if you are over-weighted in a sector, rotate out of the overweighted sector to bring your portfolio back into balance.

Tools for Determining How to Rotate

Drifting

Start with four or five funds. If you like growth, you may be more weighted to growth—let's say 20 percent large cap growth, 20 percent midcap growth, 20 percent technology index fund, 10 percent health care fund, 20 percent basic value fund, and 10 percent cash.

If one fund starts doing better than the others, you'll find that the prescribed percentage you started with in each sector changes. You may have started with 20 percent in technology, but it may do so well that it becomes 40 percent. Sector drift happens naturally and automatically, and the question is how to handle it. Here are several alternatives.

- Continue drifting. You can let your account drift and overweight in the more successful sectors. This worked well in 1998 and 1999 but can become dangerous, as it did in 2000.
- Best of the best. You can do what most investors do: sell the losers and add to the winners. As great as that may sound, ironically it is usually one of the least attractive options and is exactly why so many investors lost money in 2000 and 2001. They added money to the growth sectors that did so well in 1999 but were decimated in 2000.
- Rebalancing, or the best of the worst. You can rebalance your account by selling some of the best-performing funds and moving some of the money into funds that have not done as well.

For most investors, probably the most logical way to start using a sector rotation strategy is by drifting. With this strategy you build a core of funds or trusts as you would for a balanced or asset allocation account. For example, you may want 30 percent large cap growth, 10 percent midcap growth, 20 percent large cap value, 10 percent midcap value, 10 percent technology, 10 percent cash, and 10 percent international.

Even if this were a simple asset allocation plan, you could not stop here because your original weightings will change through drifting and you'd need to rebalance your portfolio to bring it back to the original allocation. However, you may want to allow for some drift toward better-performing sectors, so you can overweight in those sectors. Therefore, you don't rebalance but instead set acceptable maximum and minimum ranges around those weightings. Let's assume you start with 20 percent growth and feel you would still be comfortable with a little less or more at any given time; then you would set your ranges with 20 percent plus or minus 5 percent.

As you see sectors rotate, a second approach to drifting is to move, or tilt, part of your funds to overweight in the attractive sectors, keeping your core positions in place. You'll know what sectors are showing strength merely by watching your own account. You can add a little to the best-performing sectors as you see the shifts, but never increase your funds beyond the ranges you set. To add to the better-performing funds, you'll need to take money from the poorer-performing funds. However, again never let the ranges on the poorer funds fall below the ranges you set.

The key here is to only allow the drifting to occur as long as you are within your ranges. For example, if you set growth at 20 percent plus or minus 5 percent, you would start with 20 percent but let growth drift to as much as 25 percent before you started to take profits off the table. If the overweighted sectors still have good fundamentals and valuations, as measured by the PEs, PEGs, and dividend yields, you can stay with the new drifted ranges but with rigid and firm exit strategies and within the limited range. Also, don't let the poorer-performing fund fall below your established ranges because it is often the worst-performing sector that rallies strongly.

If you move into the wrong sector, you will be hurt a little but not as much as the person who rotated completely out of one sector and into another.

It is important to have ranges and not let yourself get overweighted. Again, this was the major problem in the 1999 and 2000 period. Investors became overweighted in techs and kept adding to them even as they expanded beyond their appropriate ranges. You want some drifting, but you want it only within certain ranges and only when the over-weighted sector still looks fundamentally sound and the valuations are reasonable. The mistake in 1999 was that there was no fundamental or valuation reason to add more to the techs or growth sectors.

These are a few helpful drifting rules.

- Build a balanced portfolio.
- Set targeted percentages for each sector or style.
- Set ranges that each sector can drift within, usually plus or minus 5 percent.
- Allow drifting within ranges as long as sector valuations and relative strength are positive.
- When you exit a profitable sector, add to the lowest sector, if the valuations are still attractive, with the sales proceeds of the profitable sector. Remember: add only if valuations such as PEs, PEGs, and other valuation tools are attractive.
- Use exit strategies, such as covered calls, protective puts, stop losses, and so on, whenever possible.

Best of the Best

One of the most popular quotes on Wall Street is "The trend is your friend." It is the basis for one of the popular sector rotation strategies, the "best of the best," which is an extreme case of drifting. With drifting, investors moved small amounts within well-defined ranges. With the best of the best, investors move large blocks of funds to the best-performing sectors and sell off all of the poorer-performing sectors. When rotating among funds, this strategy seeks to find and invest in the best fund in the sectors that show the best relative strength. I refine this by investing in the five sectors that are moving up in relative strength and also limit moves within ranges, keeping the core positions in place.

For most investors, using a family of sector funds, such as Fidelity's sector funds, is the easiest way to work with this strategy. Fidelity has 36 sector funds. Sector rotation is becoming so popular that there are currently over 500 sector funds. The problem with any strategy is that the more popular it becomes, the more likely the potential for outperforming diminishes. In the past, you assumed that you could change sectors quarterly, but now you often have to look at sectors weekly or in extreme markets. With this strategy, you are looking at the sectors that are moving up the fastest in relation to the market or have the best relative strength.

The easiest source for this information is *Investor's Business Daily,* which tracks 197 industries, or Standard & Poor's Web site. As soon as those fast-moving sectors show weakness and their relative strength falls below 80 percent, shift into the best fund in another sector showing the stronger relative strength. Although following trends can be a great strategy, it is time consuming and can be very dangerous. So make sure you have tough, rigid exit strategies and don't waver when you get sell signals, whether from economic data, valuations, or overweighting.

Best of the Worst

When you open your newspaper, do you look for the funds that are doing the very best and rush out to buy them, or do you look for funds that have beaten down and buy them? Investors too often have a tendency to look at all the funds that did well, wanting to experience those returns and believing blindly that "the trend is your *only* friend."

If you believe, however, that the trend is a fair-weather friend, then you may want to look at sectors that have been beaten down but are starting to show some life and moving back up slowly. If you are this investor, then you will like the best-of-the-worst strategy. The opposite of best of the best and drifting, it is based on the same premise as the Dogs of the Dow—the big losers of one year often tend to be the big winners the next year.

The strategy of best of the worst is based on the belief that it is often futile to chase performance; what was the best fund the previous year is unlikely to be the best fund the next year. For years, no mutual funds had triple-digit returns, but in 1998 six funds had over a 100 percent return. In 1999 more than 184 funds had more than a 100 percent return, almost all Internet and technology funds of course. By 2000, two funds had this kind of return, by mid-2001, there were none. No funds in 2001 had been in the top categories in 1999—none! Even worse, many of the Internet and technology stocks were bankrupt. By the third quarter of 2001, 99.3 percent of all mutual funds were down for the year, thus making bonds and cash the best funds.

Even though most investors know that sector funds tend to rotate widely, they look at mutual fund ratings and at what *was* hot the previous year. Hindsight is wonderful but of little use in finding the best funds for tomorrow. The hot funds of yesterday are almost always sector funds versus balanced or widely diversified funds. The fact that so many funds had returns so far above average was a warning signal.

With this strategy of best of the worst, investors are looking for the best fund in the bottom sectors. They usually don't select the worst sectors but rather poorer-performing sectors that are improving in relative strength and showing at least some signs of life.

For the best-of-the-worst strategy to work well, you need to be aware of the movement of sectors. This is the same premise behind the Dogs of the Dow strategy and value cost averaging, strategies that reflect our belief that sectors will revert to their mean.

As mentioned earlier, you probably want to use best-of-the-worst strategy for only part of your portfolio. You may want to keep a well-balanced core account and then work around the fringes with a strategy such as timing or sector rotation. It is important when using best of the worst to have an exit strategy for exiting sectors that are overweighted, are trading at unjustified levels, or in which you have achieved large profits. For example, when MCD gained 22 percent for one month in 2000, it was apparent that this increase could not be justified by looking at its historic averages. Being so high above the average return for blue chip stocks was a warning signal. Both the best-ranked and worst-ranked sectors reverted to their mean in subsequent years, which means the worst sectors tend to come back up to their average return and the best sectors tend to fall to their average.

Don't pick last year's winners if their valuations are high because they are likely to fall to their average return. Instead, pick losers that are undervalued as they are likely to rise to their average return.

Although sectors do tend to move to their average return, the question is when. To avoid trying to time, I suggest placing stop losses on funds and trusts to help you exit near the top and rely on valuations and relative strength to help you buy at the bottom.

Setting Up a Program

As noted earlier, you can use either funds or trusts for these strategies, but the day-to-day mechanics are different for each. Starting a program is somewhat time consuming, but it becomes relatively simple and routine once you set up an account.

Here are a few suggestions.

- Start with a wrap program at a brokerage firm where you can trade no-load and loaded funds, trusts, and stocks without commissions. You should not have to pay more than 1 percent, especially if you have other assets with the firm.
- Look at your retirement accounts and determine if you can employ these strategies. Try to use tax-deferred accounts whenever possible.
- Now look at relative strength. Look at the best-performing sectors and the worst. Watch the sectors for a few weeks to see if you can tell which of the bottom sectors are starting to move. Look for the relative strength numbers (easy to find in *Investor's Business Daily*).

- Pick two sectors that have strong relative strength. Although I am concentrating on selecting the undervalued sectors, to start with I want some sectors that are already moving strongly. Because we don't know when the top sectors will fall, we want to be in some of them just in case it takes a while for our bottom selections to move up.
- Pick three sectors that did poorly last year but are starting to show a little improvement in their relative strength. You can't pick just the bottom sectors though; sectors have to show a little movement and need to have good valuation, so check the PEGs and PEs relative to their averages, the averages of other sectors, interest rates, consumer confidence, and sector fundamentals.
- If using funds, go to Morningstar, Lipper, or another mutual fund rating service and find the best fund in the sectors you selected. If using indexes or trusts, you can eliminate this step.
- Put in place exit strategies, such as protective puts and stop losses. Also use covered calls to get you out at your targeted returns.
- Start shifting when a sector becomes overweighted, when it has risen more than 30 percent, when the valuations are weak, or when the relative strength is decreasing. When you start taking profits, add to the best fund of the last quarter's worst sectors.
- Remember that buying is only half the trick!
- If you have earned more than 20 percent, start using a few exit strategies, such as stop losses at 7 to 8 percent away and mental stops for mutual funds.
- If one of your sectors increases to over 40 percent of your portfolio, reduce it to a maximum of 25 percent, move your stop losses up to 5 percent, and start buying puts.
- If a fund drops from the top five in its category, move out—but if the sector still looks good, pick one of the better funds in the sector.
- If PEGs or PEs move 30 percent higher than average, buy tight protective puts.
- If you are conservative, especially on initial trades, buy protective puts for 20 percent of your portfolio and immediately employ stop losses at 7 to 8 percent under prices, and start to move out when a sector falls to those levels (with mutual funds you need to use mental stop losses).

When investing in mutual funds, popular approaches are families that carry many sectors, such as Fidelity Select Funds, which hold over 36 sectors, or Rydex funds. If you are using exchange-traded funds (ETFs) such as the indexes (SPY, MDY, QQQ, or iShares), you will have more flexibility in using exit strategies and valuation. These funds are actually much more attractive for sector rotation as they are "purer." If they are technology index funds, they tend to be pure technology without overlap into other sectors. If they are health care, they tend to be pure health care. Because you have a much clearer picture of what you own, I prefer exchange traded index funds. They trade just as stocks do and most have options.

Dollar Cost Averaging

Although we do not often think of dollar cost averaging as a timing strategy, it actually is. Although, adding money into the market each month over a long period has proven successful, many studies challenge the practice. Most studies show had you invested $10,000 immediately, even if the market fell slightly, in most markets you would have more money than the person who invested only $1,000 of the $10,000 quarterly. Being out of the market and in cash, even if done monthly, often hurts more than it helps. However, it is not my purpose to debate the pros and cons of dollar cost averaging. Obviously, if you were dollar cost averaging and the market was going up, you were worse off than the person who invested all the money before the market rallied. However, if the market were to fall, you would have been better off dollar cost averaging. The worth of dollar cost averaging is it reduces risk because we don't know which way the market is going. In addition, most investors have the ability to save only a little at a time instead of lump sums, so dollar cost averaging offers a disciplined approach into the market.

Entering the market slowly. Dollar cost averaging focuses on investing a fixed dollar amount on a regular basis, usually monthly. It works much better with mutual funds than with trusts or stocks because of transaction fees. When the price declines, you end up buying more shares; and when the price rallies, you buy fewer shares. Over a long period, especially in markets that move up and down dramatically, your average cost should be less.

Exiting the market slowly. We often think of dollar cost averaging as a way to get into the market, but I actually find it more useful as a way to exit. As you start to see large profits build, take a set amount out each month and move out slowly, just as you moved in slowly.

Value Cost Averaging

When my brother was teaching at West Point he told me about a young army captain, Michael Edleson, who was also teaching there and had developed an investment strategy called value cost averaging. I had thought all investment strategies came from Wall Street or academia. I became more intrigued with the idea originally because of where it was developed, but over the years I have found it helps me to take profits. Although it is easy for most investors to understand, it is a little more difficult to implement than a simple dollar cost averaging strategy.

The main reason I like this strategy is that it makes you think and gives you a sense of the market, where the money is going, and how big the moves in the market actually are. Although it is a program that has set rules and should be followed automatically without emotion or rethinking, it makes you aware of the direction of the market.

In its original format, it seemed better suited as a timing strategy, but I have adapted it to work for sector rotation because I find it even more useful in working with sectors.

Instead of trying to guess when to get in and out of the market or do the research necessary or collect all the data needed, you can use the much simpler, value cost averaging, which is a form of dollar cost averaging. With dollar cost averaging, you invest a certain amount each month. When the market is down, you purchase more shares. When the market is up, you purchase fewer shares, but you invest the same dollar amount each month.

With value cost averaging, you are attempting to increase your wealth or *increase the value of your account by a set amount* each month. Rather than investing a fixed amount each month, instead you are growing your account by a set amount. The amount you invest varies in order for the value of your account to increase by a set amount each month. When the account goes up less than your target, you invest more. When it goes up more than your target growth, you invest less. Sometimes, if the account goes up much more than your target, you sell shares.

> **Dollar cost averaging helps you invest a fixed amount monthly. Value cost averaging helps you increase your wealth or value monthly.**

For example, if you want your account to grow in each of the next six months by $500, start by investing $500 the first month. Remember that at the end of the first month you want $500; you want your account to grow in the second month to $1,000; in the third month you want your account to be at $1,500; and so on until it reaches $3,000 in the sixth month. If at the end of the first month you find your account has gone up to $600, you only need to add $400 to reach your growth of $500 a month.

Account up. Now let's say you do really well and at the end of the second month you are up to $1300; you only need to add $200 to be on target.

Account down. Then a bad month comes, and you've lost $300. But this is a buying opportunity! You want to invest more, so you add $800 while the market is low. Over a long period, value cost averaging will bring your average price down even more than dollar cost averaging because you are investing more money in the down months and less in the up markets. In this case you are investing $800 when the market is low, but if you were using dollar cost averaging you would be buying the same $500 worth of funds each month.

Account up above your target. Let's assume the market turns quickly and your account surpasses the target and grows $800 instead of $500. At this point you have a nice profit, so you should sell some of your winners; therefore you sell $300. Again you will be better off than you would by dollar cost averaging if the market continues to go up and down, as you will have taken some profits that will allow you to add more money when the market falls again.

Starting balance	Add	Grew by	TARGET BALANCE	ENDING BALANCE	Month
$ 0	$500	$100	$500	$600	January
600	400	300	1000	1300	February
1300	200	**-300**	1500	1200	March
1200	800	800	2000	2800	April
2800	-300	600	2500	3100	May
3100	-100	200	3000	3200	June

As you can see, when your investment grew less than $500, the next month you added more than $500 to the account. When it grew more than $500, you took money out of the account. As you can see in March, the account lost money and missed your $500 growth target, so you added $800 the next month. In April, it grew by $800 and so the next month you took $300 out. Remember that the target here is not to add $500 a month but to have the account *grow* by $500 a month. When it grows more than that, take some money out the next month; when it grows less, add some.

The purpose of value cost averaging is to assure that you increase your wealth each month. Sometimes the market will do most of the work, and sometimes you will have to do extra work by investing more. Sometimes you will take money off the table because the market did much better than anticipated.

With value cost averaging, you consider not only getting into the market but also getting out. The problem for most investors is not having automatic exit strategies. With dollar cost averaging, you are investing a certain dollar amount each month. With value cost averaging, you are adding more in the down months and adding less or selling in the up months. Because value cost averaging follows the rule of buying low and selling high, I prefer this over traditional dollar cost averaging strategies. Value cost averaging has offered higher returns than dollar cost averaging and allows us to be more certain of reaching our targeted returns. With dollar cost averaging, just because you invest $3,000 doesn't mean you will have $3,000 in six months. If the market falls, you will be investing but won't achieve your goal. When you want to achieve a target goal, value cost averaging is much better.

These are the arguments for and against value cost averaging.

Pros

- Results in lower average price per share than dollar cost averaging.
- More appropriate for achieving target goals
- Disciplined approach to sell at the top
- Investing more dollars at a lower price
- The American Association of Individual Investors showed in computer-simulated tests that value cost averaging outperformed dollar cost averaging 95 percent of the time.

Cons

- Involves more work than dollar cost averaging.
- Returns are not as dramatic as other sector rotation strategies.

Going one step further. This is an easy program to adapt to sectors. Set targets for each sector for the amount of growth you want over the years. Base your targeted growth on the average growth of a sector over the years. If the average growth is 12 percent per year, you would set your target for 1 percent growth per month. As a sector rises more than the average return would suggest, you either sell or add less to that sector. If sectors are moving less than their average return suggests, you add more to those weaker sectors. This is done on the assumption that the sectors that are down have value and will rise to their average return. If something is doing much better than it should, you want to take some of your money off the table, because the probability is low that it can continue to outperform for a long period.

This strategy is a good way to move from one sector to another and to time without the emotion that is so often tied to our investment decisions, especially when the market is as hot as it was in 1999. Just think of how well this strategy would have worked then. As the techs were soaring, you would have sold off your winners all year and added to sectors that had not done well in 1999, probably utilities, oils, consumer staples, or, even better, health care. You would have been adding to the sectors that turned and did well in 2000, and you would have sold off your techs, which had exploded and were performing far above their averages. At the time it might have seemed counterintuitive, but as 2000 approached, you would have been glad to be in utilities and oils instead of techs. Because utilities did the best in 2000 and performed well above their averages, you would have been selling them late in the year. By 2001 utilities were down over 20 percent, so by selling utilities in 2000 you not only were able to cash in on some of the profits but also spare yourself a large fall.

Getting started. To begin your value cost averaging, follow these steps.

- Determine how much you have to work with. Let's say $1,000.
- Determine which sectors, style, or indexes you wish to include.
- Divide your assets. Let's say you select five style categories, such as large cap growth, midcap growth, large cap value, midcap value, and international. You decide that you want each to grow by $200 per month.
- Each month, evaluate each sector. If they have grown more than their average return, reduce your investments or take some profits. Usually, if one sector is up, the others may be down, so taking profits in one will give you the additional funds to invest in the others.

Rebalancing

Remembering that our goal is to sell at the top and buy at the bottom, it seems difficult to sell your winners and add to your losers. It's emotion that keeps investors from taking profits.

When Prudential Securities developed its wrap mutual fund program, it debated whether to include an automatic rebalancing feature; not only was it time consuming to build the models but costly to maintain. However, the program's designer, Mark Rappaport, convinced Prudential to go forward with the rebalancing feature. His logic was that individuals, if given the choice to rebalance, would not have the time or the ability to make such frequent adjustments even if it could be done with a simple phone call.

I interviewed Mark for one of my radio shows, and he provided good insight into rebalancing.

Balance is the key to life. Even if not "key," we generally view balance as a good thing. Balanced diets, a balance of work and play, even balanced wheels on our car are what most of us seek. Balanced portfolios are advantageous as well—proper balance, or asset allocation, generally provides a risk/return characteristic suitable for both our temperament and goals.

When portfolios get out of balance, they need realignment and rebalancing. Historically, rebalancing has added only about 0.50 percent to returns, but, as noted earlier, 0.50 percent compounded over 20 years can make a tremendous difference.

Portfolios get out of balance because one sector tends to do better than others, and so the account is overweighted in that sector. "The practice of rebalancing (bringing the portfolio back to its original balanced weightings) holds two key benefits for us as investors—maintaining the appropriate risk characteristics and improving long-term performances," says Mark.

He continues to explain that it is important to maintain the original weighting that you select when you first establish your asset allocation.

In January, we set out to construct a portfolio in line with both our temperament for risk and our time horizon—a 60 percent stock/ 40 percent bond allocation. By the end of June, market performance had shifted our assets to 70 percent stock/30 percent bond. Hence, our allocation is now more aggressive as it is more heavily weighted in stocks, the more volatile asset class of the two. Because the original portfolio balance is now significantly imbalanced, we would seek to restore balance—and thus our appropriate risk/return allocation—by *rebalancing* the portfolio.

This was the drift I spoke about earlier; I permitted drift within certain ranges as long as the valuations were still attractive. However, rebalancing does not permit any drifting and as a result usually underperforms the drifting strategy that permits a little overweighting in the best sectors.

Mark believes that rebalancing decreases risk over the long run and prevents you from overestimating the value of new sectors. Rebalancing also can be put on automatic pilot. Most brokerage firms, through wrap programs, and almost all annuities now allow rebalancing with automatic programs. Certainly for a portion of an account, rebalancing is a great strategy because it adheres closely to an investor's risk parameters and doesn't let the account deviate from the original judgment calls that the investor made.

Mutual Funds Can Cloud Your True Allocations

Rebalancing programs are trying to eliminate drift, but mutual funds have additional problems. By maintaining the targeted risk/return allocation, we eliminate some of the drift style. However, even if we eliminate drift in a portfolio, we may find that drifting is occurring within the mutual funds. Mutual funds, especially value funds, sometimes let their portfolios drift a little to improve returns when one sector dominates but is still not overvalued. Funds will drift to growth stocks when growth appears better, and until growth looks overvalued, they will allow the drift to occur. The asset allocation study done by Professor A. Craig MacKinley of the Wharton School claimed drifting was so prevalent that you had to adjust your mutual fund selection when creating an asset allocation program. Fund titles seldom provide adequate information on the underlying stocks, so funds may have more value stocks or growth stocks than their name implies. Drifting is actually the first sector rotation strategy mentioned in this book, but you can only allow drifting when you are monitoring the drift and can never let it exceed specified ranges. Assume you want a portfolio allocation of 60 percent growth funds/ 40 percent value. However, if the value fund you use is out of balance and is 50 percent growth and 50 percent value, your actual weighting will be 80 percent growth and 20 percent value and thus out of balance. This is why I tend to prefer index trusts and exchange traded funds when looking at sector rotation; you always know exactly what you have.

Improving Returns

There is much debate on how much safety rebalancing adds as sometimes you may come out of a sector that is doing well and go back into a sector that may still underperform for awhile but in general appears to improve returns by 0.25 to 0.50 percent annually. Usually this improvement comes at no cost, although it can and does have additional tax considerations that can reduce your total returns. According to Mark:

> If maintaining the targeted risk/reward is not appealing enough (though it should be—most of the biggest mistakes in investing originate from the inability to control risk), how about the appeal of making more money? Several studies have pointed out the performance advantage of rebalancing or the "rebalancing bonus." Studies of rebalancing an equal mixture of stocks and bonds annually from 1926 to 1994 yielded average annual returns of 8.34 percent versus 7.85 percent—a pickup of about half a percentage point in return per year.

Remember that when compounded annually, 0.50 percent is very rewarding. The best part is with an array of automated rebalancing programs in most mutual fund families, wrap accounts, and annuities, you don't have to do any of the work but still get all the reward. And it is usually free!*

Other studies have come to similar conclusions. A T. Row Price study compared two $10,000 portfolios—one left unbalanced with the account drifting with the market's moves and the other rebalanced quarterly. The original allocation was 60 percent stocks,

---

*Toddi Gutner, "A Rebalancing Act to Protect Your Portfolio," *Business Week* (June 17,1996).

30 percent bonds, and 10 percent cash. The unbalanced account grew to $150,019 over a 15-year period, and the rebalanced account grew to $154,035.* Other studies have shown an even greater advantage to rebalancing. The best benefits are achieved in volatile markets such as those we have recently had. Imagine how well you would have done in 1999, 2000, and 2001 if you were automatically moved out of the overweighted tech sector at the end of 1999 into value. The difference was well over a 10 percent advantage for the rebalanced accounts versus the buy-and-hold accounts for those three years.

Most of the strategies I've discussed are essentially ways to get you out of the market, the sectors, or stocks near the top. The purpose is not to squeeze out every last penny of profit potential but instead to learn another exit strategy. Most of us have no problems buying good stocks, but we find selling difficult. Rebalancing is another tool to help you "exit gracefully." There should be no surprise that these strategies would outperform most buy-and-hold strategies. It is no surprise that these strategies do better in bear markets and in volatile markets. But what is often a surprise is that they frequently do better even in good markets.

Remember that we are usually selling our winners in these strategies and buying or adding to our losers. Again the premise is that almost everything reverts to its average, or mean. What goes up usually comes down, and what is down in the market, if it is of good quality and viable, will come back up. With rebalancing, we sell our overweighted position and buy the poorer-performing position as with the best-of-the-worst sector rotation strategy.

The main benefit of value cost averaging, rebalancing, and the best of the worst is that they force us to do what we know rationally is correct: take profits and sell part of our winners, or sell high and buy low. These programs can put us on autopilot and take out the emotion to give us attractive alternatives to buying and holding. Buying good stocks for core accounts and working around the edges with these trading strategies help to take some profits before they disappear and take small losses before they become big losses.

Most of us love the winners; we are elated to find that great stock. We are also disappointed at the prospect of adding to our losers. If you are like that, you may have to do what I do. Whenever I doubt the benefits of rotation, I hold up the Phoenix charts or think of the rotation of the Dow stocks in the 1990s or, even better, remind myself of how AT&T fell over 85 percent and Lucent over 90 percent. Immediately, I remember that selling at the top is not such a bad idea.

Watching the Seasons

Many of the strategies used in the previous chapter on timing for getting in and out of stocks and the market are applicable to sectors. In addition to seasonal trends for the market, there seem to be seasonal patterns for sectors, such as:

- Small cap value sectors tend to do better in December and January.
- Value sectors tend to do better in the summer.

---

*William J. Berstein, "The Rebalancing Bonus: Theory and Practice," *Efficient Frontier* (1996).

- Technology sectors tend to do poorly in June but do better in the last quarter of the year.
- Large cap growth tends to do well from November to April.
- 80 percent of returns come from November to May, while September tends to be one of the worst months.

How to Use This Information

I have developed rules that work well and provide a sense of discipline. You might want to look at them and adapt them to your own needs.

As April approaches, sell tight calls on most of the tech and growth sectors and bring your stop losses up to 5 percent away, especially on sectors that have over a 20 percent profit. Don't wait until June to get out of techs as it may be too late, so start your exit strategy early.

As May approaches, do the following:

- Do more calls and bring stop losses up higher on sectors with large profits to 5 percent away.
- Because most returns come between November and May, lighten up on equities from June to October.
- Buy insurance or Nasdaq puts as June seems to be weak for technology stocks.
- Collar whichever techs you are willing to sell.
- Buy puts on high PE and high PEG sectors.
- Also buy puts on high beta sectors.

This way you are protecting yourself for the downside and raising cash for dips in the market during the summer—in other words, attempting to sell at the top and buy at the bottom. This is a strategy to sell and gives you the money to buy at the bottom usually in September and October. As you sell out of the techs and growth, add to value sectors for the summer.

As August approaches, move stops up and collar a lot of positions, knowing you are going into September and October. Now start selling calls or using exit strategies for value positions because you want to be out of them by November and back into growth then.

By September and October, you should again be hedged on most of your portfolio (with stop losses, puts, or collars). You can also use calls; although calls don't protect you from large falls, they help you raise cash to buy additional shares of growth stocks. Be very defensive during these months.

Novembers tend to be strong for growth. Let your calls, collars, and puts expire in November. If it looks as though you might be getting called away, you can sell some puts to buy at lower prices. Stay fully invested from November to April. If there has been no correction by then, keep some puts and stop losses in place. Historically, this seasonal timing has worked well. It keeps you in the market for the best months and gets you out, or gives you some profits (on puts and calls), in the weak months.

Reinvest as cash you have raised during April through October.

Stay fully invested in equities from November to April.

In November, add to small cap value.

In February, start selling off some of small cap value.

Don't cut of your upside with covered calls from November to April.

Always protect half of your position if you are up more than 50 percent. Also be sure to protect 25 percent of your position if your portfolio is up more than 30 percent in a year, no matter what season it is. After November 2000, I will probably always have a little more protection and not count on seasonality as much.

What can go wrong? This strategy, I have to admit, did not work for me in November 2000. I can blame it on the Feds, the elections, or whatever, but getting back in then hurt my clients and took months to recover the losses. In spite of my concern, I decided to include it since it has worked so well for so long. Not only is November historically a good month, but in six of the seven previous election years, the market was up more than 16 percent in November alone.

Even the best strategy fails sometimes, so always have a backup, which certainly worked better than the buy-and-hold approach that many investors had in 2000. But it didn't work as well as my accounts that I kept fully protected all the time. In the future, I will always keep a few more stop loss orders and puts on my accounts, even in good months. I probably still will not do covered calls from November to March, as I don't want to cut off the upside, but I think I will use some puts and stop loss orders, which should be sufficient protection for those months. Because of one bad year, you don't want to go to extremes and overprotect everything. Ironically, had I used all the strategies I reviewed and not played with seasonality, I would have avoided the November 2000 problems. So why am I telling you about seasonal hedging? Because I think it can still work; just be a little more cautious, even going into the good months.

Back to the Basics: PEs and PEGs

It is easier and safer to have timing and sector rotation on automatic pilot. You do this by using rebalancing and value cost averaging, and you can also set some rules and criteria as I did with timing. I use the same basic valuation rules (PEGs, PEs, yields, growth); risk measurements (beta, correlation); technical, economic, fundamental, and weighting rules; and my own unique profit criteria. Once these criteria give a signal or warning, start using exiting strategies.

Look at the PEs and PEGs for the sectors and compare them to their historic average PEs and PEGs (just as you would for the stocks and timing). As these ratios get higher compared with their averages, start to use exit strategies. When you exit, look for the low PE and PEG sectors and buy those sectors back. This is similar to the best of the worst strategy that uses performance as the main criteria, whereas here we are using valuations.

In both cases buy the best undervalued sectors and sell the overvalued sectors albeit using different warning signals.

Interest Rates

As with timing, interest rate moves are one of the key factors in determining the direction of the market. When interest rates are increasing, the market is dangerous for stocks. Decreasing interest rates have historically been very good for stocks. As with timing, when you see interest rates rising, shift from your stock funds to your money market, value, or balanced funds. When interest rates have peaked and cuts look possible, move more dollars out of money market funds and more into balanced and value funds. As rate cuts continue, move back into growth sectors. *Do not move into bond funds when rates are increasing.* Because of interest rate risks, bonds can be almost as dangerous as stocks when rates are rising.

Economy in Recession

The S&P declined only nine times for a 12-month period since 1961. In eight of those nine times the market started to recover about six months before the economy recovered. Although we cannot tell when the economy will turn around, we do know that we will miss most of the runup in the market if we wait until the economy is healthy. Bob Stovall of Prudential Financial showed in a July 2001 newscast that the S&P 500 gained on average 27 percent in the two quarters before an economic turnaround and the first two months after the turnaround.

Overweighting and Profits

We can use many of the tools used in timing for sector rotation, such as support and resistance levels, earnings, yields, manufacturing statistics, employment numbers, business cycles, and political and fiscal policy as well as fundamental changes in the sectors.

But I feel that the best reason to rotate, or time, is because we do not want to be overweighted in a sector. The next best reason is that we need discipline in taking profits. Always keep these two criteria in mind, no matter what other strategies you use.

Letting the Pros Do the Work for You

We often believe in the premise of a strategy but don't have the time or patience to do the research ourselves. Some programs rotate sectors for you in addition to information in several newsletters and Web sites, or you can let funds do the rotations for you.

Fund programs. MFS Research Fund, for example, has 32 industry analysts who can buy and sell sector stocks for the fund within their areas of expertise. Meridian Investment Management of Englewood, Colorado, also offers a program with its own funds. It had a good track record for several years but was in the lower range of sector rotation groups, up only 7.93 percent in 2000. (However, anything that was up in 2000 doesn't sound all that bad to me.) State Street Research Galileo Fund also carries a mix of funds that mimics the Russell 1000 index.

Newsletters. Several newsletters inform you when and where to move. The *Hulbert Financial Digest* shows that the best track record is held by Jack Bowers' *Fidelity Monitor,* with returns averaging 20 percent over the last ten years. Bowers, who uses Fidelity funds, switched recently from a momentum strategy (similar to best of the best) to a more value-oriented strategy (similar to best of the worst). The second–best track record was awarded to Jim Schmidt, whose *Timer Digest* watches price movements. One of the more popular newswriters is Doug Fabian, who writes the *Fabian's Fidelity Sectors,* which tells you which Fidelity sector funds look the most attractive.

Web sites. Fidelity Funds has a Web site that provides information as does Standard & Poor's Web site <www.stockinfo.standardpoor.com>.

Advantages of Holding Sector Funds

Even if you don't want to move or shift from sector to sector, you still may want to build a portfolio using sector funds instead of broadly diversified funds. Typically, a group of sector funds can beat the market because of the expertise of the fund manager Martin Ratner, president of Professional Sector Management in Menlo Park, California, showed that 70 percent of Fidelity's sector funds outperformed the S&P from 1989 to 1994. The sector funds' total return was 40 percent higher than the return on the S&P fund. So simply build a portfolio of 10 to 12 sectors and let it sit.

Summary

Stocks Change and So Do Sectors

We saw how stocks rise to glory and then fall back dramatically. We also saw how sectors change. Just as we may want to time stocks or rotate stocks, we may want to consider rotating sectors. Changes in sectors and the economy create risk but also offer opportunity. The trick is, as always, learning how to control that risk. That is precisely what we are doing with sector rotation. We are limiting the damage that can be done by violent moves from one part of the economy to another.

Pay for advice; it's cheaper than you think. The cost of avoiding professional advice can be high. The bull market in 1999 made everyone think that investing was easy and everyone was a financial genius. Bernstein Research conducted a study showing that individuals trading on their own were likely to turn over their portfolios five times a year. That excessive amount of trading was good for the IRS and the discount brokers, but investors who pay for advice often are convinced by financial advisors to trade only when there is a reason to trade.

It is nice to have someone for your sector rotation accounts who can research estimated earnings, PEs, and PEGs to guide you. However, if you do work with a financial advisor on these types of accounts, still consider flat-fee accounts. You will have to communicate with your advisor, and a lot of work on your part is required if you want to be hands on.

As an alternative, you may want to consider a portfolio manager. You can work with the manager to design the kinds of accounts you want—maybe one asset allocation, one timing, one sector rotation based on valuations such as PEs, and another based on performance, such as the best of the worst. You can feel comfortable allowing the advisor discretion because you know that the account is based on a flat fee and the manager's only motivation is to do a good job for you. It may be worth another one-half of a percentage point to have someone move your stop losses up and do the rebalancing. Fees for portfolio management accounts start as low as .75 percent and go as high as 3 percent. When searching for a portfolio manager, performance as well as fees should be considered as should the willingness of the manager to adapt to your unique style and needs.

CHAPTER 15

Tax Balancing
Location, Location, Location

DEFINITION

Tax balancing is placing your investments in the proper location so that you minimize taxes and increase your returns.

KEY

Safety: ★★★★   Simplicity: ★★★

Returns: $$$$ Tax efficiency: $$$$$+

SUMMARY

Safety: Increases safety because it allows you to increase your returns with no additional risk.

Returns: Tax balancing can improve returns dramatically, usually by the amount of taxes you pay on your investments.

Simplicity: This strategy is simple to understand and, once put in place, easy to maintain.

Tax efficiency: Tax balancing is the ultimate in tax efficiency.

One of the easiest and safest ways to increase returns is to keep the money you would normally pay to the federal government in taxes. The average American works until the middle of May to pay those taxes, so if taxes can be reduced, personal wealth could increase tremendously. The purpose of this chapter is to show you how to enhance returns by placing your investments in the proper location. In my book *100 Questions Every Working American Must Ask,* I address the tax savings of retirement planning; and my previous book *The Money Manager* looks at many tax-advantaged investments and their pros and cons. Every one's tax situation is unique, so you should always, *always* discuss any tax ideas with your tax advisor.

Now let's look at placing your investments where they can improve your total return by avoiding taxes.

Putting Your Investments in All the Right Places

Of all the mistakes I have seen investors make over the years, the most common is not exiting on time. That is hard to do, though, and often understandable. The second biggest mistake is having investments in the wrong location. There is no excuse for that. It is easy to solve and takes only a little common sense, but even the brightest of investors don't take the time to evaluate the tax consequences of location. In a 1996 workshop, I asked my radio listeners to list the investments in their IRAs and individual accounts. Over 70 percent had long-term core stocks in IRAs and mutual funds in taxable accounts. This one simple mistake can be extremely costly.

Core stocks, indexes, index funds, and long-term capital gain investments don't need to be in tax-deferred accounts and should be placed in taxable accounts. When you put these investments in tax-deferred accounts, you are converting what would be low long-term capital gain rates to higher ordinary income rates when distributed.

After 2001, securities you hold for five years will be taxed at only 18 percent. Yet they will be taxed at ordinary income rates if you put them in 401(k)s and regular IRAs (not Roth) when you take distributions out.

Locate Short-Term Capital Gains and Ordinary Income in Tax-Deferred Accounts

On the other hand, mutual funds, bonds, covered calls, sector rotation programs, rebalancing programs, and the like have high ordinary income taxes and should not be held in taxable accounts and, whenever possible, should be placed in retirement accounts, annuities, private placement insurance vehicles, 401(k)s and IRAs. Any investment that has short-term capital gains, dividends, or interest has an immediate tax consequence. Every year you are sharing part of your return with the federal and your state government. You can time the taxes on long-term capital gain investments, but you cannot time or control them with these investments. Ordinary income taxes for most individuals are much higher than for long-term capital gains, and between federal and state taxes, you may have to give up as much as 45 percent in taxes.

Keep those investments that have long-term capital gains in taxable account and those taxed as ordinary income in tax-deferred accounts.

Taxable Accounts versus Tax-Deferred Accounts

On the first of the following lists, I have shown investments that are appropriate to locate in taxable accounts and accounts of children under the age of 14.

On the second chart, I have listed investments that should be sheltered or located whenever possible in annuities, low-income family member's accounts, accounts of children over age 14, tax-deferred IRAs, and retirement accounts. Often, investments are suitable in either case.

Investment for Taxable Accounts

Investments	Strategies
Long-term core stocks	Buy-and-hold
Inflation index notes	Asset allocation
Coins	Laddering
Oil and gas partnerships	Hedging
Commodities	Protective puts
Collectibles	Dollar cost averaging
Real estate	Collars
Raw land	
Home equity	
Municipal bonds	
Tax-sheltered partnerships	
Indexes	
Index funds	
Index CDs	
Principal-protected notes	
Emergency funds	
Cash, money market accounts, Treasury bills	

Aggressive Investments
Midcap and smallcap funds and stocks
International funds and stocks
Aggressive growth stocks and funds
Venture capital
Business equity

Investments for Tax-Deferred, Low-Tax Accounts

Investments	Strategies
Index CDs	Rebalancing
Inflation index notes	Sector rotation
High-yielding securities	Covered-call writing
Preferred stocks	Timing
Government bonds, mortgages	Guaranteed trusts
Bond trusts	Dogs of the Dow
Dividend-paying stocks	Protective puts
REITS	Stop losses
Mutual funds	Trading
Utilities	Collars
Zero-coupon bonds and CDs	Value cost averaging
Participating index notes	
Principal-protected notes	

Locate Cash and Emergency Funds in Taxable Accounts

On the tax-deferred list, cash and emergency funds are excluded because these should be restricted to taxable accounts and are not appropriate for tax-deferred accounts. Even though these are safe investments, they should not be used in tax-deferred accounts because retirement accounts are long term, and you should be seeking good returns. Cash should be used only in tax-deferred accounts as part of sector rotation or timing strategies when you are waiting for opportunities to buy. Emergency funds should be easily available. You should also probably not place CDs in IRAs unless you are extremely conservative or are close to retirement and due for distributions. In retirement accounts you are striving for long-term strong returns, not short-term emergency funds that offer meager returns.

Look at the tax consequences of each investment. Guaranteed equity trusts, introduced earlier, were half zero-coupon bonds and half mutual funds. Both parts of the trust have high tax consequences. The zeros have tax consequences even though you don't receive your principal back until maturity. The mutual funds can have short-term capital gains that are taxed at ordinary income rates. (Remember that between federal and state taxes, this could be as high as 45 percent). This type of investment seldom has any place in a taxable account, even in a young child's account because children are usually taxed at their parents' rate. When you invest in these types of investments, consider sheltering them in tax-deferred accounts such as IRAs, educational IRAs, and pension plans.

Place Your Sales in the Correct Location

In addition to placing investments in the correct place, it is also important to place the sales in the correct place. *Where* you sell your investments can often be as important as *when* you sell. Before you sell any investment, you should consider the possibility of shifting the sale to another location, such as your children's accounts, charitable remainder accounts, or directly to charities or family members who are in lower tax brackets. Everyone except the government usually benefits from these transfers.

Long-term capital gains investments give you flexibility. You want to keep long-term capital gains investments in your taxable accounts so you can hold them forever and possibly not pay taxes until you sell. You could theoretically never pay taxes or wait to sell until you are in a much lower tax bracket. You can also gift them to a charity and pay no taxes, or gift them to your children and family members and pay lower taxes on them, or hold them until you die and get a stepped-up cost basis. (This is changing under the new estate tax laws.)

Never Sell a Profitable Position

Well, almost never. If you have children or give to a charity or in any way help to support elderly parents or others in low tax brackets, think twice before you sell stocks. Although you can only gift $11,000 (as of 2002) per person a year, you can also pay for education, set up 529 educational accounts, pay for health care, and so on for your dependents.

Instead of gifting money for birthdays or holidays or even weddings, set up an account for that child or lower-tax-bracket-nephew or niece and gift them stocks. Have them sell the stocks if they want or need the cash. Both of you will benefit.

Don't Locate Sales in Your Account

Scenario #1. Assume you have a $10,000 stock that you paid $2,000 for six months ago. If you sell it and are in the 40 percent federal and state tax bracket, you will only net $6,800 as you will have to pay short-term capital gain taxes.

$10,000 (current value)
$ 2,000 (cost)
$ 8,000 profit = short-term capital gain

$ 3,200 taxes on $8,000 short-term capital gain

$ 6,800 net after paying taxes on your $10,000 investment

Now you only have $6,800 to give to your charity, your children, or your family members.

If you gift the cash to a charity, the charity only gets $6,800 and you get only a tax deduction of $6,800 and a possible tax savings of $2,720.

If you give the cash to your children, they will get only $6,800 of the $10,000.

Do Locate Sales in Charities Accounts

Scenario #2. Assume you have the same $10,000 stock, but now instead you gift the stock to the charity instead of giving it cash. These numbers are just to make the example simple. There are many variables related to these sales, so check with your tax advisor, but basically this example will give you an idea of the benefits of gifting securities in lieu of cash to a charity.

$10,000 (current value of gifted securities)

$10,000 (charitable deduction and a $4,000 tax savings versus $2720 in scenario #1)

Charity now has $10,000.

Charity sells, pays no taxes, and therefore benefits.

The benefit of location is that the charity has $10,000 versus $6,800, and you save $4,000 in taxes instead of $2,720 because of the larger deduction.

Locate Sales in Child's Account

Scenario #3. Instead of selling the stock and paying for your child's braces with the proceeds, assume you gift your stock to your 15-year-old child who is in the 10 percent tax bracket.

$10,000 (current value of the securities that you gift)
$10,000 (gift to child)
$ 800 (taxes paid by child at 10 percent on $8,000 profit)
$ 9,200 (net to child)

Benefit = $9,200 toward payment of braces versus $6,800 if you had sold stock.

What if you had long-term capital gains versus short-term capital gains? Would it still be beneficial to gift? Even if the stock were at a long-term capital gains federal rate of 18 percent and a state rate of 5 percent, you would still have significant advantages to gifting. Your child would net $9,200 versus the $8,160 you would net.

In addition to gifting $11,000 per person, you can also pay for your children's expenses and gift money to older children for health care premiums to pay medical bills or for education even above the $11,000 gift exclusion. However, your child's age and tax bracket must be considered.

For example, you have a six-year-old child to whom you gift stocks of XYZ that have tripled. If your tax bracket is 39.6 percent federal and 5 percent state, you could pay as much as 44.6 percent on short-term capital gains, 20 percent on long-term, and 18 percent on stocks held five years if they were purchased after January 2001. You may gift to a child but, unfortunately, if the capital gains are more than $1,500, they are likely to be taxed at your bracket because your child is under that age of 14. Until children reach 14, they are taxed at their parents' tax bracket.

Of course, in the world of taxes, nothing is so straightforward. There are hundreds of idiosyncrasies in the tax codes, so check with your tax advisor before you go ahead with any of these suggestions, especially if you are lucky enough to be one of the superrich (over $3.5 million).

Stocks You Want to Keep

What if you want to gift to a charity but have no stocks that you want to sell or give away? If you tithe or regularly gift to charities, always, always, always look at your stock portfolio before you gift. If your commissions are negligible, gift XYZ stock even if you want to keep it. Gift it to the charity and then immediately buy back the stock with the money you would have otherwise gifted. (There are no 30-day wash rules with gifting stocks at a profit.) You have now increased your cost basis so you are in a better tax position when you sell years down the road.

For example, you paid $5 a share for XYZ, which is now worth $55 a share. If you gift to charity, you get a charitable deduction of $55. If you use the dollars you would have gifted and repurchase your stock, your cost basis will then be $55, not $5.

Advantages of Gifting Stocks and Buying Back versus Cash

The pros of gifting to charities are:

- The charity gets a larger amount.
- You avoided paying capital gains. (This allows you to keep down your adjusted gross income and thus may allow you to indirectly save even more by increasing itemized deduction limits, IRA limits, and personal exemptions.)
- You receive a larger charitable deduction and save more in taxes.
- You can buy back your stock immediately and thus will have a higher cost basis.

The Gift That Keeps On Giving: Charitable Remainder Trusts

Even if you are not in a particularly charitable mood, you may want to consider a *charitable remainder trust,* remembering that where you sell can be just as important as when you sell.

These trusts allow you to gift appreciated securities, sell them in the trust often with deferred capital gains, and take income for as long as you and a joint survivor live. If you are concerned about converting stocks into income-generating investments, charitable remainders work well. They are especially attractive for individuals who have appreciated assets they have held for many years. They may now want to generate income from their portfolio. Possibly, they have retired or they may want or need to rebalance their portfolio. The higher the appreciation on the asset, the better charitable remainders work. You need to consult with your estate planner and tax advisor.

You need to look at many more variables, especially when calculating from a mortality table for your tax deductions and the tax consequences as you take distributions. However, in the 22-plus years that I have been advising individuals on finance, there has seldom been a time when higher-taxed individuals could not benefit from charitable trusts.

If you have heirs, you may want to use the tax savings to purchase life insurance to replace wealth your heirs would have otherwise received. With wealth replacement insurance, they receive a tax-free lump sum. You need to purchase only as much as the after-tax value of your estate. If you don't have heirs, you can spend and enjoy the extra income generated from the tax savings.

The advantages of a charitable remainder trust:

- Allows you to gift highly appreciated assets
- Defers capital gains taxes
- Gives you a tax deduction
- Generates income for the rest of your life and the life of a joint survivor
- Helps a charity or other good cause or may even be passed to a foundation under your family name
- Will usually net you a higher income by avoiding capital gains
- Wealth replacement insurance often paid for by tax deductions so your heirs receive the same or more wealth
- Provides asset protection (probably the best reason for many wealthy individuals) as creditors cannot touch the principal

The disadvantages of a charitable remainder trust:

- If you are young, you may have limited tax savings, depending on mortality tables and the amount of income you wish to receive. The older you are, the more you can take out and the higher the tax deductions you will receive.
- You need to work with an attorney to set up these trusts and help determine the tax deduction and most advantageous amount of income to take from the trust.
- Although all the transactions are tax free within the trust, the income you take out will be taxed when it is disbursed at ordinary income tax rates first, then capital gains, and lastly principal.

Other Placements with Positive Tax Consequences

Locate Overweighted Stocks in Exchange Funds

Employees often have an overweighting in company stock, or individuals may have accumulated large positions through inheritances or because of other reasons. You may know you are overweighted; you may know you need to sell, but the taxes may be unbearable. You may have gifted as much as you want or can to charities and children, so you can't sell by shifting to these accounts.

One solution is to locate your stocks in an exchange fund, which takes your stocks in a nontaxable exchange in return for shares in the fund.

These funds are usually limited to individuals who have a net worth of more than $5 million and can exchange at least $1 million worth of stock. At the end of a set period (usually seven years), you get your stock and, if the fund has appreciated, shares of other stocks in the fund as well.

This allows you to be more diversified without the risk associated with overweighting in one stock. Although this is an attractive strategy, it is one you definitely need to discuss with your tax advisor.

Locate Trading Strategies in Tax-Deferred Accounts

You do not benefit from a tax loss in tax-deferred account. Thus, you want to find strategies that diminish losses, such as covered calls, collars, stop losses, sector rotation, rebalancing, and the like. Although these strategies often increase safety and lessen the potential for losses, they can and usually do have high tax consequences.

There are two advantages, however, to these strategies. First, you are using the strategies that are most likely to avoid large downside losses. Second, you are sheltering those investments from likely large tax consequences.

Locate Buy and Hold Funds in Taxable Accounts

Because buy-and-hold and asset allocation strategies are intended to reduce trading and thus tax consequences, funds used for these strategies can be held in taxable accounts.

These placements have two advantages.

1. You are placing investments that could incur large losses in a place where the federal government can and does share part of the loss with you. When your loss occurs in a tax-sheltered account, no one shares that loss with you and you cannot write it off on your tax return.
2. You have eliminated one of the greatest negatives of taxable accounts by placing only investments with minimal tax consequences in these accounts.

Locate Zeros and Mortgages in Tax-Deferred Accounts

Because zero coupon bonds have phantom income, you pay taxes on income that you don't receive each year. Therefore, it is better to shelter zeros in a tax-deferred account as well as guaranteeing programs that use zeros and the guaranteed trusts that use them.

Also, when possible, place mortgages in tax-deferred accounts. Not only is the income from mortgages taxable but the monthly return of principal and interest is an accounting nightmare.

Private Placement Insurance

Charles Evangelakos of Sagemark Consulting often explains some of the new adaptations of traditional variable insurance policies. For wealthy individuals, the new private placement insurance programs allow you to trade within your insurance trusts. You can select and work with your own money manager and have him or her design a program for your specific needs. Because there are no taxes on the trades in these private placements, they are the ultimate trading vehicle.

529 Plans

We often invest for our children in Uniform Gifts to Minors Act (UGMA) accounts, but, as with all investments, there are pros and cons to these plans. Two of the biggest problems are that until the child is 14, the income is taxed at the parents' tax bracket. The second negative is that once a child reaches the age of maturity, which is 18 in most states and 21 in others, they have complete control over those funds.

One of the worst experiences of my life involved these plans. Almost 20 years ago, I had set up a UGMA account for a young widow and her 12-year-old son. Every week she came in with a $25 check. She earned less than $12,000 a year at that time, and it was difficult for her to save that much money each week. When the son reached the age of 18, he came into my office and wanted to take out a few thousand dollars. I didn't want to give it to him without talking to his mother but couldn't get in touch with her. Although I told him I couldn't give him the money without his mother's permission, he knew better and demanded the money from my manager, and he got it! Three weeks later he was killed in a motorcycle accident. His mother blamed me, and probably rightly so. I not only lost a good friend, but had I known the dangers of these accounts, I might have spared a valuable young life. Over the next ten years, three other children came in to demand money, two of whom were with religious groups. These children were kind and charitable, trying to help others in their group. No matter how great your children are, you cannot assume, though, they won't squander the money. I use these accounts with much caution now. You may have the best children in the world, but their values may not always coincide with yours, so be careful.

There are alternatives when saving for children. You can save in your accounts and use long-term capital gains investments, then gift to the children when they need the money. You may also opt to use the new 529 plans, which are especially attractive. Athol Cochrane, a financial planner at Prudential Insurance, wrote several guidelines for these 529 plans.

529 Savings Plans
Athol D. Cochrane, CLU, ChFC

College for our children! The very thought is for many an excellent means of birth control. Well, fear not, help is on the way. It is known as the 529 college savings plan. Adopted by many states, this vehicle offers many attractive options, some of which have been significantly enhanced by the tax act of 2001, fondly referred to as the Economic Growth and Tax Relief Reconciliation Act of 2001.

While most of us fear the cost of college, many also ask which is the best vehicle to use to accumulate the funds needed to pay for the expenses. We have all heard about the Education IRA (now called "education savings accounts") where we could set aside $500 per child per year. If our income was "too much," we were unable to utilize this program. Well, with the 2001 tax act, we are now able to contribute $2,000 per year to education savings accounts. There are also UGMA accounts that can be utilized and those were discussed by Carolann.

How about 529 plans? These programs are adopted by individual states and are administered by many of the large brokerage and mutual fund names you know. It is important to point out that these programs are not college pre-payment programs where you are restricted to using the money for an in-state school. Even though these 529 programs are sponsored by individual states, the funds can be used at any institution of higher learning. But you may ask what this does for me. Let's discuss some of the features.

1. We enjoy tax-deferred accumulations, and they will be tax free if used after 12/31/2001 and before the scheduled sunset provision in the new tax act of 2001, which is 2010. It is widely expected that this sunset provision will be extended for these programs—but we never know!
2. Special gift and estate tax treatment. This will be discussed later.
3. There are no income limits. Everyone is eligible to participate.
4. Contributions to the savings account offer flexibility and low contribution amounts.
5. Unlike the education savings accounts, there is a high contribution limit. You can make contributions until growth and contributions for all accounts for a beneficiary equal $246,000. Growth can continue above this amount, but no further contributions will be allowed.
6. Change beneficiaries—You can change the beneficiary; for example, if one child decided he did not want to go to college, you can change it to any member of the original beneficiary's family. You could name a grandchild—even yourself! This has been further expanded with the tax act of 2001 to include cousins.

Let's discuss some of the benefits in more detail. The special gift and estate tax treatment of 529 plans allows special gift tax exclusion. Current law allows us to make gifts not to exceed $11,000 per year per beneficiary without triggering gift taxes. The 529 plan has a special option that allows the donor a one-time option to give up to $50,000 for each beneficiary. In the case of married donors, it is $100,000 without federal gift tax consequences. The donor, however, is restricted from making any further gifts to the beneficiary for five years. If the donor dies within the five-year period, under the add back rule uncompleted gifts made to a beneficiary will be brought back into the deceased donor's estate for estate tax purposes. However, once the five years have run, the gifts and future growth of those gifts are out of the donor's estate. In addition, after the five years are up, living donors can begin making gifts to the beneficiary again. The accumulations of the 529 plan can be used for qualified expenses at any accredited institution of higher learning in the country and many foreign schools as well. The 2001 tax law changes now permit full room and board expenses for students enrolled at least half-time.

Many of the 529 programs offer flexible investment choices as well as automatic transfers from the donor to the donee's 529 account. Investment choices include aggressive, moderate, and conservative. In some cases, an "age weighted" portfolio option is available. This option automatically rebalances the account into more conservative investments as college years approach and the child nears college attendance.

With the escalation of costs associated with college projected to be in the 6 percent range annually, you owe it to yourself to check out this valuable benefit—the 529 Plan.

Annuities

One of the appropriate places to trade mutual funds and rebalance funds is in an annuity. I asked Jefrey Suyemtsu, vice president and regional coordinator of Prudential Investments, to explain annuities and their benefits.

The term *annuity* derives from the Latin term meaning "annual." So in the most basic of terms, an annuity generally refers to a series of consistent, regular payments of principal and interest over a period.

Let's look at this basic concept in real life. If you are lucky enough to work for a company that provides a defined benefit pension plan, the company, based on several factors including your years of service and income, will calculate a retirement benefit that is paid to you at retirement in "consistent, predictable streams of income payments for a period of time." These payments usually continue over your lifetime and if you're married, your surviving spouse can also receive part or all of this benefit during his or her remaining lifetime should you die. In essence, the company has either purchased from an insurance company an annuity or created an annuity to provide for this type of benefit.

What about Social Security? How many retirees or future retirees look at Social Security as part of a "guaranteed" retirement benefit they expect to receive the rest of their life? Who doesn't want to retire and know with certainty they will always receive a guaranteed amount of income for the rest of their life? If you thought you didn't like the annuity concept, maybe you didn't realize just how much you depend on it to provide not only income but peace of mind. Annuities can be classified into two types: immediate and deferred.

What Is a Tax-Deferred Annuity?

A *tax-deferred annuity* is a contract between you (the contract owner) and an insurance company. It is used to accumulate wealth on a tax-deferred basis. The money you deposit into the contract is allowed to grow over a period and the interest or earnings on your deposit(s) are not reportable as taxable income while they remain in the contract. This tax-deferred growth is the most important feature of a deferred annuity. Because you do not pay taxes on the earnings until you withdraw the money from the contract, you have the benefit of all your money working for you, and as a result the compounding effect on tax-deferred accounts can help build wealth significantly faster than in a taxable account. This is an especially effective approach when you allow money to grow at compound rates over 10-year to 25-year periods.

Types of Tax-Deferred Annuities

Fixed annuities. *Fixed annuities* provide a minimum guaranteed interest rate by the issuing insurance company.

Variable annuities. *Variable annuities* have often been described as mutual funds with an insurance wrapper. They have all the basic features of a fixed annuity: tax-deferred growth, guaranteed death benefits for the beneficiaries, income features, and flexibility. But a significant benefit of a variable annuity is its allowing you to create a personal investment strategy by choosing among a range of investment options. You can usually select from a broad range of stock and bond funds that cover all asset classes as well as money markets and a fixed account.

Is an Annuity Right for Me?

As you can see, annuities can be a good "location" for sector rotation strategies. Just as there is no perfect investment, there is no perfect answer to this question. Annuities play an important role in many people's lives for different reasons and can be an integral part of an overall investment and retirement strategy. Used correctly, annuities can fulfill the needs of investors in a variety of ways as well as, and sometimes better than, any other alternative.

Although *Safer Investing in Volatile Markets* gives you a glimpse of many different strategies, it in no way can make you an expert. If you are serious about any of these strategies, dig a little deeper and work with your financial advisor. This book should get you started and give you a solid understanding of which strategies will best suit you.

Some Tips to Remember

Buy and Hold

- In buy-and-hold accounts, try to hold positions for three to five years, especially if the account is well diversified. If you hold a security for five years, the new capital gains rate is 18 percent. If your securities become less attractive for valuations, technical, or fundamental reasons, however, be aware of sell signals!
- In buy-and-hold accounts that are well balanced, don't panic sell on market falls. In 1987, 44 percent of investors sold after the crash, only to regret it a year later.
- If you have a buy-and-hold account make sure you consider the strategies for asset allocation and divide your assets among value, growth, inflation, and deflation hedges.
- Consider having two portfolios: a core asset allocation (buy and hold) in taxable accounts and a TAA (tactical asset allocation portfolio) in tax-deferred accounts. Use tax-free municipal bonds, trusts, passive index funds, and stocks for your core asset allocation. Use sector or style mutual funds, highly taxed instruments such as government bonds, sector rotation, and trading strategies for TAA.
- Consider tax-managed mutual funds to limit taxable capital gains.

Reducing Risk

- Shop for guaranteed trusts on the secondary market; not only do they have better guarantees, but also shorter maturities than new trusts.
- Invest in mutual funds or managed investments for the riskier investments, such as mid-cap, small cap, international, or emerging growth.
- *Never* put more than 10 percent of your money in any one trust or fund, with the possible exception of the broad S&P index trusts.
- *Never* invest more than 5 percent in any one stock.
- *Never* invest more than 20 percent in any one sector—unless you are trading.
- Balance the risks of one investment with another investment that moves in a different direction or has low correlation.
- Concentrate on selecting sectors, not stocks.

- Understand your own risk tolerance, remembering that the market has always come back up after large falls in the past, but it also has gone down more than 10 percent over 109 times and it can stay there for a long time.
- Don't take more risk than you need to achieve your goals. If you only need a 6 percent return to retire comfortably, then maybe skip the stock market.
- If you are more aggressive, consider the Nasdaq's QQQ. Because these are so much riskier than the S&P 500, always consider insurance or stop loss orders on them.
- When markets are extremely volatile, one strategy that really works is buying insurance and collars. However, insurance costs can eat into your returns, so use them sparingly and don't insure things of little value.
- Buy insurance when the market is high, not after it has crashed.
- If you are willing to take more risk, you can invest in high beta stocks with betas higher than 1, and if you are more conservative, invest in low beta stocks less than 1. A high beta stock will move up faster but also fall faster.
- When looking at risks, also look at Section IV in Value Line Investment Survey, which shows the price stability, earnings predictability, and price growth persistence. Look for companies that are buying back their own stocks. Historically, these stocks outperform the market. It is usually a good sign and can be helpful in selecting stocks.

Buying Stocks

- Remember the stock market usually moves about six months before the economy recovers. You cannot wait till the recession is over to get back in the market.
- Although no one has a crystal ball, if there is any light at the end of the tunnel, start buying, not selling, during recessions. Since World War II, most business cycles have been one year recessions followed by four-year expansions. However, these are averages. In reality, there are no neat little packages. Some contractions have been as short as six months, some as long as five years. In general, these averages give us some hope that no matter how long or how painful, there always has been a recovery.
- Don't buy mutual funds at the end of the year in taxable accounts. They may be liable for capital gains distributions that you did not receive.
- If you believe in seasonal rotation, be invested from November to May. Invest in growth for the last quarter of the year and in value or cash from April through October.
- Watch the Purchasing Managers Index for the best clues on the current economy. The Index of Leading Economic Indicators also gives clues on the direction of the economy in the future. My husband used to watch what he called the "cardboard box" indicator. He would call packaging companies that made cardboard boxes every quarter and see how many boxes were shipped. His theory was that if production was picking up, companies would need boxes to ship the product. It seemed to work well for us.

- If a stock has a history of stock splits, as it approaches the $80 to $100 trading range, consider purchasing it for a short-term trade.
- If you have limited patience, time, and interest in the market, consider SPY, spiders, with some stop loss orders and protective puts. They offer great downside protection, yet give you an opportunity to share in the unlimited returns of the market.
- Remember selling put options is dangerous, but if you are interested in buying at a lower price, consider selling puts and letting someone pay you for your patience.
- Don't look at price when buying stocks, look at value. Buy 10 shares of a good $50 stock instead of a 100 shares of a poor performing $5 stock.
- Momentum investing is attractive in bull markets. In bear markets, watch valuations instead. If you do not want to sell immediately when you get a sell signal, use some of the other exit strategies we discussed: stop losses, covered calls, put insurance, collars, sector rotation, dollar cost averaging out, value cost averaging out, or rebalancing.
- For growth stocks, look for low PEGs, (price to earnings to growth ratios). However, low PEGs no longer necessarily mean a strong buy because the current ability to forecast earning and growth rates is dubious. Use low PEGs for the first screen, but then also look at other factors, such as price to sales ratios.
- When seeking value, look for low PEs (price to earning ratios).

Selling Stocks

- Bottom-up investing may often lead to finding the best "neglected" stocks, but also it often leads to many wasted hours that can be used more wisely in developing an overall strategy and top-down plan that focuses on your goals and risk tolerance.
- Don't sell profitable positions; gift them away to lower tax-bracketed family members if you can. You can gift in addition to $11,000 per person, the costs for education, and medical expenses.
- Don't wait until December to sell stocks for losses. Everyone else will be selling then. Start liquidating in August, and buy back in November and December when everyone else is selling.
- Remember, if you write off a stock as a loss, you have to wait over 30 days to buy it back in order to avoid the IRS wash rules.
- *Always have an exit strategy.* Set a target to get out at the top and a floor that you do not want your investment to fall below.
- If your profits are greater than 20 to 30 percent in one year, think about selling part of your position. Remember, historic returns in the market are much lower than that, and the market usually reverts to its averages.
- When you get a sell signal, do not let emotion prevent you from acting.
- Always monitor the PEs and PEGs of the sectors as well as of each stock in your portfolio. Use them as clues for selling.
- When PEs and PEGs are higher than average, start using some of your exit strategies

- Although it is often debatable whether watching when insiders sell is a good indicator of the company's strength, it can be used as a signal of weakness. If the owners are selling, you may want to consider putting some exit strategies in place.
- Although you may not be able to use low PEGs as main criteria to buy growth stocks, you can still use high PEGs as sell signals and warning to exit.

Tax-Deferred Accounts

- Look at how much you can save and determine the best place to locate it; e.g., taxable or tax-deferred accounts. Save as much as possible in tax-deferred accounts if you are young.
- In tax-deferred accounts, concentrate on safer investments and consider protective puts, collars, and covered calls for individual stocks. Remember that the government does not share your losses because they are not tax deductible.
- Be careful of zero-coupon bonds; they have hidden taxes. Even though you receive no income, you pay taxes each year on the income that you will receive at maturity. So whenever possible hold in tax-deferred accounts.
- Consider sector rotation and trading strategies to strive for higher returns, but try to limit their use to tax-deferred accounts.

Measuring Returns

- It is difficult to outperform the market over the long run. However, by avoiding some of the downside you can outperform by small amounts that can compound to increase your wealth dramatically.
- When measuring performance, look at the time-weighted returns versus dollar weighted.
- Compare your returns to a benchmark, such as your targeted returns or the market. If you are aggressive and have all small cap stocks, do not compare your returns to the Dow, instead compare to a small cap index.
- The stock market is considered a good inflation hedge over a long time, but it tends to respond very poorly to inflation or inflation news over the short term, so consider rising inflation as a sell signal. (Remember, when inflation is high, it is likely the Fed will raise interest rates, and increased interest rates are bad for stocks, businesses, and bonds.)
- Be realistic when you are estimating returns for financial and retirement plans. Historically, the stock markets perform twice as well the growth in the GDP (gross domestic product).* If you go back to when records are first available on the market, approximately 200 years ago, you find that "real" (after inflation is taken out)

---

*Similar to the GNP (gross national product) but determined by the location of the facilities doing the production, instead of the ownership as with GNP. GDP are domestic locations. This ratio 2:1 seems to hold true for most of the world's markets.

returns on the stock market averaged about 6 percent. This is approximately two times the average annual real growth for GDP.

- Although it can be more volatile and fraught with more risks, consider the international market for part of your portfolio if you are young and seeking to outperform the indexes. Not only has the international market outperformed U.S. markets historically, but some international positions actually decrease portfolio volatility over the long run. Also consider international bonds. Usually, they have low correlation relative to the U.S. markets.

Overweighted

- If you are overweighted in a stock, consider Exchange Funds.
- If you are overweighted in a company stock, remember that loyalty risk is extremely dangerous and gradually sell off your positions or gift them to charitable remainder trusts.

Miscellaneous

- Understand the risk, the standard deviation, the beta, and the resistance of every investment and write it down.
- Consider utilities. They have only underperformed the S&P by .5 percent and are often safer.
- Write down the expected returns of every investment. Find the expected returns from Value Line Investment Survey or Standard & Poor's Stock Reports.
- Remember, if it looks too good to be true, it probably is. Be very careful when you see stocks that are getting a lot of hype without sound fundamentals. Remember that analysts love to recommend stocks, but are very hesitant to downgrade them.
- Write down economic factors that are likely to impact your portfolio; e.g., if you have a lot of bonds, be wary of interest rate moves; if you have a lot of retail stock, worry about consumer confidence.
- Remember PEs and PEGs are estimates. Therefore, do not base your buy decisions solely on these valuations, but look further at event risks and fundamental, economic, and political factors.
- If you do not know how to evaluate the information in Value Line, call for their free booklet, "How to Invest in Common Stocks," at 800-833-0046.
- The best values are often the neglected small companies that get little press. They might go years without being noticed, so watch relative strength as well as value measurements for these stocks.
- Watch business cycles. At the top of the cycle the market tends to be strong. At the bottom, the market tends to be weak, but also tends to be undervalued and to offer the best bargains. Remember you want to buy low. *Stocks are one of the few items that when they go on sale no one wants to buy.*

- When you want guarantees, invest in participating index CDs, S&P indexes with puts, guaranteed trusts, and bonds. If you want growth, invest in stocks, funds, and trusts.
- Check your old U.S. Savings bonds. Even they have risk. If they were purchased before the 1970s, they may not be paying interest. They usually only pay for 30 years.
- In general don't invest in bond funds. Bond funds do not have guarantees as bonds do and the funds have higher fees than purchasing individual bonds. If you need diversification, use trusts.
- Have money set aside in emergency funds and cash that is equivalent to two to three months' worth of income.
- Don't forget inflation protection. Check your pensions for Cost of Living Indexes (COLAs). Even in retirement, if you do not have adequate COLAs, make sure you plan for inflation in your investments.
- Be careful of costs for trading accounts. Consider flat or wrap fee accounts. However do not use wrap accounts for core portfolio—why pay a fee when you will not be trading?
- Don't chase performance. The best funds one year, tend to be the most vulnerable for large falls the next year. Consider instead investing in undervalued sectors.
- Use midcap instead of small-cap funds. They have returned nearly the same and are much safer.

Some Tips on Life

- Don't pray for blue eyes, brown eyes work just as well. It is more important sometimes to be grateful for what we have than to take the risk of striving for more.
- Life is short, enjoy it.
- Always wear your seat belt.

My husband and I were speaking at a radio seminar. As we left, someone asked me what my best investment was. I said, "Cisco Systems." Then my husband said, "my family." Those were the last words he ever said to anyone other than me. Put life in perspective. Your family is the most important thing. No material investment can ever compete.

For those who want to know more, consider these sources of information:

- Benjamin Graham's *The Intelligent Investor* and David Dodd's work on PE and growth measures
- Sidney Cottle for security analysis
- Jeremy J. Siegel, *Stocks for the Long Run: A Guide to Selecting Markets for Long-Term Growth*
- AAII—American Association of Individual Investors. 312-280-0170
- *Barron's.* 800-544-0422

- *Investor's Business Daily.* Probably the best daily source for growth oriented investors
- *Wall Street Journal.* Of course. However, provides a little less in-depth financial information, but still probably one of the best sources of overall general information on the markets, economy, individual stocks, and industries. 800-778-0840
- *U.S. Financial Data.* Important for anyone investing in bonds, and interested in monitoring interest rate moves. Published by St. Louis Federal Reserve Bank. 314-444-8808
- *Standard & Poor's Stock Reports.* Covers more stocks than any other research report
- *Value Line Investment Survey.* Provides reports on fewer companies (1,700) than S&P stock report, but are usually more current. Often some of the data is more accurate and applicable, and a little more user friendly. *Value Line* also follows another 1,800 companies but not as frequently. 800-833-0046

GLOSSARY

ADR American Depositary Receipt. ADRs are receipts issued against a deposit of a foreign stock. These securities trade on U.S. exchanges and afford a convenient way to purchase international securities.

beta A measure of a stock's risk relative to the market. High betas imply securities will move faster than the market; low betas imply securities will move slower than the market, and betas equal to 1 imply securities will move in line with the market.

cash flow Earnings plus noncash items, usually depreciation.

callable security A security that the issuer may call or redeem at a predetermined price prior to its maturity date. Bond, CDs, principal protected notes, and exchange traded trusts, preferred stocks, all can have call features.

CDs Certificates of deposit are issued by banks and are insured by the Federal Deposit Insurance Corporation (FDIC) up to $100,000 per depositor, per institution. The interest can be at a fixed rate or indexed to a benchmark.

CPI Consumer price index, which is prepared by the Department of Labor and measures inflation; over the last 20 years, it has averaged 3.8 percent.

DPS Dividends per share.

EPS Earnings per share.

fundamental value The economic value of a stock based on its product, people, and monetary flows.

growth investing An investment style that attempts to find stocks when they are young with potential for strong future growth.

IPO Initial public offering.

mean Average.

Nasdaq National Association of Securities Dealers Automated Quotations. Often called the OTC, or over-the-counter stock market.

net income A company's earnings or profit calculated as revenue after deducting all operating and financial expenses and before dividend payments; basically, what is left after all bills are paid.

PE Price per share divided by earning per share; price-earnings ratio.

relative PE A company's PE divided by the industrywide or marketwide PE.

revert to the mean Move back to previous average returns.

ROE Return on equity; earnings divided by shareholder equity.

stepped-up CDs Coupon rates that are stepped up or increased over time.

undervalued Stock whose price is below the value range.

zero-coupon bonds Debt purchased at a discount to its face value that will mature at par. Eliminates the reinvestment risk but increases interest rate risk. Interest from zero-coupon bonds is subject to taxation annually as ordinary income, even though no income is received until maturity.

Future Value Table

The Effects of Saving and Inflation on Your Dollars' Lump Sump Investment

This table shows the future of a single investment or deposit (lump sum) of one dollar ($1.00). Use the table when you are trying to calculate the value of $1.00 invested at the yields listed below or at an inflated value. Look down the column that shows the interest rate or inflation rate. Stop at the row that shows the number of years you can invest. Always use after-tax yields, the yeilds you receive after you deduct the taxes due. For example, if you expect inflation to be 6 percent, simply look down the 6 percent column until you reach the year row that you are interested in. This figure shows you the value your dollar must grow to in order to keep up with inflation. Whenever you are planning your future goals, you should use inflated dollars.

Example: You invest $20,000. What will the value be in 15 years at 10 percent? Look at the column for 10 percent and stop when you reach the 15-year row. Each dollar will be worth $4.18, or $20,000 will be worth 4.18 × 20,000 = $83,600.

						Interest or inflation rate						
Years	4%	5%	6%	7%	8%	9%	10%	11%	12%	13%	14%	15%
1	1.04	1.05	1.06	1.07	1.08	1.09	1.10	1.11	1.12	1.13	1.14	1.15
2	1.08	1.10	1.12	1.14	1.16	1.18	1.21	1.23	1.25	1.27	1.29	1.32
3	1.12	1.16	1.19	1.22	1.25	1.29	1.33	1.36	1.40	1.44	1.48	1.52
4	1.17	1.22	1.26	1.31	1.36	1.41	1.46	1.51	1.57	1.63	1.68	1.74
5	1.22	1.27	1.33	1.40	1.46	1.53	1.61	1.68	1.76	1.84	1.92	2.01
6	1.27	1.34	1.41	1.50	1.58	1.67	1.77	1.87	1.97	2.08	2.19	2.31
7	1.32	1.41	1.51	1.61	1.71	1.82	1.94	2.08	2.22	2.35	2.50	2.66
8	1.37	1.47	1.59	1.72	1.85	1.99	2.14	2.30	2.47	2.66	2.85	3.05
9	1.42	1.55	1.69	1.84	1.99	2.17	2.35	2.56	2.77	3.04	3.25	3.52
10	1.48	1.63	1.79	1.96	2.16	2.37	2.59	2.84	3.11	3.39	3.70	4.05
11	1.54	1.71	1.89	2.11	2.33	2.58	2.85	3.15	3.48	3.86	4.22	4.65
12	1.60	1.80	2.01	2.25	2.52	2.81	3.14	3.49	3.90	4.34	4.81	5.35
13	1.67	1.89	2.13	2.41	2.72	3.05	3.45	3.88	4.36	4.89	5.49	6.15
14	1.73	1.98	2.26	2.57	2.94	3.34	3.80	4.31	4.89	5.55	6.26	7.08
15	1.80	2.08	2.39	2.75	3.17	3.64	4.18	4.78	5.47	6.25	7.13	8.14

Interest or inflation rate

Years	4%	5%	6%	7%	8%	9%	10%	11%	12%	13%	14%	15%
16	1.87	2.18	2.54	2.92	3.43	3.97	4.60	5.31	6.13	7.06	8.13	9.36
17	1.95	2.29	2.69	3.16	3.70	4.32	5.05	5.89	6.87	7.98	9.27	10.77
18	2.03	2.41	2.85	3.38	4.00	4.72	5.56	6.54	7.68	9.02	10.57	12.38
19	2.11	2.53	3.02	3.62	4.32	5.14	6.12	7.26	8.61	10.19	12.06	14.23
20	2.19	2.65	3.20	3.87	4.66	5.60	6.73	8.06	9.65	11.52	13.74	16.31
25	2.67	3.39	4.29	5.42	6.85	8.60	10.83	13.58	17.00	21.23	26.46	32.90
30	3.24	4.32	5.74	7.61	10.06	13.27	17.45	22.89	29.96	39.11	50.95	66.22
35	3.95	5.52	7.68	10.67	14.79	20.41	28.10	38.57	52.80	72.06	98.10	133.18
40	4.80	7.04	10.29	14.97	21.72	31.41	45.26	65.00	93.05	132.78	188.88	267.88
45	5.84	8.99	13.76	21.00	31.92	48.33	72.89	109.53	163.99	244.64	363.68	538.77

Present Value Table: Saving for the Future

Lump Sum Savings (Single Deposit) Needed to Acquire $1,000

Use this table when you want to find how much you have to save today to receive $1,000 in the future. If you have specific goals that you want to achieve, such as saving for your children's college education or purchasing a new home, this table will show you how much you need to put aside now to have the money you want in future years. Example: If you need $50,000 in 20 years and you can earn 10 percent on your money, find the intersection of the number of years you can save and the yield you can earn after taxes. At the intersection of the 10 percent column and 20-year row, you will find the number 148. You need $148 for each $1,000. For $50,000 you will need to set aside today $7,400 (50 × 148).

							Yield									
Years	1%	2%	3%	4%	5%	6%	7%	8%	9%	10%	11%	12%	13%	14%	15%	16%
1	990	980	970	960	951	942	932	923	914	905	896	887	878	869	861	852
2	980	961	942	923	905	887	870	853	836	820	804	788	773	758	743	728
3	970	942	915	888	863	837	813	789	766	744	722	701	681	661	642	623
4	960	923	888	854	822	792	763	735	708	683	659	636	613	592	572	552
5	951	906	863	821	784	747	713	681	650	621	594	567	543	519	497	476
6	942	887	837	790	746	705	666	630	596	564	535	507	480	456	432	410
7	932	870	813	760	711	665	623	584	547	513	482	452	425	400	376	354
8	923	853	789	731	676	627	582	540	502	466	434	404	376	351	327	305
9	914	836	766	703	645	592	544	500	460	424	391	361	333	308	284	263
10	905	820	744	676	613	558	508	463	422	386	352	322	295	270	247	227
11	896	804	722	650	585	527	475	429	388	351	317	287	261	237	215	195
12	887	788	701	624	557	497	444	397	356	319	286	257	231	208	187	168
13	878	773	681	601	530	469	415	368	326	290	258	229	204	182	163	145
14	869	758	661	577	505	442	388	341	299	263	232	205	181	160	141	125
15	861	743	641	555	481	417	362	315	275	239	209	183	160	140	123	108
16	852	728	623	534	458	394	339	292	252	218	188	163	142	123	107	93
17	844	714	605	513	436	371	317	270	231	198	170	146	125	108	93	80
18	836	700	587	494	416	350	296	250	212	180	153	130	111	95	81	69
19	827	686	570	475	396	330	277	232	195	164	138	116	98	83	70	60
20	819	673	554	456	377	312	258	215	178	148	124	104	87	73	61	51

Years	1%	2%	3%	4%	5%	6%	7%	Yield 8%	9%	10%	11%	12%	13%	14%	15%	16%
22	803	646	522	422	342	278	226	184	150	123	101	83	68	56	46	38
24	787	622	492	392	310	247	197	158	124	102	82	66	53	43	35	28
26	772	598	464	361	281	220	172	135	106	84	66	53	42	33	26	21
28	756	574	437	333	255	196	150	116	90	69	54	42	33	26	20	16
30	742	552	412	308	231	174	131	99	75	57	44	33	26	20	15	12
32	727	531	388	285	210	155	115	85	63	47	35	27	20	15	11	9
34	712	510	366	264	190	138	100	73	53	39	29	21	16	12	9	6
36	699	490	345	244	173	123	88	63	45	32	23	17	12	9	7	5
38	685	471	325	225	157	109	76	54	38	28	19	13	10	7	5	4
40	672	453	307	208	142	97	67	46	32	22	15	11	8	5	4	3

INDEX